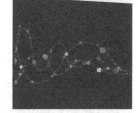

Foundations of Data Intensive Applications

Large Scale Data Analytics under the Hood

Supun Kamburugamuve
Saliya Ekanayake

Published by John Wiley & Sons, Inc., Hoboken, New Jersey.
Published simultaneously in Canada.

ISBN: 978-1-119-71302-9
ISBN: 978-1-119-71303-6 (ebk)
ISBN: 978-1-119-71301-2 (ebk)

For general information on our other products and services or for technical support, please contact our Customer Care Department within the United States at (800) 762-2974, outside the United States at (317) 572-3993 or fax (317) 572-4002.

Wiley also publishes its books in a variety of electronic formats. Some content that appears in print may not be available in electronic formats. For more information about Wiley products, visit our web site at www.wiley.com.

Library of Congress Control Number: 2021942305

Cover images: © Makstorm/Getty Images
Cover design: Wiley

SKY10028708_080421

To my wife Chathuri, son Seth, daughter Nethuki, and our parents.

—Supun Kamburugamuve

To my wife Kalani, and two sons, Neth and Senuth, and our parents.

—Saliya Ekanayake

About the Authors

Supun Kamburugamuve has a PhD in computer science from Indiana University – Bloomington. For his thesis, he researched improving the performance of data-intensive applications with Professor Geoffrey C. Fox. Supun created Twister2 and co-created Cylon projects that are aimed at high-performance data-intensive applications. His research work is published in recognized conferences and journals. Supun is an elected member of the Apache Software Foundation and has contributed to many open source projects including Apache Web Services projects and Apache Heron. Before joining Indiana University, Supun worked on middleware systems and was a key member of the WSO2 ESB project, which is a widely used open source enterprise integration solution. Supun has presented his ideas and findings at research conferences and technical conferences including Strata NY, Big Data Conference, and ApacheCon.

Saliya Ekanayake is a senior software engineer at Microsoft. He is part of the Cloud Accelerated Systems & Technologies (CAST) group that is developing high-performance machine learning systems. Before joining Microsoft, Saliya was a postdoctoral fellow at Berkeley Lab, specializing in improving the performance of large-scale machine learning systems. He holds a PhD in computer science from Indiana University – Bloomington, where his research contributed to the development of SPIDAL, a scalable, parallel, and interoperable data analytics library that outperformed existing big data systems on several machine learning applications. After his PhD, Saliya also worked on designing large-scale graph analytics systems and algorithms at Virginia Tech. His work has been published in recognized conferences and journals, with more than 20 publications to his name. Saliya is also an Apache committer for the Apache Synapse project.

About the Editor

Thomas Wiggins is a freelance proofreader and editor. He holds a BA in fine arts and theatre/drama from Indiana University, as well as an MS in media arts and science from Indiana University/Purdue University – Indianapolis. For the past nine years, Mr. Wiggins has done proofreading work on scientific papers submitted to conferences and journals around the world, as well as offering his services pro bono for amateur writers. In 2011, he helped in the creation of e-humanity.org, a federal grant-funded online repository for the Native Tribal collections of several museums, including the Smithsonian. He currently is an employee of Cook Inc.

Acknowledgments

This book presents the ideas and work of countless software engineers and researchers over many years. We thank them for their hard work that helped us to write this book. The open source software community has made data-intensive applications popular and easily accessible to the public. We would like to thank the Apache Software Foundation for producing some of the best open source communities that have built wonderful frameworks for data-intensive applications. Many other open source communities are building these amazing products; some notables ones are Pandas, Numpy, PyTorch, Tensorflow, OpenMPI, and Kubernetes.

Our thanks also go out to members of the digital science center at Indiana University, whose work has influenced the content of this research. We both had the privilege to work with our thesis advisor, Distinguished Professor Geoffrey C. Fox at Indiana University – Bloomington, who has been a key driving force behind high-performance data-intensive computing. The work we did with him was a great inspiration for the book.

We would like to thank Chathura Widanage, Niranda Perera, Pulasthi Wickramasinghe, Ahmet Uyar, Gurhan Gundez, Kannan Govindarajan, and Selahattin Akkas at the Digital Science Center of Indiana University. The work we did and the software we developed together were a great motivation for the book. We would like to thank Thejaka Kanewala for the wonderful conversations we had on data-intensive applications. We would like to thank Thejaka Kanewala for the wonderful conversations we had on data-intensive applications and Jaliya Ekanayake for the feedback on the book.

Finally, we would like to thank our families for the extraordinary sacrifices they've made so that we could make this book a reality.

Contents at a Glance

Contents

Introduction

Many would say the byword for success in the modern era has to be *data*. The sheer amount of information stored, processed, and moved around over the past 50 years has seen a staggering increase, without any end in sight. Enterprises are hungry to acquire and process more data to get a leg up on the competition. Scientists especially are looking to use data-intensive methods to advance research in ways that were not possible only a few decades ago.

With this worldwide demand, data-intensive applications have gone through a remarkable transformation since the start of the 21st century. We have seen wide adoption of big data frameworks such as Apache Hadoop, Apache Spark, and Apache Flink. The amazing advances being made in the fields of machine learning (ML) and deep learning (DL) are taking the big data era to new heights for both enterprise and research communities. These fields have further broadened the scope of data-intensive applications, which demand faster and more integrable systems that can operate on both specialized and commodity hardware.

Data-intensive applications deal with storing and extracting information that involves disk access. They can be computing intensive as well, with deep learning and machine learning applications that not only consume massive data but also do a substantial number of computations. Because of memory, storage, and computational requirements, these applications require resources beyond a single computer's ability to provide.

There are two main branches of data-intensive processing applications: streaming data and batch data. Streaming data analytics is defined as the continuous processing of data. Batch data analytics involves processing data as a complete unit. In practice, we can see streaming and batch applications working together. Machine learning and deep learning fall under the batch application category. There are some streaming ML algorithms as well. When we say machine learning or deep learning, we mostly focus on the training of the models, as it is the most compute-intensive aspect.

Users run these applications on their laptops, clouds, high-performance clusters, graphic processing unit (GPU) clusters, and even supercomputers. Such systems have different hardware and software environments. While we may be developing our applications to deploy in one environment, the framework we use to construct them needs to work in a variety of settings.

History of Data-Intensive Applications

Data-intensive applications have a long history from even before the start of the map-reduce era. With the increasing popularity of internet services, the need for storing and processing large datasets became vitally important starting around the turn of the century. In February 2001, Doug Laney published a research note titled "3D Data Management: Controlling Data Volume, Velocity, and Variety" [1]. Since then, we have used the so-called "3 Vs" to describe the needs of large-scale data processing.

From a technology perspective, the big data era began with the MapReduce paper from Jeffrey Dean and Sanjay Ghemawat at Google [2]. Apache Hadoop was created as an open source implementation of the map-reduce framework along with the Hadoop Distributed File System following the Google File System [3]. The simple interface of map-reduce for data processing attracted many companies and researchers. At the time, a network was often a bottleneck, and the primary focus was to bring the computation to where the data were kept.

A whole ecosystem of storage solutions and processing systems rose around these ideas. Some of the more notable processing systems include Apache Spark, Apache Flink, Apache Storm, and Apache Tez. Storage system examples are Apache HBase, Apache Cassandra, and MongoDB.

With more data came the need to learn from them. Machine learning algorithms have been in development since the 1950s when the first perceptron [4] was created and the nearest neighbor algorithm [5] was introduced. Since then, many algorithms have appeared steadily over the years to better learn from data. Indeed, most of the deep learning theory was created in the 1980s and 1990s.

Despite a long evolution, it is fair to say that modern deep learning as we know it spiked around 2006 with the introduction of the Deep Belief Network (DBN). This was followed by the remarkable success of AlexNet in 2009 [6]. The primary reason for this shift was the increase in computational power in the form of parallel computing that allowed neural networks to grow several orders of magnitude larger than what had been achieved in the past. A direct consequence of this has been the increase in the number of layers in a neural network, which is why it's called *deep learning*.

With machine learning and deep learning, users needed more interactive systems to explore data and do experiments quickly. This paved the way for Python-based APIs for data processing. The success of Python libraries such as NumPy and Pandas contributed to its popularity among data-intensive applications. But while all these changes were taking place, computer hardware was going through a remarkable transformation as well.

Hardware Evolution

Since the introduction of the first microprocessor from Intel in 1972, there have been tremendous advances in CPU architectures, leading to quantum leaps in performance. Moore's law and Dennard scaling coupled together were driving the performance of microprocessors until recently. Moore's law is an observation made by Gordon Moore on the doubling of the number of transistors roughly every two years. Dennard scaling states that the power density of MOSFET transistors roughly stays the same through each generation. The combination of these two principles suggested the number of computations that these microprocessors could perform for the same amount of energy would double every 1.5 years.

For half a century, this phenomenon has helped speed up applications across the board with each new generation of processors. Dennard scaling, however, has halted since about 2006, meaning clock frequencies of microprocessors hit a wall around 4GHz. This has led to the multicore era of microprocessors, where some motherboards even support more than one CPU or multisockets. The result of this evolution is single computers equipped with core counts that can go up to 128 today. Programming multicore computers require more consideration than traditional CPUs, which we will explore in detail later.

Alongside the multicore evolution came the rise of GPUs as general-purpose computing processors. This trend took a boost with the exponential growth in machine learning and deep learning. GPUs pack thousands of lightweight cores compared to CPUs. This has paved the way for accelerated computing kernels available to speed up computations.

GPUs were not the only type of accelerator to emerge. Intel KNL processors came out initially as accelerators. Field Programmable Gate Arrays (FPGAs) are now being used to develop custom accelerators, especially to improve deep learning training and inference. The trend has gone further, with the development of custom chips known as Application Specific Integrated Circuit (ASIC). Google's Tensor Processing Unit (TPU) is a popular ASIC solution to advance the training of large models.

The future of hardware evolution is leaning more toward accelerators, to the point where devices would carry multiple accelerators designed specifically for different application needs. This is known as *accelerator level parallelism*.

For instance, Apple's A14 chip has accelerators for graphics, neural network processing, and cryptography.

Data Processing Architecture

Modern data-intensive applications consist of data storage and management systems as well as data science workflows, as illustrated in Figure I-1. Data management is mostly an automated process involving their development and deployment. On the other hand, data science is a process that calls for human involvement.

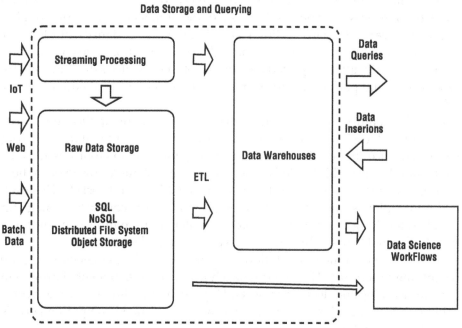

Figure I-1: Overall data processing architecture

Data Storage and Querying

Figure I-1 shows a typical data processing architecture. The priority is to ingest the data from various sources, such as web services and devices, into raw storage. The sources can be internal or external to an organization, the most common being web services and IoT devices, all of which produce streaming data. Further data can be accumulated from batch processes such as the output of an application run. Depending on our requirements, we can analyze this data to some degree before they are stored.

The raw data storage serves as a rich trove for extracting structured data. Ingesting and extracting data via such resources requires data processing tools that can work at massive scale.

From the raw storage, more specialized use cases that require subsets of this data are supported. We can store such data in specialized formats for efficient queries and model building, which is known as *data warehousing*. In the early stages of data-intensive applications, large-scale data storage and querying were the dominant use cases.

Data Science Workflows

Data science workflows have grown into an integral part of modern data-intensive applications. They involve data preparation, analysis, reflection, and dissemination, as shown in Figure I-2. Data preparation works with sources like databases and files to retrieve, clean, and reformat data.

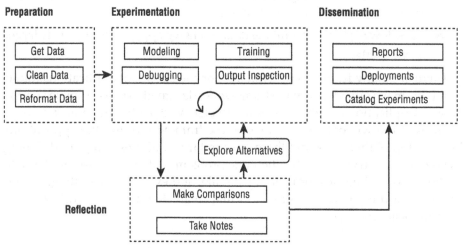

Figure I-2: Data science workflow

Data analysis includes modeling, training, debugging, and model validations. Once the analysis is complete, we can make comparisons in the reflection step to see whether such an analysis is what we need. This is an iterative process where we check different models and tweak them to get the best results.

After the models are finalized, we can deploy them, create reports, and catalog the steps we took in the experiments. The actual code related to learning algorithms may be small compared to all the other systems and applications surrounding and supporting it [7].

The data science workflow is an interactive process with human involvement every step of the way. Scripting languages like Python are a good fit for such interactive environments, with the ability to quickly prototype and test various hypotheses. Other technologies like Python Notebooks are extensively used by data scientists in their workflows.

Data-Intensive Frameworks

Whether it is large-scale data management or a data scientist evaluating results in a small cluster, we use frameworks and APIs to develop and run data-intensive applications. These frameworks provide APIs and the means to run applications at scale, handling failures and various hardware features. The frameworks are designed to run different workloads and applications:

- **Streaming data processing frameworks**—Process continuous data streams.
- **Batch data processing frameworks**—Manage large datasets. Perform extract, transform, and load operations.
- **Machine/deep learning frameworks**—Designed to run models that learn from data through iterative training.
- **Workflow systems**—Combine data-intensive applications to create larger applications.

There are many frameworks available for the classes of applications found today. From the outside, even the frameworks designed to solve a single specific class of applications might look quite diverse, with different APIs and architectures. But if we look at the core of these frameworks and the applications built on top of them, we find there are similar techniques being used. Seeing as how they are trying to solve the same problems, all of them use similar data abstractions, techniques for running at scale, and even fault handling. Within these similarities, there are differences that create distinct frameworks for various application classes.

There Is No Silver Bullet

It is hard to imagine one framework to solve all our data-intensive application needs. Building frameworks that work at scale for a complex area such as data-intensive applications is a colossal challenge. We need to keep in mind that, like any other software project, frameworks are built with finite resources and time constraints. Various programming languages are used when developing them, each with their own benefits and limitations. There are always trade-offs between usability and performance. Sometimes the most user-friendly APIs may not be the most successful.

Some software designs and architectures for data-intensive applications are best suited for only certain application classes. The frameworks are built according to these architectures to solve specific classes of problems but may not be that effective when applied to others. What we see in practice is frameworks are built for one purpose and are being adapted for other use cases as they mature.

Data processing is a complicated space that demands hardware, software, and application requirements. On top of this, such demands have been evolving rapidly. At times, there are so many options and variables it seems impossible to choose the correct hardware and software for our data-intensive problems. Having a deep understanding of how things work beneath the surface can help us make better choices when designing our data processing architectures.

Foundations of Data-Intensive Applications

Data-intensive applications incorporate ideas from many domains of computer science. This includes areas such as computer systems, databases, high-performance computing, cloud computing, distributed computing, programming languages, computer networks, statistics, data structures, and algorithms.

We can study data-intensive applications in three perspectives: data storage and management, learning from data, and scaling data processing. Data storage and management is the first step in any data analytics pipeline. It can include techniques ranging from sequential databases to large-scale data lakes.

Learning from data can take many forms depending on the data type and use case. For example, computing basic statistics, clustering data into groups, finding interesting patterns in graph data, joining tables of data to enrich information, and fitting functions to existing data are several ways we learn from data. The overarching goal of the algorithmic perspective is to form models from data that can be used to predict something in the future.

A key enabler for these two perspectives is the third one, where data processing is done at scale. Therefore, we will primarily look at data-intensive applications from a distributed processing perspective in this book. Our focus is to understand how the data-intensive applications run at scale utilizing various computing resources available. We take principles from databases, parallel computing, and distributing computing to delve deep into the ideas behind data-intensive applications operating at scale.

Who Should Read This Book?

This book is aimed at data engineers and data scientists. If you develop data-intensive applications or are planning to do so, the information contained herein can provide insight into how things work regarding various frameworks and tools. This book can be helpful if you are trying to make decisions about what frameworks to choose in your applications.

You should have a foundational knowledge of computer science in general before reading any further. If you have a basic understanding of networks and computer architecture, that will be helpful to understand the content better.

Our target audience is the curious reader who likes to understand how data-intensive applications function at scale. Whether you are considering developing applications using certain frameworks or you are developing your own applications from scratch for highly specialized use cases, this book will help you to understand the inner workings of the systems. If you are familiar with data processing tools, it can deepen your understanding about the underlying principles.

Organization of the Book

The book starts with introducing the challenges of developing and executing data-intensive applications at scale. Then it gives an introduction to data and storage systems and cluster resources. The next few chapters describe the internals of data-intensive frameworks with data structures, programming models, messaging, and task execution along with a few case studies of existing systems. Finally, we talk about fault tolerance techniques and finish the book with performance implications.

- **Chapter 1: Scaling Data-Intensive Applications**—Describes serial and parallel applications for data-intensive applications and the challenges faced when running them at scale.

- **Chapter 2: Data and Storage**—Overview of the data storage systems used in the data processing. Both hardware and software solutions are discussed.

- **Chapter 3: Computing Resources**—Introduces the computing resources used in data-intensive applications and how they are managed in large-scale environments.

- **Chapter 4: Data Structures**—This chapter describes the data abstractions used in data analytics applications and the importance of using memory correctly to speed up applications.

- **Chapter 5: Programming Models**—Discusses various programming models available and the APIs for data analytics applications.

- **Chapter 6: Messaging**—Examines how the network is used by data analytics applications to process data at scale by exchanging data between the distributed processes.

- **Chapter 7: Parallel Tasks**—Shows how to execute tasks in parallel for data analytics applications combining messaging.

- **Chapter 8: Case Studies**—Studies of a few widely used systems to highlight how the principles we discussed in the book are applied in practice.

- **Chapter 9: Fault Tolerance**—Illustrates handy techniques for handling faults in data-intensive applications.

- **Chapter 10: Performance and Productivity**—Defines various metrics used for measuring performance and discusses productivity when choosing tools.

Scope of the Book

Our focus here is the fundamentals of parallel and distributed computing and how they are applied in data processing systems. We take examples from existing systems to explain how these are used in practice, and we are not focusing on any specific system or programming language. Our main goal is to help you understand the trade-off between the available techniques and how they are used in practice. This book does not try to teach parallel programming.

You will also be introduced to a few examples of deep learning systems. Although DL at scale works according to the principles we describe here, we will not be going into any great depth on the topic. We also will not be covering any specific data-intensive framework on configuration and deployment. There are plenty of specific books and online resources on these frameworks.

SQL is a popular choice for querying large datasets. Still, you will not find much about it here because it is a complex subject of its own, involving query parsing and optimization, which is not the focus of this book. Instead, we look at how the programs are executed at scale.

References

At the end of each chapter, we put some important references that paved the way for some of the discussions we included. Most of the content you will find is the result of work done by researchers and software engineers over a long period. We include these as references to any reader interested in learning more about the topics discussed.

References

1. D. Laney, "3D data management: Controlling data volume, velocity and variety," *META group research note*, vol. 6, no. 70, p. 1, 2001.

2. J. Dean and S. Ghemawat, "MapReduce: Simplified Data Processing on Large Clusters.," *Sixth Symposium on Operating Systems Design and Implementation*, pp. 137–150, 2004.

3. Sanjay Ghemawat, Howard Gobioff, and Shun-Tak Leung, "The Google File System," presented at the 19th ACM Symposium on Operating Systems Principles, 2003.

4. F. Rosenblatt, *The perceptron, a perceiving and recognizing automaton Project Para. Cornell Aeronautical Laboratory*, 1957.

5. T. Cover and P. Hart, "Nearest neighbor pattern classification," *IEEE transactions on information theory*, vol. 13, no. 1, pp. 21–27, 1967.

6. A. Krizhevsky, I. Sutskever, and G. E. Hinton, "Imagenet classification with deep convolutional neural networks," *Advances in neural information processing systems*, vol. 25, pp. 1097–1105, 2012.

7. D. Sculley et al., "Hidden technical debt in machine learning systems," *Advances in neural information processing systems*, vol. 28, pp. 2503–2511, 2015.

Data Intensive Applications

They say it takes a village to raise a child. Developing data-intensive applications is no different. Coming up with an algorithm that can utilize the abundance of data is just one part of the ecosystem needed. In this chapter, we start with a simple data analytics example to dive into the anatomy of data-intensive applications. Then we look at the steps to scaling an algorithm so it can utilize distributed resources in parallel. We end the chapter with a discussion on some of the challenges faced when developing large-scale systems.

Anatomy of a Data-Intensive Application

Data-intensive applications are designed to run over distributed resources, such as on a cluster of computers or a cloud. Also, these applications are developed based on supporting frameworks both to reduce the development time and to keep the application logic simple without having to deal with the intricacies of distributed systems. These frameworks provide the necessary components to create and execute data-intensive applications at scale. When an application written using a framework is deployed to a cluster, the framework and the application become a single distributed program. Therefore, we will consider the framework as part of the application for our discussion. To understand what is under the hood of a data-intensive application, let us try to write one from the ground up.

A Histogram Example

Imagine we have many CSV files with data about users. For our purposes, let us assume the CSV files have the format described in Table 1-1 where it has an ID, name, and date of birth (DOB) for each record.

Table 1-1: CSV File Structure for User's Data

ID	NAME	DOB
001	John Adel	2000-Jan-03
003	Susan Smith	1980-Jun-05
008	Adam Voker	1991-Feb-20

We are interested in producing a histogram of users by their birth year. The following code snippet is what we would need if our data were in a single file. It will produce an array of counts for each year that is present in the data, which can be used to create a histogram.

```
while ((line = read_line(file)) != null)
year = extract_year(line)
      counts[year]++
```

However, assume the individual files are small, but collectively they are large, and it takes too much time for a single serial program to process them. Now let us look at a single query to count the people who were born in each year. To get an answer quickly, we are going to divide the files into multiple computers and do the file reading and computations in parallel using multiple instances of a program.

Say we have a distributed file system where all the relevant files are in a shared directory. The processes are going to pick an equal number of files from this folder to process. For example, if we assume 1,000 files and we have 10 computers (or processes), each program can process 100 files, as shown in Figure 1-1.

Program

Even though we partition files among 10 processes, we do not need to develop 10 separate programs to run in each of our computers. Since every process in this scenario is doing the same thing, we can write a single program to accomplish this task and create many instances of it. In short, this program will read a set of files from a shared directory and process them. The overall structure of our program is as follows:

```
map<int, int> counts;
for f in assigned_files
   while ((line = read_line(f)) != null)
        year = extract_year(line)
          counts[year]++
```

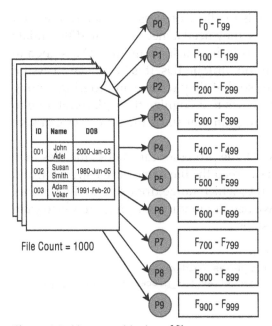

Figure 1-1: Linear partitioning of files among processes

Process Management

The next question is, how are we going to start these processes in the 10 machines? Manually logging into them and starting 10 processes is not a scalable solution. One basic solution is to start the processes using a simple bash script that will initiate an SSH connection for each machine to start the processes. Alternatively, one could even use the parallel distributed shell (PDSH) to spawn processes similar to using SSH in a shell script.

Still, there are two issues we have not yet solved with this program. First, how is each process going to know which files to process among the many available? Second, how do we calculate the total sum of the entries using the counts in each process? Let us look at the options available to solve the first problem.

There are two approaches we can use for the work assignment issue. First, imagine our launcher program (`shellscript`) knows about the folder and files in it so it can read the files and assign them to processes before starting them. In our case, we can give them as command-line arguments to each process. According to this option, our launch script will look like what is shown here in pseudocode. The program we wrote will need to take a set of filenames as command-line arguments.

```
List<string> all_files = read_file_names(folder)
For p = 0; p < num_proceses; p++
    list<string> files_for_process = getfiles_for_proc(all_files, p)
    start_process(p, files_for_process)
```

The second approach we can use is to allow processes to determine their share after they are started. To do this, they need a mechanism to differentiate themselves from each other. Often this is done using a unique ID assigned to a process. Instead of assigning random unique IDs, it is beneficial to assign sequences of numbers to processes so that they receive an ordering among themselves. This will help the processes to recognize their place relative to other processes. For example, the program that starts the processes can give them numbers beginning from 0.

Now equipped with this unique ID, the processes can choose the files they will work on. For instance, they all can read the file names as a list, sort it, and assign the names according to the IDs, which range from zero to the number of processes. With this approach, we need to modify our program (histogram program) to include the following steps:

```
r = process_id // id starts from 0
List<string> all_files = read_file_names(folder)
list<string> files_for_process = get_files_for_process(all_files, p)

map<int, int> counts;
for f in files_for_process
    while ((line = read_line(f)) != null)
year = extract_year(line)
        counts[year]++
```

As we can clearly see, having a sequence of numbers helps us to assign the filenames. If we had random unique numbers, this would have been much harder.

Communication

At the end of the calculation, each process is left with a set of counts for every year they have seen. These numbers are local to each process. To calculate the total count for each year, the processes need to send their counts to a single process. Since we are working on a distributed environment, the only way for them to do this is by using the computer network. In general, we use messages to send data among processes.

To make things simpler, assume we have a library to send and receive messages from between processes, and we are going to do this summation in the 0th process. We need to modify our program so that the end of every program other than the 0th process will send a message to the 0th process. As such, the complete program will have the following structure:

```
r = process_id // id starts from 0
List<string> all_files = read_file_names(folder)
list<string> files_for_process = get_files_for_process(all_files, p)
```

```
map<int, int> counts;
for f in files_for_process
   while ((line = read_line(f)) != null)
year = extract_year(line)
       counts[year]++


If (r == 0) {
   List<map<int, int>> process_counts
   Process_counts[0] = counts
   For p = 1; p < num_processes; p++
      map<int, int> c = receive_from_process(p)
      process_counts[p] = c;
   /// calculate global counts from all process counts
   map<int, int> global_counts = aggregate_counts(process_counts)
} else {
   send_to(p, counts)
}
```

Instead of sending counts to the 0th process, every process can send the count to the one that submitted the application as well. In our case, it is a bash program, so we cannot easily send a message there. But if it were a Python script, we could have proceeded that way as well.

Another option is to avoid communication and write local counts to a file unique to each process. This would leave the aggregation of results to the launcher script to be carried out as a post-processing step. Local data can also be sent to a network endpoint if an aggregation service exists, but that is out of the scope of this example as we are interested in producing the histogram locally.

In this example, the aggregated results were required only at the 0th process or the launcher script. However, a common pattern with results aggregation is that all processes may require the collected results to a future computation step. This can be achieved in several ways. For example, the results can be collected at the 0th process as suggested here, but the 0th process can then broadcast the results back to each process.

It can also be done by each process pushing the local results to a server, followed by a synchronization step and pulling results from other processes again from the same server. A parameter server [1] is an example of this pattern. A more efficient way, however, is to perform an `allreduce` collective communication.

Execution

At this point, the question arises of how we can further improve our processing. A computer has many CPUs, and it would be best if we could utilize them for our calculations. We can run multiple threads inside our process to handle multiple files at the same time. Furthermore, we can do optimizations such as loading part of a file, which is an input/output (I/O)-intensive operation, while processing another part already loaded into memory.

Data Structures

Our earlier example is a simple one where we read a line of text, parse the attributes to find the year, and count the records for each. We can do this just by reading data one line at a time. But there are operations that require us to look at the complete dataset instead of simply going through one line at a time. One example is a sorting operation. Assume we want to reorder our data using the birthday attribute. One way to do this is to load the data into a list and sort it. If we create objects for each record in heap memory and keep references to those objects in the list, the sort can be inefficient due to cache not being applied properly. To avoid this, we use data structures that can store data efficiently in-memory.

Putting It Together

With our example, we identified some key requirements in a data-intensive application executing in multiple computers. If we look at any large-scale application running in parallel, at the center is a set of tasks distributed across computers doing computations and exchanging messages among them. How these tasks are programmed and connected to work together is defined by a programming model adopted by the application.

   We always use a framework that provides a programming interface to develop a data-intensive application. Depending on the framework, they hide various details of the application from the user to make it easier to develop, test, and deploy. When we execute an application, the framework and the application become one program code at runtime. So when we talk about runtime characteristics, we will use application and framework interchangeably.

   Now let us look at different components that are part of a data-intensive application at runtime, as shown in Figure 1-2. These will be described in greater detail in the next few chapters.

Application

The application is the entity programmed by the user. We use an API provided by a framework of choice to access the critical functions needed to run in a distributed environment. Various frameworks designed to handle different application classes provide the necessary APIs. We will go into the details of programming models in Chapter 5.

Resource Management

To execute an application using multiple computers, we must first distribute it to these computers and monitor them while they are executing. Since the

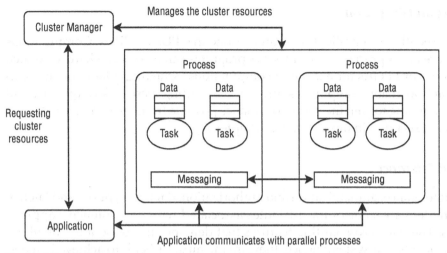

Figure 1-2: Runtime components of a data-intensive application

clusters can be shared among many other programs at the same time, they often have programs specifically designed to manage resources so that they can be allocated to applications without conflicts. These are called *cluster resource management software*. Data-intensive applications need to work with them to acquire the required resources, spawn the parallel processes, and manage them. Chapter 3 will give an introduction to various computing resources and how they are managed.

Messaging

Messaging between parallel tasks is one of the most important aspects when scaling applications to a substantial number of nodes. After we have the processes and establish messaging between them, we can run any distributed application. So along with cluster resource acquisition, message passing provides a minimal API to run any distributed application. The only question is how hard it is to write different classes of applications with this model. This is where the other higher-level abstractions and frameworks come in. We dive into these complex communication patterns in Chapter 6.

Data Structures

Efficient and compact storage of in-memory data is critical to application performance. Depending on the application classes, we require different data structures. Some of the data structures used commonly in data-intensive applications are tables, tensors, matrices, vectors, and graphs. In Chapter 4 we will go into more detail about data structures.

Tasks and Execution

The execution of parallel tasks can be done in CPUs or GPUs. Computations use threads or processes on CPUs. So, programs can use special hardware such as GPUs or FPGAs for executing computations. Scheduling tasks of an application to available compute resources and executing these tasks require careful programming to gain the best performance possible from the hardware. We will look at execution in more detail in Chapter 7.

Fault Tolerance

Fault tolerance, authentication and authorization, data encryption, and latency guarantees are some of the attributes associated with data-intensive applications. These are cross-cutting features that demand the cooperation of all the components in a system; hence, they are the most difficult to achieve in a distributed environment.

Fault tolerance is an integral aspect of many data-intensive applications that perform critical computations at large scale. Thanks to improvements in hardware, the importance of fault tolerance has declined over the years. Some applications rarely consider faults, as it can hinder their performance, while for others it is critical to provide continuous processing amidst failures. Fault handling techniques for data processing applications are discussed in Chapter 9.

Remote Execution

Imagine our application can be divided into multiple computations that need to be executed at scale. Every computation can output some data that later computations depend on. The output data can be small or large depending on the computations.

Data analytics frameworks commonly take the approach of submitting computations from a driver program to the cluster. This is commonly referred to as *remote execution*. This method has parallels to classic workflows, where different computations are orchestrated by a workflow manager. The assumption here is that computations have specific compute resource requirements and thus cannot execute as a single program with the same resources.

This method is mostly popular with exploratory data analytics. The data and work distribution of the program is done at the central server. In our previous example, we discussed the option of submitting script assigning the files to the workers. This method is equal to that task.

Parallel Applications

Data-intensive applications can take considerable time to execute as a serial application. Often we do not have enough memory to load data and execute applications in a single computer. To reduce the time and to solve problems that are too big for one computer, we need to execute them using parallel computers. We cannot simply take a serial application and run it in parallel. Instead, we need to design and develop a parallel version of the algorithm. Let us start with a serial application and discuss how we can make a parallel version from it.

Serial Applications

Serial execution is still the preferred choice for most applications in existence. Despite being complex, they are much easier to write, debug, and understand than parallel applications. To better understand this in the context of data analytics applications, let us look at the K-means clustering problem.

Simply put, the task here is to classify a group of data points into k clusters. However, finding an exact solution can be extremely difficult due to combinatorial explosion, yet there is an elegant approximate algorithm, Lloyd's algorithm, that is commonly used in practice.

Lloyd's K-Means Algorithm

This is an iterative algorithm that continuously tries to improve the cluster assignment for points [2]. It is comprised of four steps:

1. **Initialize cluster centers**—Given N number of D dimensional data points and a value k, the algorithm first initializes k vectors each of D dimensions. These act as the initial centroids for the k clusters. There are several initialization methods available, such as K-means++ [3], Gonzales method, and random points. Here we use random initialization for the sake of brevity.

2. **Assign points to clusters**—Iterating over the data points and centroids, the algorithm assigns each point to the nearest centroid. Typically, the Euclidean distance between a point and centroid is taken as the distance.

3. **Update cluster centers**—Once all points are assigned to clusters, the next step is to compute the mean point of each cluster, which will be taken as the centroid of that cluster for the next iteration.

4. **Iterate until convergence**—The algorithm repeats steps 2–4 until all the newly calculated centroids differ less than a given threshold to their previous values.

```cpp
std::vector < Coord > points;
std::vector < Coord > centers;

Initialize(points, numPoints, numDims, rng);
Initialize(centers, numCenters, numDims, rng);

bool converged = false;
while (!converged) {
  std::vector < Coord > newCenters(numCenters);
  for (const Coord & p: points) {
    double minDist = DBL_MAX;
    uint32_t minDistClusterIdx;
    uint32_t clusterIdx = 0;
    for (const Coord & c: centers) {
      auto dist = p.DistanceTo(c);
      if (dist < minDist) {
        minDist = dist;
        minDistClusterIdx = clusterIdx;
      }
      ++clusterIdx;
    }
    newCenters[minDistClusterIdx].AddPoint(p);
  }

  for (Coord & c: newCenters) {
    c.Normalize();
  }
  converged = TestConvergence(newCenters, centers);
  centers.swap(newCenters);
}
```

The preceding code starts with two vectors (the C++ method of handling dynamic arrays) for points and centers. For the sake of simplicity, the centers are randomly initialized here, but note there are other clever initialization algorithms used in the literature, as mentioned earlier.

The outer loop in line 10 follows step 2 of assigning each point to the closest center. The assignment happens in line 22, after the inner loop that iterates over all centers for a given point. These points are accumulated to a new centroid vector.

Updating cluster centers occurs in the loop in line 25. The fourth step, which tests for convergence, comes right after this when the old centers are replaced by new ones before starting the next iteration of the algorithm.

The immediate advantage of this serial code is its comprehensibility. The flow of the code maps one to one with the execution flow. Also, it is easier to debug a single thread than multiple threads or processes. All the integrated development environments (IDEs) support debugging with breakpoints that allow them to step through the code at runtime. In a multithreaded environment, this means stopping all threads and stepping through, but the ordering is not guaranteed. In addition, developing serial applications is more productive than parallel applications in terms of both development effort and time.

The limitations of serial applications lie in scalability and performance. For example, the *K-means* example presented here has an asymptotic complexity in the order of $O(NkD)$ for the convergence loop. As such, it soon becomes prohibitively expensive to run the serial implementation for larger numbers of $N, k,$ or D.

Parallelizing Algorithms

To harness the power of more compute resources, the algorithms must be parallelized. They often need to run over distributed resources as well. Parallelizing algorithms requires several steps, from identifying parts that can be run in parallel to assigning them to programming tasks and orchestrating the communication between tasks. Once a parallel program is laid out, the implementation may choose to map it onto either distributed or nondistributed physical computing units.

Figure 1-3 presents the steps taken to transform an algorithm from serial to parallel and map it onto physical computing units, whether distributed or nondistributed. We explain these steps in the following sections.

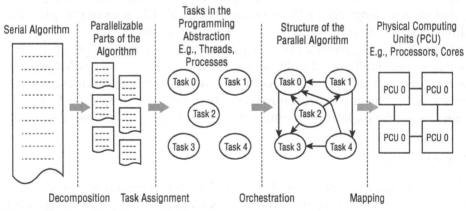

Figure 1-3: Steps in making a parallel program

Decomposition

Algorithms operate over data domains such as a range of values, list of files, table of columnar data, and graph of connections. The famous *wordcount* algorithm, for example, works over a list of words as its data domain. Also, the representation (list, table, matrix, graph) and the number of domains an algorithm may use can be more than one.

The task of decomposition is to identify subdomains of data, where the actions on each of them can happen concurrently with synchronization at the boundaries. Going back to the same *wordcount* example, the list of words could be split into multiple lists such that counting of words can be carried out over these subdomains independently.

A careful reader may notice that a synchronization step is required to arrive at the final output. We elaborate on this in the orchestration phase.

Task Assignment

Once the subdomains are identified, the next step is to pick suitable asynchronous constructs offered in the chosen programming language or framework. Multithreading is one such parallel construct supported by almost all programming languages. Using threads can become tedious, but it allows for sharing the address space of the parent process. This makes it easier to share boundary conditions or perform synchronizations.

Subprocesses are another way to parallelize parts of the algorithm. This would follow the opposite end of the memory model, where nothing is shared between processes unless through explicit message passing. We defer the discussion of such differences in memory models to a later section of this chapter.

While threads and processes can be thought of as low-level concurrency constructs, there are many other high-level idioms available depending on the programming language or the framework. OpenMP,[1] for example, provides directives such as `#omp parallel for` to control concurrency.

Message Passing Interface (MPI)[2] exposes processes as the unit of concurrency and provides a multitude of methods to communicate between them. MapReduce frameworks such as Apache Hadoop[3] utilize two concurrent primitives, *map* and *reduce*, with a specific synchronization pattern between them. Apache Spark[4] provides similar high-level primitives that are more general than *map* and *reduce*.

Orchestration

This step is tightly connected with the previous task assignment. The idea is to synchronize control and data between various tasks in the parallel algorithm. To illustrate this, consider a *wordcount* process carried out by N tasks, where the original wordlist is split equally among them. Each task will independently produce a table of words with counts for the respective sublist of words.

---

[1] https://www.openmp.org/
[2] https://www.mpi-forum.org/
[3] https://hadoop.apache.org/
[4] https://spark.apache.org/

At the end of this computation, the count tables need to be merged to get the global word count. This step introduces a synchronization point, which is an essential part of the parallel program. In a distributed setting, one such orchestration could be as simple as gathering all individual tables in a single place and performing a *hashtable* update over all of them. Note, this approach may require improvements to scale well if the number of unique words exceeds the memory limits of a single machine.

While the previous example is about synchronizing data, orchestration could also be done to synchronize control. A simple *fork-join* region is a good way to highlight this. In this common pattern, a single task would come to a point and spawn several other tasks to perform a parallel region in the code. Once the parallel tasks are complete, the control falls back to a single task. The parallel program needs to guarantee this control synchronization for the correct execution of the parallel algorithm.

Like task assignment, the choice of programming language or framework may provide the building blocks to perform synchronization between tasks. In fact, they may even allow for high-level constructs such as *parallel for*, *fork-join*, *reduce*, *gather*, *broadcast*, etc.

Mapping

The final stage when developing a parallel program is to map its execution onto physical computing units such as CPU or accelerator cores (GPU, FPGA, TPU). It should be noted here that the choice of mapping should not affect the correctness of the program unless owing to erroneous programmer assumptions on the task placement. What it could affect, though, is the performance, primarily due to nonuniform memory access (NUMA) costs and intercore data transfer costs.

For instance, in a compute-intensive multithreaded region of the code, it would be better to bind individual threads to separate CPU cores accessing memory local to them, as opposed to letting the OS determine thread placement, as well as using shared data structures across threads. As such, while the scheme of task mapping may not change the correctness, it is important to bear these nonuniform performance costs in mind when structuring the program and its execution.

K-Means Algorithm

Previously we mentioned the steps necessary to make a parallel application from a serial one. Let us apply this method to our *K-means* example and derive a parallel version from it.

The first step is to identify the things we can do in parallel. The core of the program revolves around the convergence loop in line 8. The resulting iterations are dependent on previous ones, so we cannot run them in parallel. However, the loop that runs over points in line 10 is easily parallelizable. In fact, the body of that loop is independent for each point, so we call it *pleasingly parallelizable.* Thus, we can use independent tasks to compute the body for each point.

There are a few other places where we can parallelize in this program, such as the distance computing loop in line 14, initialization operations in lines 4 and 5, and center update loop in line 25. However, we will continue providing a *parallel* loop to replace line 10. In pseudocode, the following replacement is what we want:

```
for (const Coord & p: points)  →  parallel for (const Coord & p: points)
```

The next step is to determine tasks. Even though we can execute the logic for each point in parallel, it is not advantageous to have separate tasks for each point. Instead, it is usually best to split the number of points among a set of tasks much smaller than the total points.

We determine communication among these threads in the third step. Examining the body of the loop reveals that centers have read-only access, so we do not need to synchronize their usage. Adding to the newCenters vector, however, needs to be synchronized as multiple threads will be accessing this.

The fourth step will determine how these tasks are mapped onto hardware. As we are using threads for tasks, we can let the OS take care of thread placement for this example.

Now, with our understanding of how to replace the serial for loop with a parallel equivalent, we present a simple implementation here. Lines 10 through 23 in the serial example can be replaced with the following:

```
std::mutex mtx;
uint32_t numPointsPerThread = numPoints / numThreads;
std::vector<std::thread> tasks;

for (int idxT = 0; idxT < numThreads; ++idxT)
{
    uint32_t pointOffset = idxT * numPointsPerThread;
    tasks.push_back(std::thread([&] {
        for (int idxP = pointOffset; idxP < numPointsPerThread; ++idxP)
        {
            for (const Coord& c : centers)
            {
                auto dist = points[idxP].DistanceTo(c);
                if (dist < minDist)
                {
                    minDist           = dist;
                    minDistClusterIdx = clusterIdx;
                }
                ++clusterIdx;
            }
            std::lock_guard lock(mtx);
            newCenters[minDistClusterIdx].AddPoint(points[idxP]);
        }
    }));
}
```

```
for (auto& task : tasks)
{
    task.join();
}
```

The first line declares a mutex, which we will later use to guarantee mutually exclusive access to the `newCenters` vector. The second line splits the number of points among threads, assuming divisibility without fractions. This is not necessarily required but makes the code easier to present.

Line 3 introduces a vector to the threads to keep track of our tasks. We push a new thread to it in line 8. The work carried out by each task is presented as a lambda function, the body of which (lines 9 through 22) is like the original `for` loop we had in the serial code. However, each task is now responsible for only a chunk of the total points. Line 21 is where we use the mutex to safeguard the access of the shared `newCenters` vector.

The advantage of this parallelization is that the code can now deal with larger numbers of points than the serial code, as multiple threads will be handling the points' space in parallel. The extra burden on the developer to carefully orchestrate the tasks is a downside. This is amplified when parallelization happens over distributed tasks, and with complex communication among them. For example, the same *parallel for* loop using distributed processes would have required explicit messaging to exchange process-local updated centers. Also, phases such as initialization would need to broadcast the same random seeds to preserve the validity of the algorithm.

The approach taken here to mutually exclude threads is not the most efficient, as threads must go through this lock for each point. A better method would have been to have thread-local vectors keep track of updated centers. Then at the end of the *parallel for* loop, the main thread could reduce these local vectors to get the final `newCenters` vector.

It is also worth mentioning that this is not the cleanest way to introduce a *parallel for* loop using threads. OpenMP, for example, provides a more streamlined directive-based parallelization of loops, which would have simplified the code. Still, the intention here is to present the basics of parallelization for a serial code and understand its pros and cons.

Parallel and Distributed Computing

An often overlooked distinction is the difference between parallel and distributed computing. Parallel computing is commonly associated with scientific applications running on high-performance computing (HPC) clusters. By contrast, applications like airline ticketing systems and messaging applications that run over loosely coupled distributed computing resources are presented as canonical examples for distributed computing applications.

While it may seem that parallel and distributed computing are worlds apart, we want to bring to your attention that such differences are because these examples tie an application or use case to a system that supports its implementation. To elaborate, let us take the same *K-means* example. If one were to parallelize it following the steps given earlier in Figure 1-1, that would only produce the parallel *K-means* application. We would need the underlying distributed system, be it Apache Spark or MPI, to execute this application over distributed resources.

This notion of a separate parallel program and its backend system blurs when we move on to regular distributed computing applications such as airline ticketing systems. There, the entire system is designed to do one application or use case, which in this instance is to let people reserve airline tickets. If we were to separate this use case from its implementation, we would begin to see similarities between such distributed systems and those systems that support parallel computing applications. Fundamentally, they both are distributed computing systems, except the former is designed to run parallel applications over distributed resources, while the latter is a distributed system targeting a specific use case.

Memory Abstractions

Developing and working with parallel programs can be quite challenging. Even a single application can have multiple parallel implementations. Moreover, a single parallel implementation can follow many patterns in different parts of the program. In this regard, a fundamental factor that helps to decide the "shape" of parallel tasks is the choice of memory model. This entails how parallel tasks access data among themselves or how the logical address space is split among tasks. In this regard, there are four fundamental memory abstractions.

Shared Memory

Shared memory provides a unified view of the memory for all the parallel tasks of a program. This enables data sharing across tasks directly without requiring special data-sharing function calls.

Each task in a shared memory model perceives the same logical view of a continuous and shared address space as depicted in Figure 1-4. Typically, shared memory systems are implemented within a single computer, where CPUs share a memory bus with the system memory.

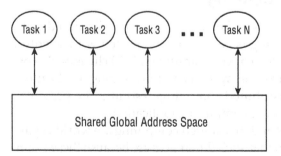

Figure 1-4: The logical view of the shared memory model

It is also possible to implement the same memory abstraction over distributed memory as shown in Figure 1-5. However, such distributed shared memory systems are not often used in practice.

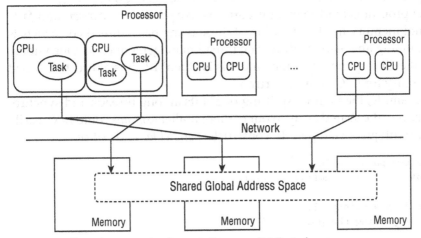

Figure 1-5: Shared memory implementation over distributed resources

We will focus on the shared memory model within a single device, as it is the most common. Threads are the typical implementation of this model. As shown earlier in the parallel *K-means* code, a thread is created by passing a function that it will execute during its lifetime.

The following snippet shows thread creation in C++ using an anonymous function. This will cause the operating system to schedule another instruction stream corresponding to the body of the lambda.

```
std::thread t([]
{
    std::count << "Hello from thread "
            << std::this_thread::get_id() << std::endl;
});
```

The syntax looks similar in Java as well, despite minor differences. One thing to note is that in Java, an explicit start() call is required to schedule the thread, whereas in C++, creation of the thread with a function automatically schedules its execution.

```
Thread t = new Thread(() ->
{
    System.out.println("Hello from thread " + Thread.currentThread
.getName())
}, "1").start();
```

Every program has at least one thread that runs the `main()` method. Therefore, if the main thread or any other thread needs to wait until the completion of another thread, it must issue a `join()` call on the target thread. For instance, assuming the main thread wants to wait on `t`, it needs to do `t.join()`.

Parallel programs tend to exhibit patterns like *parallel for, barrier,* and *fork-join.* Shared memory implementation of these using basic thread constructs is time-consuming and leads to duplicate thread management code. One widely used parallel library meant to alleviate this is OpenMP.[5] It is a directive-based parallel library for C, C++, and Fortran.

As an example, the manual splitting of points among threads and synchronizing access to the shared array in our earlier parallel *K-means* could have easily been done with just two OpenMP constructs: *parallel for* and *critical*.

```
#pragma omp parallel for
for (int i = 0; i < numPoints; ++i)
{
    Coord& p = points[i];
    /* body using the point p */
    ...
#pragma omp critical
    newCenters[minDistClusterIdx].AddPoint(p);
}
```

In this listing, `#pragma omp parallel for` is shorthand for creating both a parallel region and a loop. OpenMP will spawn multiple threads and split the `for` loop among these threads. The number of OpenMP threads can be set using runtime arguments. Since we access a shared vector, we can use `#pragma omp critical` to indicate serialized access to this vector.

While libraries such as OpenMP ease the development of multithreaded programs, there are still many general challenges with parallel and distributed computing. We will explore some of them in a later section.

Distributed Memory

Distributed memory plays the opposite role as shared memory, in that it shares nothing between tasks by default. Any kind of data sharing must be explicitly communicated via messages. Figure 1-6 shows the logical view of distributed memory model.

Figure 1-7 shows an implementation of this over distributed resources. The immediate effect of a distributed memory model is the segmented address space. Moreover, as tasks share nothing, the programmer is presented with a local view of computing that, when run as a collection of cooperating processes, needs to yield the expected global view of the computation.

---

[5]https://www.openmp.org/

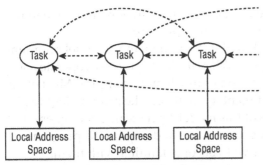

Figure 1-6: The logical view of the distributed memory model

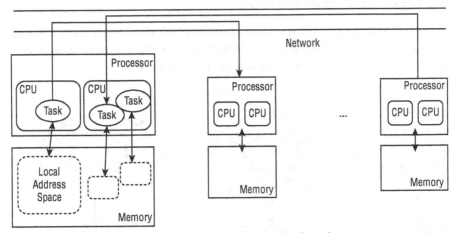

Figure 1.7: Distributed memory implementation over distributed resources

The main advantage of this model is that it is not restricted to a single machine like the shared memory model. Therefore, distributed parallel applications always use a form of distributed memory model. It also removes the lock-based synchronization in shared memory. Moreover, issues such as false sharing [4] do not happen with this model as nothing is shared.

From the discussion up to this point, it may seem that distributed memory model is superior to the shared memory model. However, it also comes with its own set of complications, especially given that it is used in computation models such as bulk synchronous parallel (BSP) [5] or task graphs (TGs). We go into detail about BSP and TGs in Chapter 5.

A primary shift in programming paradigm is the loss of a global view of computing. For example, in the *parallel for* exercise, the main thread had all the knowledge about the complete dataset and the total iterations needed. If we were to do something similar with distributed memory, we would find a set of independent processes that are programmed to operate on a chunk of the loop iterations and arrays local to them. There is no entity that has global knowledge of the program except for the programmer. If these processes need to capture the global view of, for example, the local arrays, then they would have to use explicit messaging to share that state with other processes.

The next issue that comes up is debugging. Shared memory model programs can be debugged using a local debugger. When multiple processes operate using the distributed memory model, this becomes much more complex. Most often, programmers would fall back to rudimentary methods like printing logs to pinpoint issues coming from programs of this model. Specifically, debuggers such as TotalView and DDT exist, but they are not free and require the programmer to go through a separate learning curve to become familiar with them.

Hybrid (Shared + Distributed) Memory

Despite the programming complexities, the distributed memory model is still widely used. Moreover, it is often combined with shared memory model, creating a hybrid memory model as represented in Figure 1-8.

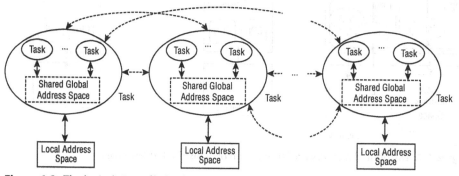

Figure 1.8: The logical view of hybrid memory model

This type of hybrid model is commonly used to achieve shared memory intranode parallelism while having internode distributed memory. In implementation terms, this is commonly referred to as an MPI+X model, where X stands for the shared memory parallelism implementation. A popular pattern is to use MPI+OpenMP.

One compelling reason to favor a hybrid model is that it reduces the number of communicating processes. For example, if there were 12 cores in a CPU and 128 of such machines, an all-MPI collective will have 12 × 128 = 1,536 processes communicating with each other. In an MPI+X implementation, communications typically happen only within internode MPI processes, so if we were to spawn a single process on each core, we would only have 128 communicating processes. This is an order of magnitude less than the previous case. This does not necessarily mean the overall performance will be better. Getting the best of both worlds in terms of performance in this model requires intricate work from the programmer.

Partitioned Global Address Space Memory

A key advantage of shared memory is the ability to share data between tasks without explicit messaging. The Partitioned Global Address Space (PGAS) [6] model provides a variant of this model over distributed resources.

Each parallel task in the PGAS model has two separate address spaces visible in Figure 1-9. The first is local to the task, and the second is shared among all tasks. The shared space is partitioned, meaning that data that a particular task allocates in the shared memory is assigned to that task.

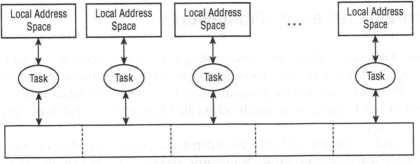

Partitioned Shared Address Space

Figure 1-9: The logical view of PGAS memory model

To better understand the details of these two different memories, let us look at the example shown in Figure 1-10. Tasks 1, 2, and 3 each allocate a private variable x. Task 1 additionally has another private variable y. Task 3 has allocated a shared variable z. All three tasks have access to a shared array *arr*. The variable z is assigned to the partitioned memory of Task 3. Similarly, chunks of *arr* are assigned to corresponding Tasks 1 through 3.

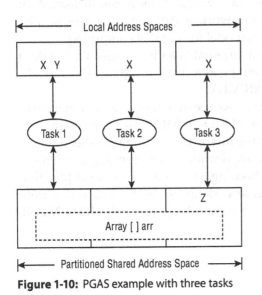

Figure 1-10: PGAS example with three tasks

There are several languages and libraries that implement this model. Unified Parallel C (UPC) [7] is one of the most familiar implementations. A variant of the PGAS model, called Asynchronous PGAS (APGAS), is also available in the literature. Chapel [8] is the only actively developed APGAS language.

While there is merit and productivity aspects to both the PGAS and APGAS models, they are not as popular among industry users as the other three models. Data-intensive systems use a simplified version of the PGAS model with distributed data abstractions seen in frameworks like Apache Spark and Flink.

Application Classes and Frameworks

We can think of batch and streaming processing as two broader classes of data-intensive applications. A stream processing application can be thought of as an assembly line where different stages do different tasks while the data is moving through it. A batch application, on the other hand, works on a batch of data already collected.

There are many subclasses of batch data-intensive applications such as machine learning, deep learning, and extract, transform, and load. These require frameworks and APIs optimized for their domains. Streaming applications tend to be more general, and we do not see subclasses that demand different types of processing. Within a streaming application, however, we can run batch processing by collecting data records.

Parallel Interaction Patterns

In our histogram example, we were running the same program multiple instances. It turns out that doing so is one of the ways we can achieve parallelism. As in our example, instances of these programs work on different data. This is called the *single program multiple data* (SPMD) model for parallel computing.

In some applications, we need to run different tasks in parallel. We can think of this as multiple SPMD programs running as a single program. This model is called *multiple program multiple data* (MPMD).

Beneath the APIs and execution models we see in data-intensive frameworks, we can still classify them as running in SPMD- or MPMD-style programs. We categorize applications depending on the interactions among parallel tasks [9]. Figure 1-11 shows four data-intensive application classes ranging from simple to complex parallel patterns. When choosing a framework for an application, we have to identify whether that framework supports the required parallel pattens by the application. These patterns are orthogonal to SPMD or MPMD as we can use them for all varieties.

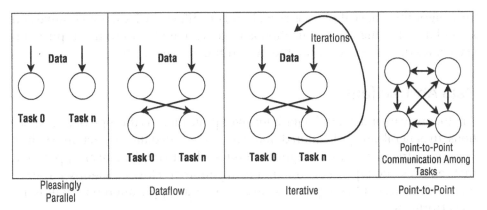

Figure 1-11: Four application classes

Pleasingly Parallel

Pleasingly parallel applications consist of tasks that do independent work without any coordination between them. This is the simplest form of parallel processing possible and the easiest to implement. Any data processing framework capable of spawning tasks can support pleasingly parallel applications.

Since tasks are independent, they can be scaled easily to many nodes. Fault tolerance is easy because if a task fails, we only need to restart that task to a previous state.

Dataflow

These are applications with some form of coordination between tasks achieved by exchanging data between them. Streaming applications and batch extract, transform, load (ETL) applications fall under this class. Streaming applications have some differences compared to batch ETL applications.

Iterative

Iterative applications possess what we call *parallel loops*. Inside a parallel loop, the tasks need to coordinate, and the output of each loop is fed back into the next. Mathematical optimization problems require such parallel loops. Many machine learning algorithms need iterations. Usually these algorithms are executed using main memory compared to disk-based computations. These are harder to support at scale compared to the dataflow and pleasingly parallel options.

Irregular

Irregular applications have point-to-point communication between tasks that are highly uncoordinated. Graph algorithms can be implemented in this fashion.

Such algorithms have iterations as well. So, the difference between iterative and irregular is that the communication is uncoordinated. Out of the application classes we discussed, these are the most difficult to get right.

Data Abstractions

Another way to understand data-intensive applications is through data abstractions. In general, an application domain needs certain data abstractions such as tensors, matrices, vectors, and graphs. It is not ideal to implement an application that requires one type of abstraction using another. How efficiently a framework can represent the required abstraction for an application will determine its performance.

To write applications, we need operations around data abstractions. For example, deep learning frameworks are implemented on tensor abstraction by implementing operations necessary for them. Frameworks like Spark are built around table abstractions with the required operations for manipulating tabular data. So, it is not just the data abstraction but the operations around it that make a framework useful.

Data-Intensive Frameworks

Data-intensive frameworks are designed to support various application classes. They provide abstractions to hide the details such as resource management, parallel process spawning, running tasks, and messaging. The application programming interface (API) of a framework provides data abstractions and operations. Depending on the applications a framework is built for, they can handle a subset of the parallel patterns we described earlier.

Components

A data-intensive framework consists of a set of components to provide the functionality of an application as mentioned earlier. They are:

- **API**—Data abstractions and operations to develop applications.
- **Resource management**—Acquire resources, spawn processes to do the computations in parallel.
- **Messaging**—Provide communication between parallel processes.
- **Tasks**—Schedule and execute the user program on the processes.
- **Fault tolerance**—Failure handling.
- **Monitoring**—Provide statistics and monitoring of applications.

Not every framework has all the abstractions we discussed here, as a certain number of them left out some functionality. For instance, a few frameworks do not provide fault tolerance or monitoring capabilities. Others do not offer task-based executions and allow users to program them as needed.

Ideally, we need frameworks that support required parallel patterns and data abstractions to develop our applications. Most frameworks include ways to develop custom data abstractions. When dealing with these abstractions, we need to think about how efficiently we can use them over the network to scale our applications to many computers. Some frameworks provide the needed functions to define data abstractions not supported by default, but they do not allow users to develop custom network operations.

Unlike data abstractions, if some parallel patterns are not supported by a framework, it is harder to implement algorithms requiring them. When developing a data-intensive application using a programing API provided by a framework, we may not be exposed to the details about how tasks interact with or communicate each other. But still, they will use these components out of sight to execute the applications.

Workflows

A real-world data processing application consists of many smaller programs to perform tasks such as data preprocessing, machine learning, data post-processing, and visualization. These programs are developed using different frameworks and programming languages, possibly by different teams within an organization. The data dependencies between these individual programs tie them together.

We can define a workflow as a sequence of programs (tasks) connected by data dependencies. Given such a set of programs, a workflow engine orchestrates the execution in the available computing resources according to data dependencies. Workflow systems for scientific computing applications [10] have been around for some time, and they are becoming an integral component in data-intensive applications as well. Data pipelines is another term used for identifying data-intensive workflows. Systems such as Kubeflow[6] and Apache Airflow[7] are some examples of workflow systems that support data-intensive applications.

An Example

Figure 1-12 shows an example workflow where we run a model training using both deep learning and machine learning libraries. The initial program in the workflow loads a dataset, cleans it, and transforms it. The next two programs transform this initial data so that we can train a deep learning system and machine learning system. Afterward, we train the two models and at the end, choose the best of the two.

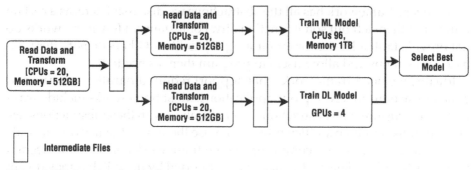

Figure 1-12: An example workflow

Applications running in a workflow can be written in different programming languages and may need specific resources to execute at runtime. For example, deep learning systems need GPUs, while a machine learning system runs on CPUs. Each application can have its own CPU and memory requirements. Workflow systems provide mechanisms to specify applications using domain-specific languages (DSLs) and graphical user interfaces. We can use general-purpose programming languages such as Python to specify workflows as well.

Workflow systems can persist the data after each application finishes. It is a clean separation between tasks with an external storage for holding the intermediate data. Depending on the available compute resources, workflow engines can choose optimal plans to execute the tasks in parallel or sequentially according to the data dependencies.

It is important to make the distinction between tasks of a parallel program and those of a workflow. A task for a workflow system is usually a program such as a machine learning algorithm. This algorithm may need to run in multiple computers, and it may internally run as a set of tasks. These internal tasks to the machine learning algorithm are fine-grained and are usually developed using a programming API supporting parallel execution. As a result of the central coordination of workflow systems, it is not efficient to use them for programming such detailed tasks.

What Makes It Difficult?

Despite their performance benefits, parallel data-intensive applications can be challenging to implement. Producing a parallel algorithm itself is a daunting task even for moderately complex applications. We will take a step forward

---

[6]https://www.kubeflow.org/
[7]https://airflow.apache.org/

and look at some of the implementation challenges, both when running locally using multiple threads as in a shared memory model and when running on distributed resources.

Developing Applications

Designing and developing parallel applications to get good performance requires skill and experience. We may not get the desired performance due to the characteristics of the algorithm or load imbalances.

Concurrency

The concurrency available within an algorithm might be limited, and we may get the desired performance when running in parallel. This can be due to high communication overheads between parallel workers, or we may not be able to divide work equally to parallel processes. The overheads in some frameworks for different classes of algorithms can also make it harder to develop efficient parallel applications.

Realistically speaking, extracting concurrency of an application is more than just applying a veneer over the serial code. It could require redesign of the algorithm, which at the end would result in parallel code that might not even resemble the serial algorithm. A good example of this is the popular parallel prefix operation implemented in GPUs. In serial code, this could be expressed simply as $B[i] = B[i-1] + A[i]$ for $1 < i < N$ elements, where N is the total number of elements. However, parallelizing this operation is not straightforward due to the data dependency of a previously computed value ($B[i-1]$). For instance, NVIDIA GPU kernels follow a sophisticated parallelization introduced by Blelloch,[8] which is drastically different from the serial code.

In many cases, we cannot directly parallelize the serial code. Instead, we may need to select approximation algorithms that have better parallel performance. Even data parallel deep learning training can be thought of as a relaxation over the batch size to yield better parallelism.

Developing parallel applications requires extensive experimentation to measure performance and make improvements. Even for the best parallel algorithms, when we increase the parallelism beyond certain limits, they do not increase the performance compared to the resources we add.

---

[8]https://developer.nvidia.com/gpugems/gpugems3/part-vi-gpu-computing/chapter-39-parallel-prefix-sum-scan-cuda

Data Partitioning

We need to divide the data among parallel processes equally to balance the load. If data is not partitioned correctly, some parallel processes may have more work assigned to them, reducing the performance of the entire application. Trying to divide the work equally can be a costly operation for some applications.

Debugging

Finding software bugs is one of the biggest challenges in large-scale applications. Timing issues that can occur only when running at scale are the hardest to pinpoint. There can be deadlocks that prevent applications from progressing. Most of these bugs are difficult to catch with regular debugging methods and need special tools that can work in parallel settings. We often rely on experience and improvised methods such as printing values when debugging such applications.

Diverse Environments

Public clouds and bare-metal hardware clusters are the main computing platforms available for data-intensive applications. Within these environments there are many hardware and software options available that make it challenging to build applications working across them.

There are numerous mechanisms available to manage computer resources, such as container-based systems, virtual machines, and bare-metal clusters. Additionally, various programming languages, data storage systems, and data formats are among the many technologies that data-intensive applications need to work effectively. Providing performance and usability while working across a diverse set of resources is one of the biggest obstacles data-intensive frameworks face.

On the one hand, these details are somewhat hidden from data-intensive application programmers, as frameworks take care of the details. But we need to configure the systems, deploy them, and make sure they run correctly in these environments.

On the other hand, as a framework developer, this means the framework design must be extensible to support various backends, communication libraries, schedulers, and job managers, all while providing best performance for the applications developed on top of it. We can see that early big data frameworks such as Hadoop tend to be a monolithic provider for all these aspects, which is inefficient and hard to maintain. Nowadays these frameworks employ more pluggable designs where one might use different job managers with the same framework.

Computer Networks

Communication overheads are one of the biggest factors that reduce the performance of parallel applications. Using correct communication operations that can optimally deploy the networking hardware available increases the performance of applications.

There are various networking hardware solutions available that offer different performance and services to the applications. Programming high-performance data-intensive applications utilizing the full power of these networking services is a challenge. Fortunately, most of the networking details are hidden, but still we need to find the best configurations and choose the correct primitives for our applications.

A messaging implementation can be synchronous or asynchronous. Synchronous messaging operations such as send/receive wait until they complete. Messages are guaranteed to be delivered within a time limit. In such a system, we can develop applications much more easily. Asynchronous operations immediately return before they complete at the other end. Mechanisms such as callbacks are used to determine their completion. We cannot guarantee messages will be delivered within a time limit.

Data-intensive systems use asynchronous messaging to achieve high performance. In such a system, messages can arrive arbitrarily late. This makes it harder to detect and handle faults.

Synchronization

When multiple processes or threads work in a single application, we need ways to access shared resources without conflicts, as well as keeping data used by distributed parts of the applications synchronized. Synchronization is the general term used to describe a set of techniques to achieve this.

There are two main types of synchronization in parallel programs. First, when data in memory is shared with multiple threads, we can use signaling between threads to synchronize access to data. Second, when data is distributed among processes, we depend on messages to pass data between the processes and keep data coherent or protect their integrity. Let us look at these two approaches in a bit more detail to understand why they are important. We will also dive more deeply into these in later chapters.

Thread Synchronization

Thread programming is a valuable addition to any programmer's toolbox. Threads are used in hybrid memory applications as described earlier. When programming with threads, synchronization is an essential aspect. Without synchronization, a program that accesses/modifies shared variables using threads can produce different answers based on the operating system's choice of thread scheduling at a given time. This is known as a race condition, which is notoriously hard to track down because reproducing the same execution order of threads is not possible. It is also worth noting that thread synchronization can be hard to get right for complex programs while preserving the performance.

A region of the program that needs exclusive execution by a single thread at a time is called a *critical region*. To ensure this exclusive access, programming languages and frameworks provide certain techniques and abstractions. Mutexes, semaphores, spinlocks, and monitors are the most commonly available. Depending on the way threads are used, several types of mutual exclusion primitives should be set up. Chapter 7 goes into greater depth about threads and how they affect data-intensive applications.

Data Synchronization

Imagine we are doing a computation using n parallel processes. Every process is assigned an exclusive dataset and performs the calculation on this dataset. After the calculation finishes, each process has a variable C that is local to it. Now, assume every process needs to get the sum of these local variables in different processes. This is data synchronization to get a global view of all the variables. In a distributed setting, the only way to achieve this is to use messaging. We have seen two methods for this in our current systems.

- **Parameter server**—This is a technique designed to achieve distributed synchronization by keeping the data that is shared among parallel processes in a central server. Owing to the single point, parameter servers do not scale well when a substantial number of compute nodes are used.

- **Collective communication**—Instead of using a central server to synchronize the data, the parallel processes can work together to share the data. There are efficient methods designed around this approach to make it scale to thousands of parallel processes [11]. We will discuss collective communication operations further in Chapter 6.

To explain the parameter server approach at large scale, imagine C in our example is an array of size 100MB and we have 1,000 processes (n). When they need to synchronize the local updates to this data, they must send them to the parameter server, which amounts to 100MB × 1,000, or 100GB. If the machine hosting the parameter server has a 100Gb/s network connection, in the best case, it will take about 8 seconds to send the data. Furthermore, a parameter server needs to process the 100GB of data it receives. Nowadays, parameter servers are rarely used for large-scale parallel computing problems. As an alternative, we rely on collective communications.

Ordering of Events

Compared to our clocks at home, computer clocks are highly accurate, but even this accuracy is not enough for us to rely on when dealing with multiple computers. When working on a single computer, we always have a single clock as a reference, and this clock can only increase the time it keeps, allowing us to have a total ordering of events. But even this argument can be incorrect when used in machines with multiple cores.

In distributed systems, we rely on causal ordering of events. We can only reason about ordering of events among parallel processes if there are messages between them. Let us assume we have two processes. Event A happens in Process 0 and sends a message to Process 1. Upon receiving this message, Process 1 does Event B. Now we know that Event A happened before B. If there was no messaging between Processes 0 and 1, we cannot guarantee the ordering of the events and need to consider them as concurrent.

Faults

A distributed system consists of many components, any one of which can fail independently of the others and cause the entire application to crash. For some applications, failure upon a fault is not acceptable. To handle faults, a distributed system needs to detect and handle them appropriately.

- **Detect the failure**—Because of the distributed nature, it is harder to determine whether a component failed or is just slow, making failure detection a challenging issue. We need to employ many different mechanisms, such as monitoring and messaging, to detect a failure.

- **Recover from failures**—Once a failure is detected, a distributed system needs to either terminate or continue to work. To continue executing under a failure, it must make many other choices. For example, can it continue to process with data loss or not? It will need to make sacrifices in some aspects of the system functionality to continue to work, such as performance.

There are many techniques available to detect failures and still run despite them. Popular methods used by data processing systems are discussed in Chapter 9.

Consensus

When multiple processes work on a single problem, they sometimes need to come to an agreement about a single data value. This is called the *consensus problem*. If there are no failures in the system and everyone is behaving as expected, it is an easy matter. But if some of the processes fail or are unreliable (provide false information), the algorithms used for achieving consensus must be failure resistant. The only way to achieve consensus in a distributed setting is through messaging. A consensus algorithm inherits all the other challenges we have discussed, such as asynchronous messaging and not being able to rely on clocks.

A consensus algorithm should have the following three properties:

- **Termination**—The system must agree on the correct value eventually.

- **Validity**—If all the correctly functioning processes propose a value, they should choose that value.

- **Agreement**—Every correct process should agree on the same value.

Data analytics is done with secure computer clusters inside organizations. These computers are not exposed to the outside world, and it is rare to see such machines be compromised and act incorrectly, producing bogus values. Because of this, most data analytics systems do not consider rogue processes in the system. Many algorithms have been developed to achieve consensus; Paxos [12] and Raft [13] are two of the most widely used practical examples.

Summary

Whether it is learning from data or simply querying or transforming data, we need to harness the power of many computers working together to efficiently execute them in a timely manner. This involves designing parallel versions of algorithms and executing them in multiple computers. Efficiently executing data applications at scale can be a challenging task. Many of the details are abstracted out in frameworks and libraries. We need to have a better understanding of what happens underneath these implementations to fully decide about our applications.

In this chapter, we introduced you to serial applications and the challenges in making them run in a distributed parallel setting. The next chapters will go through each of the areas we discussed that are critical to running data-intensive applications at scale.

References

1. M. Li et al., "Scaling distributed machine learning with the parameter server," in *11th {USENIX} Symposium on Operating Systems Design and Implementation ({OSDI} 14)*, 2014, pp. 583–598.

2. G. A. Wilkin and X. Huang, "K-means clustering algorithms: implementation and comparison," in *Second International Multi-Symposiums on Computer and Computational Sciences (IMSCCS 2007)*, 2007: IEEE, pp. 133–136.

3. D. Arthur and S. Vassilvitskii, "k-means++: The advantages of careful seeding," *Stanford*, 2006.

4. J. Torrellas, H. Lam, and J. L. Hennessy, "False sharing and spatial locality in multiprocessor caches," *IEEE Transactions on Computers*, vol. 43, no. 6, pp. 651–663, 1994.

5. T. Cheatham, A. Fahmy, D. Stefanescu, and L. Valiant, "Bulk synchronous parallel computing—a paradigm for transportable software," in *Tools and Environments for Parallel and Distributed Systems*: Springer, 1996, pp. 61–76.

6. M. De Wael, S. Marr, B. De Fraine, T. Van Cutsem, and W. De Meuter, "Partitioned global address space languages," *ACM Computing Surveys (CSUR)*, vol. 47, no. 4, pp. 1–27, 2015.

7. T. El-Ghazawi and L. Smith, "UPC: unified parallel C," in *Proceedings of the 2006 ACM/IEEE conference on Supercomputing*, 2006, pp. 27–es.

8. B. L. Chamberlain, D. Callahan, and H. P. Zima, "Parallel programmability and the chapel language," *The International Journal of High Performance Computing Applications*, vol. 21, no. 3, pp. 291–312, 2007.

9. J. Qiu, S. Jha, A. Luckow, and G. C. Fox, "Towards hpc-abds: An initial high-performance big data stack," *Building Robust Big Data Ecosystem ISO/IEC JTC*, vol. 1, pp. 18–21, 2014.

10. Y. Gil *et al.*, "Examining the challenges of scientific workflows," *Computer*, vol. 40, no. 12, pp. 24–32, 2007.

11. R. Thakur, R. Rabenseifner, and W. Gropp, "Optimization of collective communication operations in MPICH," *The International Journal of High Performance Computing Applications*, vol. 19, no. 1, pp. 49–66, 2005.

12. L. Lamport, "Paxos made simple," *ACM Sigact News*, vol. 32, no. 4, pp. 18–25, 2001.

13. Z. Wang, C. Zhao, S. Mu, H. Chen, and J. Li, "On the Parallels between Paxos and Raft, and how to Port Optimizations," in *Proceedings of the 2019 ACM Symposium on Principles of Distributed Computing*, 2019, pp. 445–454.

Data and Storage

Modern computing is a data-driven undertaking, with global enterprises accumulating petabytes of data that need to be stored and queried to extract valuable knowledge. Before the advent of big data technologies, we used file systems or relational databases for this purpose, but with datasets now in the petabytes scale and beyond, relational database management systems and traditional file systems cannot scale. Distributed file systems, NoSQL databases, and object storage systems are used today to handle these large datasets.

In this chapter, we will go through important concepts for data and storage. Since the main focus of this book is on data processing, we will keep our discussion limited to cover the most important topics.

Storage Systems

Storage systems are the platforms on which modern enterprises are built. They contain petabytes of data serving applications running nonstop. We have seen many types of storage systems over the years developed to support specific use cases and the demands of various applications. Because of this, we must consider many factors when choosing storage systems. In the era of large data, the first factor we need to take into account is how much data we are going to handle along with cost versus performance considerations.

There are numerous storage media available, including tape drives, hard disks, solid-state drives (SSDs), and nonvolatile media (NVM). Hard disks can be in disk arrays in RAID configurations to provide fault tolerance and increased I/O performance. A hard drive in our laptop is a block storage device that stores data in blocks of 512 bytes. As users, we never see the blocks because we access it through a file system created on top of the hard drive. The file system abstracts the block storage and provides a uniform API to facilitate data retrieval.

Furthermore, the type of access pattern we use for our data plays an important role. We may need to access data all at once, sequentially, randomly, or in a streaming fashion part by part. Also, we need to consider the type of data we store such as binary files (video, photos), text files, and whether we need to update the data after storage. Another aspect of a storage system is choosing between local and network storage. Local storage is attached to a computer, while in network storage the data can be in another computer that we access through the network. It all comes down to whether we need to share data among applications and users.

Storage for Distributed Systems

A computer cluster can be configured to access storage using three different methods. They are direct-attached storage (DAS), network-attached storage (NAS), and storage area networks (SAN). Figure 2-1 shows how these different storage systems are attached to a computing cluster.

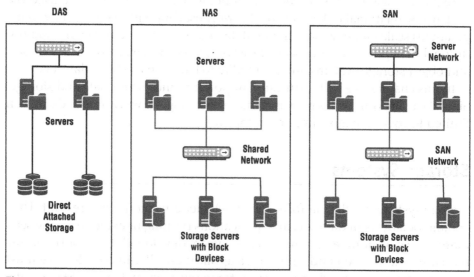

Figure 2-1: Three ways to connect storage to computer clusters: direct-attached storage (left), network-attached storage (middle), storage area networks (right).

Direct-Attached Storage

Direct-attached storage is where a disk is attached to a computer directly. A laptop hard drive is a DAS storage. There are many protocols and hardware needed to attach disks to a computer, such as SATA, eSATA, NVMe, SCSI, SAS, USB, USB 3.0, and IEEE 1394.

If the server holding direct-attached storage goes down, that storage is no longer accessible to the other nodes. To avoid this problem, network-attached storage systems were developed. In NAS, multiple storage servers are connected to the compute servers using the regular network. Since NAS systems use a regular network, the data movement can create a bottleneck. As a result, storage-attached networks were developed with separate network access.

Hadoop File System (HDFS) is a distributed file system specifically designed to run on servers with direct-attached storage. In-house big data systems still find direct-attached storage-based clusters the most cost-effective solution for handling large amounts of data.

Storage Area Network

Instead of managing hard drives in each machine, we can put them in a central server and attach them to multiple computers through the network as block devices. In this mode, the individual machines will see storage as block storage devices, but how they are matched to the actual hard drives can be hidden. This method of attaching block storage through the network is called storage area network (SAN).

SAN uses dedicated networks from the storage to the compute nodes to provide high-speed access. The storage space is seen by the host as a block device. We can create a file system and store data here similar to a local hard drive. SAN storage servers come with sophisticated options that allow automatic replication and failure recovery. They can use disk arrays to speed up the I/O speeds. A SAN can be divided into the host layer, fabric layer, and storage layer, as shown in Figure 2-2.

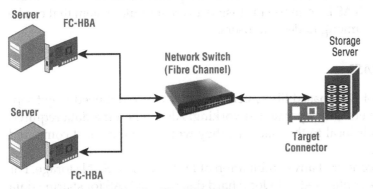

Figure 2-2: SAN system with a Fibre Channel network

- **Host layer**—The host layer resides in the servers that use the SAN storage. These servers are equipped with network devices called host bus adapters that connect the server to the SAN.

- **Fabric layer**—The fabric layer is responsible for bringing data from a host (initiator) to a target such as a port on a storage server. The fabric layer consists of network devices such as switches, routers, protocol bridges, gateway devices, and cables. There are many methods available to transfer data from host layer to storage layer, and while some of these are specific to SANs, sometimes they can use generally available networks as well. Depending on the network interfaces there are several protocols available to transfer the data between host and storage. Table 2-1 lists the different network channels and the protocols available.

Table 2-1: Storage Area Network Channels and Protocols

CHANNEL	PROTOCOLS	SPEED
Fibre Channel	Fibre Channel Protocol, NVMe-oF	32 Gbps
InfiniBand	iSER, NVME-oF, SRP	100 Gbps
Ethernet	iSER, NVME-oF, iSCSI	100 Gbps

- **Storage layer**—The storage layer consists of the servers that host the storage devices of the SAN. Usually, many disks are combined in RAID configurations to provide both redundancies and high throughput. A SAN can have many types of storage systems in it such as NVMs, tape storage, and hard disk drive storage.

Network-Attached Storage

Compared to SAN, with network-attached storage [1] the user sees the remote storage as a mounted file system rather than a block device. NAS uses regular network hardware to connect to the storage servers. Network File System (NFS) and Server Message Block (SMB) are two of the protocols made to access files over the network. NAS is common in clusters to create a file system that can be used to share files among nodes and users.

DAS or SAN or NAS?

The advantages of DAS-based file systems are that we do not need to get separate storage servers and separate networking. Also, when the data required by computations is local to the machine, they work extremely fast compared to a NAS or SAN.

A cluster may consist of any combination of DAS, NAS, or SAN storage. For example, it can be configured with local hard disks and a NAS for sharing data among users. Another option could be a DAS/NAS/SAN hybrid where SAN is used to host the data for a relational database management system (RDBMS). Compared to NAS, SAN solutions provide high-bandwidth and low-latency access, but they are usually expensive as opposed to having local hard disks in machines or NAS systems. But the lines between NAS and SAN can be blurred due to various hardware options available. For instance, NAS can run on high-speed networks that are equal to a network you might see in a SAN system.

Storage Abstractions

Depending on the requirements, servers can access the storage using a block abstraction, a file system, or as objects (Figure 2-3). Usually, file systems are created on top of block storage, and object storage can use a file system or block storage to access the data.

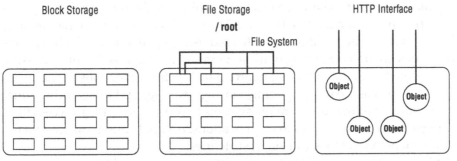

Figure 2-3: Storage abstractions: block storage (left), file storage (middle), object storage (right)

Block Storage

This manner of storage saves data blocks. A block storage can place the data blocks into different hard drives. Depending on the abstractions, the user may not notice where they are physically present. Block storage is normally associated with SAN and DAS systems. On-premises clusters use SAN technologies to create block devices in the compute nodes or use directly attached hard drives. Directly using the block storage is done only in special applications that require the best performance possible.

Block storage is popular in cloud environments for hosting persistent data from virtual machines. Without persistent storage, a virtual machine would lose all its work when it is terminated. In clouds, technologies such as SAN used by block storage are not visible to the users. Here are some examples of block storage services in cloud environments:

- **AWS Elastic Block Storage (EBS)**[1]—EBS is raw storage exposed as a block device to virtual machines. We can create these devices with personalized configurations (size, etc.) and attach them to EC2 instances, or even create a file system on the attached storage device and use it from the EC2 instances to store data.

- **Azure Disk Storage**[2]—The same as EBS, premium storage is low-latency disk support for I/O intensive workloads in Azure virtual machines.

- **Google Persistent Disks**[3]—As with other services, Google Persistent disks provide a network-attached block storage for virtual machine instances.

File Systems

File systems are by far the most popular abstraction for storing data. There are hundreds of file systems available that work inside a single machine, across many machines, or even between machines in different data centers. A file system gives a file abstraction to store the data. The data is organized into hierarchical folders and stored in files that are addressed using a path name, which is a hierarchical designation consisting of the folders and the name of the file. File APIs are associated with the POSIX standard, which defines functions for basic file operations such as creating, opening, closing, reading, updating, and writing. POSIX standard allows different file systems to use similar APIs to access files, making it easier to create portable applications. An application can access a file as a stream of bytes, blocks, or set of structures.

A file system is divided into logical, virtual, and physical layers.

- **Physical layer**—This layer provides access to specific storage media such as hard disk and tape.

- **Virtual layer**—At this level, different file systems are developed to organize and manage the data in the physical layer. There are many file systems including EXT4, NTFS, etc.

- **Logical layer**—Many virtual file systems can be combined in a single file system view (root) to give access to files.

We are all familiar with the file systems at work in our local machines allowing access to the internal hard drives of the computer. A file system can be created on top of storage devices residing in a networked set of machines. NAS systems expose files through the network.

---

[1] https://aws.amazon.com/ebs
[2] https://azure.microsoft.com/en-us/services/storage/disks/
[3] https://cloud.google.com/persistent-disk

In cloud environments, there are virtual file systems that can be attached to virtual machines. Here are some of the file services available:

- **AWS Elastic File System (EFS)**[4]—EFS is a virtualized networking file system (NFS) available to virtual machines.

- **Azure Files**[5]—This is a virtualized networking file system available over the SMB protocol.

Object Storage

Object storage [2] stores data in a flat structure compared to the hierarchical structure in file storage. Object storage is used for storing large amounts of unstructured data such as text files, audio files, sensor data, and video files. These data do not have any structure associated with them to put them in places such as databases. Object storage has become the standard for keeping backups and archiving the data. Thanks to their flat structure, they can scale to store petabytes of data, and compared to file storage, they are easy to manage at that scale.

The storage unit in an object storage is called an *object*. An object stores the actual data along with metadata and has a unique identifier in the form of a URL or a text string. Object storage allows a rich set of metadata to be associated with the objects, and this information can be used for searching. There is no hierarchical structure in object storage systems such as folders as seen in file systems because everything is in a flat structure.

Clients typically use an HTTP-based RESTful API to access the objects. A RESTful API has methods such as PUT, POST, GET, and DELETE. The API uses the PUT and POST methods to create new objects, GET to retrieve them, and DELETE to delete objects. Usually, clients are provided to hide some of these details. RESTful APIs allow object stores to be accessed from anywhere with an internet connection such as a mobile device. Object storage is usually categorized as write once read many (WORM) storage as they do not allow updates to the existing objects.

Object storage is common in public and private clouds. There are object stores that can be deployed in in-house clusters as well. For the user, it is not obvious how the objects are stored on the disks. Object storage can use file systems or block storage to house data.

Data Formats

We encounter data in many different formats. Some common examples are CSV, JSON, XML, Text, and Binary types. Every format has a defined storage structure.

---

[4]https://aws.amazon.com/efs/
[5]https://azure.microsoft.com/en-us/services/storage/files/

CSV, JSON, and XML are all text-based formats. They define the structure using other text elements. For example, in a CSV file, the attributes are separated by a marker such as a comma. Most data formats have some mechanism to define a schema. Schemas provide a mechanism to understand a document.

JSON and XML are two of the most popular data formats used for transferring data among distributed systems like web-based services and clients. Text formats take more space to store and more processing power to parse but are easier to work with because they can be inspected by regular text editing tools. For larger files that require more compact and efficient storage mechanisms with the ability to search faster, there are binary file formats such as Parquet and Avro.

XML

XML stands for Extensible Markup Language. It has a hierarchical format for storing data. XML documents contain elements, attributes, and values. An element can contain other elements as well as attributes. The following is a simple XML document. In this example, the top element is called message and is enclosed in <>. Every element has an ending tag with the syntax </>. The header element has an attribute called contentType.

```
<message>
  <header contentType='text'>
  <to>serviceX</to>
  <from>clientY</from>
</header>
<body>Hello from client</body>
</message>
```

XML can optionally have a schema attached to a document. The schema specifies the structure of the document and constraints on the data. For instance, it can specify that the document has a message element with two elements called header and body one after another (in order). Furthermore, it can specify constraints such as how a name cannot contain special characters. If a document is presented with only one element inside the message element, we can reject it as an invalid document according to the schema. Here is the corresponding schema for the previous XML document:

```
<xs:schema attributeFormDefault="unqualified" elementFormDefault="qualified"
xmlns:xs="http://www.w3.org/2001/XMLSchema">
  <xs:element name="message">
    <xs:complexType>
      <xs:sequence>
        <xs:element name="header">
          <xs:complexType>
            <xs:sequence>
              <xs:element type="xs:string" name="to"/>
```

```
            <xs:element type="xs:string" name="from"/>
          </xs:sequence>
          <xs:attribute type="xs:string" name="contentType"/>
        </xs:complexType>
      </xs:element>
      <xs:element type="xs:string" name="body"/>
    </xs:sequence>
  </xs:complexType>
</xs:element>
</xs:schema>
```

XML was the dominant method of data transfer in the early days of web-based services. Many companies joined together to create a set of specifications around XML to shuttle data between services and client programs. SOAP [3] and WSDL [4] were some of the standards created around XML with this initiative. SOAP defines a message format with a header and a body for encapsulating a network message. WSDL is a specification to describe a service along with the request and response formats of the messages. These standards allowed any framework to read messages originating from a client as long as they adhered to the standard specifications. There are many other standards such as Extensible Stylesheet Language Transformations (XSLT) [5] for specifying transformations on XML data and XPath [6] for addressing parts of XML documents.

XML parsing is a relatively time/resource-consuming task because of its verbosity as well as the constraint enforcement. As a result, it requires more space to store it, and people have moved away from XML to a much simpler JSON format that is easier for machines to parse and humans to understand.

JSON

JavaScript Object Notation (JSON) is the most popular data format used in web services. Compared to XML, JSON is less verbose, but some can argue it is still complicated. JSON is used mostly with REST services on the web, which is the dominant form of defining services. A JSON document has two main structures. The first is a collection of name-value pairs, and the second is an ordered list of values. The following is a JSON document for the same XML message we described earlier. Note that the root message element is no longer needed, and the end tag is simplified to a closing bracket. header is an object that has a set of key-value pairs. body has only one value.

```
{
    "header": {
        "@contentType": "",
        "to": "serviceX",
        "from": "clientY"
    },
    "body": "Hello from client"
}
```

In most cases, the raw data coming from a user or an application will be in JSON or XML format. These data formats are not designed to be queried at large scale. Imagine having a large number of JSON objects saved in the file system. To get useful information, we would need to parse these files, which is not as efficient as going through a binary file.

CSV

Comma-separated values (CSV) is a text file format for storing tabular data. A table is a set of rows with columns representing individual attributes of rows. In a CSV file, each data row has a separate line. For every row, the values of columns are separated by a comma. Values are stored as plain text. The following is a comma-separated CSV file that shows the grades of students for different subjects they have taken. There is a header in the CSV file to label each column in the table.

```
"Name",  "Subject-1", "Subject-2", "Subject-3", "Subject-4"
"Joshua Johnson",   A+,   B+,   A,   B-
"Harry Wilson", A+,  A+,  A,  B
"Gerty Gramma", A+,  A+,  A,  A-
"Android Electric", A-,  B+,  C+,  B+
```

CSV is a popular data format for storing small to medium-scale data. Popular spreadsheet tools all support the loading and saving of CSV files as tabular data. Even though everyone is using CSV files, it is not a full standard. Different implementations can choose a host of methods to handle edge cases.

As an example, since CSV files are comma separated, a comma inside an attribute value needs to be handled independently. An implementation can choose to wrap values in quotation marks to handle commas inside a value. The same is true for line breaks within values. Some CSV implementations support escape characters to handle such cases as well. Other separators such as tabs, spaces, and semicolons are used in CSV files to separate the attributes. There is a specification called RFC4180 developed to standardize CSVs, but in practice, it is not 100 percent followed by the tools.

Since CSV is a text representation, it can take up a large amount of space compared to a compact binary format for the same data. We can have a CSV file with two integer columns to make our point. Assume our row has the following two integers:

```
7428902344, 18234523
```

To write that row as plain text, we need to translate each character into a character encoding value. If we assume ASCII format and allocate 1 byte for each character, our row will require 21 bytes (for each digit, line end character, delimiter, and space). By using a binary format, we need only 8 bytes to write the integer values, a reduction of more than half. Additionally, we cannot look up a value in a CSV file without going through the previous lines since every-thing is text. In a structured binary file, the lookups can be much more efficient. Nevertheless, CSV files are widely used because humans can read them and the rich set of tools available to generate, load, visualize, and analyze CSV files.

Apache Parquet

We can break up a table of data by storing the rows and columns in contiguous spaces. When storing rows, we refer to it as *row-wise storage*, and when storing columns, we call it *column-wise storage* or *columnar storage*. Parquet stores the data in the columnar format. It is a binary storage file format for tabular data. Let's take a look at a simple example to understand the columnar option.

Assume we have a table with two columns and five rows of data. The first column is holding a 32-bit integer value, and the second column has a 64-bit integer value.

```
First, Second
10, 123045663
23, 123043265
21, 145663663
22, 123063662
12, 123046362
```

In the case of CSV, we store this file as a plain text file. For binary we need to decide in what order we are going to store the data. Assume we choose row-wise. Figure 2-4 illustrates how this would look. Each row has 12 bytes with a 4-byte integer and an 8-byte integer. The values of each row are stored contiguously.

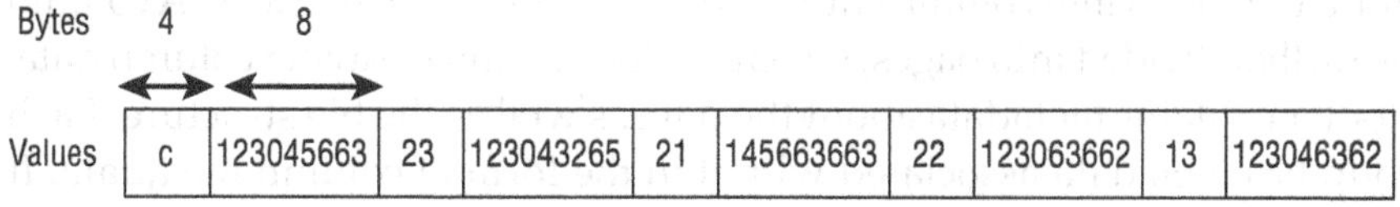

Bytes   4   8

| Values | c | 123045663 | 23 | 123043265 | 21 | 145663663 | 22 | 123063662 | 13 | 123046362 |

Figure 2-4: Storing values of a row in consecutive memory spaces

We can store the values of columns contiguously as well. Figure 2-5 shows the bytes when storing in this format.

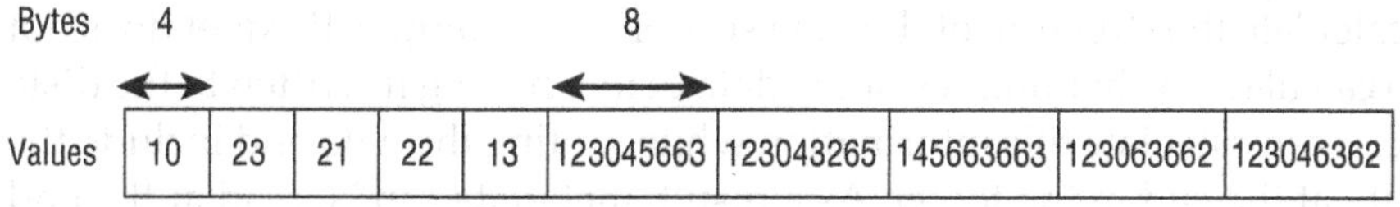

Bytes   4   8

| Values | 10 | 23 | 21 | 22 | 13 | 123045663 | 123043265 | 145663663 | 123063662 | 123046362 |

Figure 2-5: Storing values of a column in consecutive memory spaces

Both formats have their advantages and disadvantages depending on the access patterns and data manipulation requirements of the applications. For example, if an application needs to filter values based on those contained in a single column, column-based representation can be more efficient because we need to traverse only one column stored sequentially in the disk. On the other hand, if we are looking to read all the values of each row consecutively, row-based representation would be preferable. In practice, we are going to use multiple operations of which some can be efficient with row-wise storage and others with column-wise storage. Because of this, data storage systems often choose one format and stick to it while others provide options to switch between formats.

Parquet[6] supports the following data types. Since it handles variable-length binary data, user-defined data can be stored as binary objects.

- Boolean (1 bit)
- 32-bit signed integer
- 64-bit signed integer
- 96-bit signed integer
- IEEE 32-bit floating-point values
- IEEE 64-bit floating-point values
- Variable-length byte arrays

As shown in Figure 2-6, a Parquet file contains a header, a data block, and a footer. The header has a magic number to mark the file as parquet. The footer contains metadata about the information stored in the file. The data block forms the actual data encoded in a binary format.

The data blocks are organized into a hierarchical structure with the topmost being a set of row groups. A row group contains data from a set of adjacent rows. Each group is divided into column chunks for every column in the table. A column chunk is further divided into pages, which is a logical unit of saving column data.

The footer contains metadata about the data as well as the file structure. Each row group has metadata associated with it in the form of column metadata. If a table has N columns, there is N number of metadata inside the row group per column chunk. The column metadata contains information about the data types and pointers to the pages.

Since the metadata is written at the end, it allows Parquet to write the files with a single pass. This is possible because we can write the data without needing to calculate the structure of the data section. For example, Parquet does not need to calculate the boundaries of the data before having it written to the disk. Instead, it can calculate this information while writing the data and include the metadata at the end in the footer. As a result, metadata can be read at the end of the file with a minimal number of disk seeks.

---

[6]`https://parquet.apache.org/`

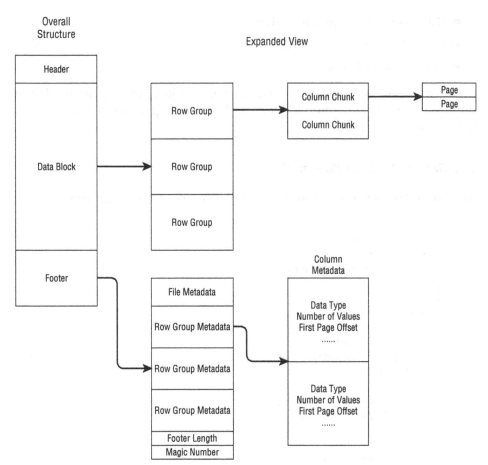

Figure 2-6: Parquet file structure

Apache Avro

Apache Avro[7] (or simply Avro) is a serialization library format that specifies how to pack data into byte buffers along with data definitions. Avro stores data in a row format compared to Parquet's columnar format. It has a schema to define the data types. Avro uses JSON objects to store the data definitions in a user-friendly format and binary format for the data. It supports the following data types similar to Parquet:

- Null having no value
- 32-bit signed integer
- 64-bit signed integer
- IEEE 32-bit floating-point values

---

[7]https://avro.apache.org/

- IEEE 64-bit floating-point values
- Unicode character sequence
- Variable-length bytes

We can use the Avro schema to code generate objects for easy manipulation of our data. It has the option to work without code generation as well. Let's look at the Avro schema.

Avro Data Definitions (Schema)

Here we can see a simple Avro schema to represent our message class:

```
{
  "name": "Message",
  "type": "record",
  "namespace": "org.foundations",
  "fields": [
    {
      "name": "header",
      "type": {
        "name": "header",
        "type": "record",
        "fields": [
          {
            "name": "@contentType",
            "type": "string"
          },
          {
            "name": "to",
            "type": "string"
          },
          {
            "name": "from",
            "type": "string"
          }
        ]
      }
    },
    {
      "name": "body",
      "type": "string"
    }
  ]
}
```

We first set the name, type, and namespace of the object. Our object's fully qualified name would be org.foundations.Message. Then we specify the fields. We have a header field and a body field. The header field is another record with three fields. The body field is of type string.

Code Generation

Once we have the schema defined, we can generate code for our language of choice. The generated code allows us to easily work with our data objects. Code generation is excellent when we know the data types up front. This would be the approach for custom solutions with specific data types. If we want to write a generic system that allows users to define types at runtime, code generation is no longer possible. In a scenario like that, we rely on Avro without code generation.

Without Code Generation

We can use Avro parsers to build and serialize Avro objects without any code generation. This is important for applications with dynamic schemas that are only defined at runtime, which is the case for most data processing frameworks where a user defines the type of data at runtime.

Avro File

When serialized, an Avro file has the structure shown in Figure 2-7. It possesses a header with metadata about the data and a set of data blocks. The header includes the schema as a JSON object and the codec used for packing the values into the byte buffers. Finally, the header has a 16-byte sync marker to indicate the end. Each data block contains a set of rows. It has an object count and size of total bytes for the rows (objects). The serialized objects are held in a contiguous space followed by the 16-byte marker to indicate the end of the block. As with Parquet, Avro files are designed to work with block storage.

Schema Evolution

Data can change over time, and unstructured data is especially likely to change as time goes by. *Schema evolution* is the term used to describe a situation in which files are written using one schema, but then we change the schema and use the new one with the older files. Schema evolution is something we need to carefully plan and design. We cannot change the old schema arbitrarily and expect everything to work. Some rules and limitations define what changes are possible for Avro:

- We can add a new field with a default value.
- We can remove a field with a default value.
- We can change, add, or remove the doc attribute.

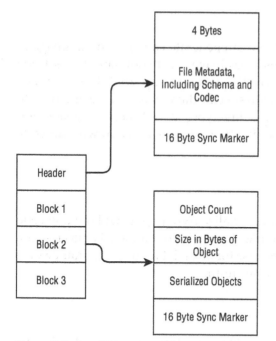

Figure 2-7: Avro file structure

- We can change, add, or remove the order attribute.
- We can change the default value for a field.
- We can change a nonunion type to a union that contains only the original type.

To change the schema like this, we need to define our original schema fields susceptible to change with the previous modification rules. For example, we must set default values if we are hoping to change a field.

Protocol Buffers, Flat Buffers, and Thrift

Protocol buffers,[8] Flat buffers,[9] and Thrift[10] are all language-independent, platform-neutral binary protocols for serializing data. Users of these technologies must define a schema file with the data structure of the objects they need. All these technologies have a compiler that generates source code in the programming language of choice to represent the objects defined.

---

[8] https://developers.google.com/protocol-buffers
[9] https://google.github.io/flatbuffers/
[10] https://thrift.apache.org/

We can use these as regular objects in our code. Once it becomes necessary to save or transfer them through the network, we can convert the objects into binary formats. The schema is embedded directly into the code generation and enforced by the program at runtime.

Here we have a definition for our message object with protocol buffers. The other formats all follow the same process.

```
message "header" {

  message HEADER {
    required string @contentType = 0
    required string to = 1
    required string from = 2
  }

  required HEADER header = 0
  required string body = 1
}
```

In the previous code snippet, we define a protocol buffer message with several fields. The next step is to generate a set of source files with our programming language of choice from these definitions. Once the files are generated, we use them in our program as regular objects. We can create our object, set values to it, and read values from it.

Data Replication

Replication is a technique used for keeping copies of the same data in multiple computers. We call a copy of the data in a computer a replica. We use replication to achieve the following:

- **Fault tolerance**—If one replica is not available, systems can continue to process requests from the other replicas.
- **Increased performance**—We can keep replicas in multiple regions as well as multiple computers within a single cluster. By staying close to the computers that access it, data can be served faster.
- **Scaling**—When data is in multiple computers, it can be simultaneously accessed by many users.

Keeping replicas is not as simple as copying data to multiple computers. If we have static data that does not change after the initial write, all we need to do is copy them to multiple computers at the initial write. We call such data *unimmutable* data. Some systems support this model, the most notable of which is the Hadoop File System. Even in these systems, the data needs to be rebalanced in case there is more load on one computer or when nodes fail. If we allow data to be modified, we will need to keep the replicas consistent when updates occur.

On the surface, it seems if a writer of a dataset takes t time units, it will require $3t$ time for replicating the data to three machines. Replicating the data can be done in a pipelined way that reduces this time drastically. This is shown in Figure 2-8 where a client usually sends data in some form of data chunks (streams), which can be pipelined through the replicas along with acknowledgments.

A system can choose synchronous or asynchronous replication. It can also

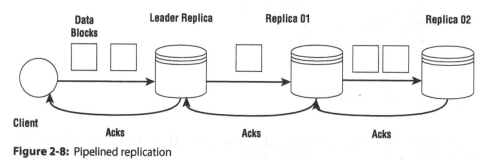

Figure 2-8: Pipelined replication

be designed as a single leader replication or multileader replication system. We may create a system with any of these combinations.

Synchronous and Asynchronous Replication

In synchronous (eager) replication systems, the system makes sure the replication is complete before sending a response back to the client for a write request. This means the client needs to wait until the replication is done, which can take time. For asynchronous replication systems, the server can immediately respond after the update is applied to the leader replica. With asynchronous replication, if an error occurs during replication, the client has no way of knowing whether its write has failed. Asynchronous replication is fast compared to synchronous, and with asynchronous replication, clients might see stale data when some replicas are not updated in time.

Single-Leader and Multileader Replication

In single-leader replication systems, the updates are controlled by a lone server acting as the leader. The replicas are called *followers*. Clients always connect to the leader to update the data. A client sends a request to update the data to the leader that in turn updates its copy. Now the leader needs to update the followers. A single leader may act as a bottleneck for handling large workloads, and if the data store expands across multiple data centers, single-leader replication systems will not scale.

As the name suggests, multileader systems can have multiple leaders at the same time. They permit simultaneous updating of the replicas. Allowing multiple clients to update different replicas is a complex process that requires careful coordination between the leaders. It can take a significant amount of resources and slows down the systems in general. Because of this, multileader replication is mostly used in systems that expand across multiple data centers. Replicating data across data centers in separate regions is a widespread practice for serving far-flung users.

If data is replicated in machines close to each other, a network failure or a power failure can make the data inaccessible, defeating one purpose of replication. To avoid such situations, data can be replicated in a way that reduces the probability of failures. For example, it can be replicated in multiple data centers.

Data Locality

Data locality comes from the general principle of the owner-computes rule in parallel computing. The owner-computes rule states that when a data partition is assigned to a computer, that computer is responsible for all the computations associated with the partition.

For a computer to work on a data partition, we need to load the data into the main memory of that computer. But what happens if the data is in another computer accessible only through the network? We would have to move that data through the network to the relevant computer. At the dawn of the big data revolution, network speeds were limited, and moving large amounts of data between computers was a time-consuming operation. It was much easier to move the computations to the computers with the data that they were going to operate for the sake of performance. This process of trying to reduce data movement is called *preserving* the data locality.

Data locality can come in many levels. The best-case scenario is that relevant data required by every task is in the computer that it runs on, thus having no need to move data through the network. But in practice this is harder to achieve. If the data is not in the same computer, it is better to at least store it in the same server rack where network speeds are faster.

Hard disk speeds have not increased as much as network speeds over the past decade. Current networks can send data much faster. Because of this, the value of data locality is greatly reduced in modern clusters. Furthermore, preserving data locality in a cluster shared with multiple applications is hard. Cloud-based object storage services that provide data as a service have further reduced the importance of data locality. Nevertheless, if conditions permit, preserving data locality can reduce the data read time significantly for applications.

Disadvantages of Replication

Even though replication has many advantages and is often used in distributed systems, it does come with some caveats.

- **Additional disk space**—Replicating data requires additional disk capacity. To add capacity, not only do we need more disks, we have to acquire additional computers and network bandwidth and extend the cluster to host the disks. Also, when more and more nodes are added to a cluster, distributed operations that span more nodes can become slow due to network communication overhead.

- **Updates are slow**—Multiple replicas need to be kept up-to-date. When an update happens to data, that update replication process can take considerable time depending on the type of replication chosen.

Data Partitioning

Imagine a large data collection we intend to process using multiple computers. We must first divide the data among computers so that they can work on part of the dataset. Data partitioning is the process of distributing data among multiple computers so that different computers/processes can act on them separately but simultaneously. When we consider data processing, partitioning comes under the broad umbrella of load balancing. Load balancing is always a hard problem to tackle in distributed computing.

Reasons for partitioning data include the following:

- **Scalability**—The data is distributed among many computers, allowing larger data sizes that do not fit into one machine to be processed in parallel.

- **Performance**—The data can be processed in parallel using multiple computers, reducing the overall compute time and increasing the amount of data processed per unit.

- **Provide operational flexibility**—Data can be partitioned according to different needs of the applications. One example is to partition data according to how old they are. New data can be given more priority in both processing and storage, while old data can be stored using cheaper methods.

- **Availability**—When data is present in multiple computers, even if part of a machine goes down, other parts of the data can be still available.

Depending on the data abstraction like a table or an array, different data partitioning techniques can be used. Because most data are stored as tables, let's look at horizontal, vertical, and functional partitioning methods for table data. We will use Table 2-2 as an example.

Table 2-2: Original Dataset with Four Rows

ID	DATE	CONTENT	URL	AUTHOR
984245	2020-01-13	{json content}	http:://jsonc.io/one	Ted Dunken
245213	2019-11-02	{json content}		AB Foundation
532134	2019-12-05	{json content}	http:://jsonc.io/now	Nethan Salem
556212	2020-02-09	{json content}	http:://jsonc.io/oxy	

Vertical Partitioning

Vertical partitioning divides the data table vertically into different sets of columns and stores them separately. Tables 2-3 and 2-4 show a vertical partitioning of our table where we included the first three columns in one table and the first column along with the last two columns in another.

Table 2-3: First Table with Only First Three Columns of Original Table

ID	DATE	CONTENT
984245	2020-01-13	{json content}
245213	2019-11-02	{json content}
532134	2019-12-05	{json content}
556212	2020-02-09	{json content}

Table 2-4: Second Table With The First Column and the Last Two Columns from the Original Table

ID	URL	AUTHOR
984245	http:://jsonc.io/one	Ted Dunken
245213		AB Foundation
532134	http:://jsonc.io/now	Nathan Salem
556212	http:://jsonc.io/oxy	

Vertical partitioning can help to isolate data attributes that are used infrequently in queries from the ones that are used frequently.

Horizontal Partitioning (Sharding)

Horizontal partitioning (also known as sharding) is used extensively for partitioning data. Here we partition by the rows of the table. Tables 2-5 and 2-6 show how the data is partitioned according to the year.

Table 2-5: Horizontal Partition with the Year 2019

ID	DATE	CONTENT	URL	AUTHOR
245213	2019-11-02	{json content}		AB Foundation
532134	2019-12-05	{json content}	http:://jsonc.io/now	Nathan Salem

Table 2-6: Horizontal Partition with the Year 2020

ID	DATE	CONTENT	URL	AUTHOR
984245	2020-01-13	{json content}	http:://jsonc.io/one	Ted Dunken
556212	2020-02-09	{json content}	http:://jsonc.io/oxy	

The attribute or set of attributes used for partitioning the data is called the *partitioning key*. There are many strategies available in this respect. According to the requirements of the applications, we can choose from various partitioning schemes, and we describe a few here:

- **Hash partitioning**—Done by applying a hash function to the partitioning key. The simplest hash partitioning mechanism is to get the hash and then use the modules of the number of partitions. However, this method can produce imbalanced partitions for most practical datasets.

- **Range partitioning**—If a record is within a range, it is assigned to the partition for that range. For instance, in our previous example, we partitioned the data according to the date attribute. If we are using a numerical key for partitioning, it can be based on numerical ranges.

- **List partitioning**—This keeps a list of values for each partition. If an attribute has a value that belongs to a list, it is assigned to the corresponding partition. For example, if a city belongs to the list of cities in a country, the record is assigned to a partition for that country.

- **Composite partitioning**—We can use a combination of the previous strategies. We might first partition the data according to range partitioning, and within those partitions we use list partitioning to separate the data further. The same key or different keys can be used for composite partitioning.

- **Round-robin partitioning**—Consecutive records are assigned to consecutive partitions in a round-robin manner. This is one of the easiest ways to partition the data as no consideration is given to the data properties.

Hybrid Partitioning

Both vertical and horizontal partitioning are used on the same dataset. As such, we can partition data horizontally according to the year and vertically to separate the content column. This is shown in Tables 2-7 through 2-10.

Table 2-7: First Horizontal Partition of 2019

ID	DATE	URL	AUTHOR
245213	2019-11-02		AB Foundation
532134	2019-12-05	http:://jsonc.io/now	Nathan Salem

Table 2-8: Second Horizontal Partition of 2020

ID	DATE	URL	AUTHOR
556212	2020-02-09	http:://jsonc.io/oxy	
984245	2020-01-13	http:://jsonc.io/one	Ted Dunken

Table 2-9: First Vertical Partition

ID	CONTENT
245213	{json content}
532134	{json content}

Table 2-10: Second Vertical Partition

ID	CONTENT
556212	{json content}
984245	{json content}

Considerations for Partitioning

When multiple computers work on a single problem, it is important to assign an equal amount of work to each machine. This process is called *load balancing*. It is a concept applied to many distributed systems including services, data analytics, simulations, etc. Load balancing is especially important when multiple computers execute tasks in parallel.

In distributed data processing systems, one significant concern about data partitioning is how to distribute the data equally among machines. Without balanced partitioning, valuable computing resources can be wasted, and applications may take longer than necessary to complete. Load balancing the partitions is tied to both data and the algorithms used.

The following is a hypothetical example of four processes doing the same computation in parallel. Say we have a large dataset filled with numbers, and we are going to multiply individual elements of this dataset by a number and get the sum. Unfortunately, we did not divide the dataset equally among the four processes, and instead assigned 50 percent, 15 percent, 15 percent, and 20 percent to four processes. Assume it takes time *t* to process 1 percent of the dataset. As we can see, the work is not load-balanced across the four processes.

The processes take $50t$, $15t$, $15t$, and $20t$ time to complete. Since they are running in parallel, the application takes the slowest process's time to complete; in our example, it is $50t$. Now assume we instead divided the work equally among the processes, 25 percent apiece. In this case, each process will take $25t$ time to complete, a two times speedup over the previous work assignment.

For data applications, load balancing is closely associated with partitioning. Parallel processes in data processing systems work on partitions of the data. So, it is important to keep the data partitions roughly the same size.

NoSQL Databases

NoSQL database is a broad term used to identify any data storage that is not a relational database. Some NoSQL databases support SQL queries, so the term should not be confused with SQL. Even though there were databases not designed according to the ACID principles of RDBMS from the very early days of computing, NoSQL databases became mainstream with the big data movement starting in the early 2000s. NoSQL databases [7] are all developed to optimally store and query data with specific structures. Some are designed to scale to petabytes of storage, while others support specific data types in a much smaller scale.

Data Models

We can classify NoSQL data stores according to the data models they support. There are key-value databases, document databases, wide column databases, and graph databases.

Key-Value Databases

These databases store key and value pairs with unique keys. The model is quite simple and can store any type of data. They also support create, read, update, and delete (CRUD) operations and are referred to as *schema-less*. The datastore does not know about the data it has, and it is only available to the application. As a result, these data stores cannot support complex queries that require knowledge of the structure of the data stored. Nevertheless, many data problems fit into these data stores owing to their simplicity. Table 2-11 shows a sample data store with few key value pairs.

Table 2-11: Key Value Data Store

KEY	VALUE
K1	Data bases
K2	\<t>data\</t>
K3	{a: "1", k: "2"}

Document Databases

A document database stores data using semistructured formats like JSON documents. They can be thought of as key-value stores with a semistructured value. Since the data store has knowledge about the structure of the values, it can support complex queries. For example, we can query these databases with an internal attribute of a JSON object, which is not possible in a key-value database. Table 2-12 shows the data store for a document database with a JSON document.

Table 2-12: Document Store

KEY	VALUE (JSON DOCUMENT)

K1	{
	
	  "header": {
	
	    "@contentType": "", "to": "serviceX", "from": "clientY"
	
	  },
	
	  "body": "First message"
	
	}

K2	{
	
	  "header": {
	
	    "@contentType": "", "to": "serviceX", "from": "clientY"
	
	  },
	
	  "body": "Second message"
	
	}

Wide Column Databases

Wide column databases [8] have table-like structures with many rows each possessing multiple columns. Wide column databases should not simply be thought of as RDBMS tables with a lot of columns. Instead, they are more similar to multilevel maps, as shown in Table 2-13. The first level of the map is the key that identifies the row. The columns are grouped into column families. A column family can have many columns and is identified by a column key (which can be dynamic). Since columns are dynamic, different rows may have a different number of columns.

Graph Databases

Graph databases are designed to represent and query graph structures efficiently and in an intuitive way. We can use relational databases, document databases, and

Table 2-13: Wide Column Store

| KEY | FIRST COLUMN FAMILY | | SECOND COLUMN FAMILY | | |
	COLUMN KEY1	COLUMN KEY2	COLUMN KEY3	COLUMN KEY 4	COLUMN KEY 5
K1	--	--	--	--	--
K2	--	--	--	--	--

key-value databases to store graph data. But the queries as implemented on these databases are more complex. To simplify the queries to be more suitable for graph data, different query languages are used. Some popular query languages include Gremlin [10] and Cypher [9]. At the present time there is no standard query language such as SQL available for graph databases. A graph database can use a table structure, a key-value structure, or a document database to actually store the data.

CAP Theorem

CAP is a broad theorem outlining a guiding principle for designing large-scale data stores. It specifies a relationship between three attributes of a distributed data store called consistency, availability, and partition tolerance [11]:

- **Consistency**—Every read request will give the latest data or an error.
- **Availability**—The system responds to any request without returning an error.
- **Partition tolerance**—The system continues to work even if there are network failures.

Large-scale data stores work with thousands of computers. If a network failure divides the nodes into two or more subsets without connectivity between those subsets, we call it a *network partition*. Network partitions are not common in production systems, but they still need a strategy when one occurs. The theorem states that a distributed data store needs to pick between consistency and availability amid a network partition. Note that the system must select between the two only when a failure happens. Otherwise, the data store can provide both consistency and availability to its data. The original goal of CAP theorem was to categorize data stores according to two attributes they support under failure, as shown in Figure 2-9.

Let's examine why a system needs to pick between availability and consistency. Should a network partition occur, the system is divided into two parts that have no way to communicate with each other. Say we choose to make the system available during the network partition. While the network partition is present, a request comes to update a data record that is fed into a machine in one side of the partition. We wanted to make the system available, so we are going to update the data. Then another request comes to a machine on the other side of the network partition to read the same data. This machine has a copy of the

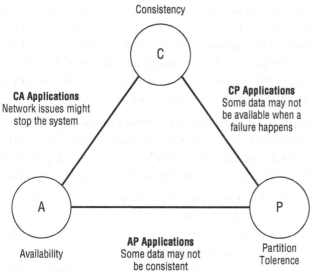

Figure 2-9: CAP theorem

data, but it is not updated with the latest version because we could not propagate the update. Since the second partition does not know about the update, it will return an old data record to the client, which makes the system inconsistent. Now if we choose to make the system consistent, we will not return the data for the second request because we do not know whether the data is consistent, making our system in violation of the availability constraint.

In practice, things are much more complicated than what the CAP theorem tries to capture, so CAP is more of a guiding principle than a theorem that clearly describes the capabilities of a system [12]. Some systems only have consistency guarantees in a network partition situation when operating under certain configurations. Most practical databases cannot provide either consistency or availability guarantees as stated in the theorem amidst failures. Furthermore, the CAP theorem is valid only under network partition scenarios, and there are many other failures possible in distributed systems. There is another theorem called PACELC [13] that tries to incorporate runtime characteristics of a data store under normal circumstances. The PACELC theorem states that under network partitions there is the consistency-availability trade-off, and under normal operation there is the latency-consistency trade-off.

Message Queuing

Message queuing is an integral part of data processing applications. Message queues are implemented in message broker software systems and are widely used in enterprises, as shown in Figure 2-10. A message broker sits between the data sources and applications that consume the data. A message source can be any number of things such as web users, monitoring applications, services, and devices. The applications that consume the data can again act as a data source for other applications. Because of this, message queuing middleware is considered the layer that glues together enterprise solutions. Message queuing is used in data processing architectures for the following reasons.

■ **Time-independent producers and consumers**—Without message queues, the producing applications and consuming applications need to be online at the same time. With message queues in the middle, a consuming application may not be active when the sources start producing the data and vice versa.

■ **Act as a temporary buffer**—Message queues provide a buffer to mitigate the temporal differences between message producing and message consuming rates. When there is a spike in message production, data can be temporally buffered at the message queue until the message rate drops down to normal. Also, when there is a slowdown in the message processors, messages can be queued at the broker.

■ **Transformation and routing**—Messages are produced by a cloud of clients that make a connection to the data services hosted in a different place. The clients cannot directly talk to the data processing engines because different clients produce different data, and these have to be filtered and directed to the correct services. For such cases, brokers can act as message buses to filter the data and direct them to appropriate message processing applications.

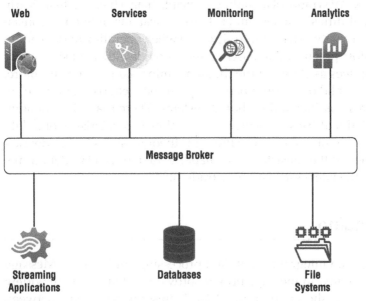

Figure 2-10: Message brokers in enterprises

Message queuing systems provide many functions to integrate different systems. These functions depend on specific implementations, but there are some attributes common in all message brokers such as message durability and transactional processing, to name a few.

Figure 2-11 shows a message queue in its most simplified form. There is a single producer and a consumer for the message queue. All the messages produced are received in that order by the consumer. But in reality, the picture is more complicated. There can be multiple consumers and producers, and the queue can be replicated across multiple nodes.

Figure 2-11: Message queue

The producers push (send) messages to the queue. Consumers can be pulling messages from the queue, or it can be pushing messages to the consumer. This choice of push or pull at the consumer affects how many consumers a queue can have. If the queue is pushing to the consumer, there can be multiple consumers in a load balancing group. When the consumers are pulling messages, it is harder to have multiple consumers. This happens because consumers do not work in synchronization to get the messages from the queue.

Message Processing Guarantees

A message broker can provide delivery guarantees to its producers and consumers. These guarantees include the following:

- **At least once delivery**—Messages are never lost but can be processed multiple times.

- **At most once delivery**—Messages may get lost, but they will be delivered only one time at most.

- **Exactly once delivery**—Messages are delivered exactly once.

Delivery guarantees are closely related to the fault tolerance of the system. If a queuing system is not fault tolerant, it can provide only at most once delivery guarantees. To be fault-tolerant, the systems can replicate messages and save them to persistent storage. The producers connecting to the message queue need to adhere to a protocol that transfers the responsibility of the messages to the queuing system. Also, the consumers need a protocol to transfer the responsibility of the messages from the queue. It is extremely difficult to provide exactly-once delivery guarantees in message queues.

Durability of Messages

Message queuing systems can store the data until they are successfully processed. This allows the queuing systems to act as fault-resilient temporary storage for messages. By saving messages to the persistent storage, they can keep more messages than otherwise permitted on the main memory. If the messages are kept in the disk of a single server and it goes down, the only way to recover those messages is by restarting that node.

Another way to ensure the durability of the messages is to replicate them to multiple nodes running the brokers, as shown in Figure 2-12. If the replicas are saved to persisted storage, it provides robust durability for the messages. Replication comes at a cost here as message systems expect to provide low-latency operations.

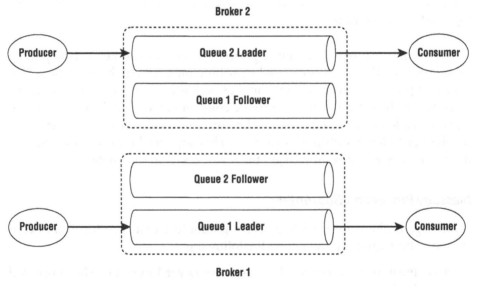

Figure 2-12: Message queue replication

Acknowledgments

An *acknowledgment* is a response message that indicates the processing status of a message. Acknowledgments help the producers and consumers of the messages to safely transfer the message responsibility. We can send acknowledgments for every message or for several messages at once.

Producers can choose among a few options:

- **Fire and forget**—The producer does not receive an acknowledgment after it sends the message to the broker. The message may get lost at the broker. This method offers the best performance.

- **With acknowledgments**—A positive acknowledgement from the broker means the message has been safely accepted by the broker and the client is no longer responsible for the message. A negative acknowledgment means the broker could not accept the message.
  Message consumers can also choose different types of acknowledgments to the broker:

- **No acknowledgments**—This offers at most once delivery to the consumers. The messages may get lost if errors such as network connection failures or consumer failures occur after the broker sends the message.

- **Auto-acknowledgments**—Messages are acknowledged without considering the processing at the consumer. If the message is acknowledged and the consumer fails before processing the message, it can lead to a lost message.

- **Manual acknowledgments**—Messages are acknowledged after they are processed by the consumer. If the consumer fails after processing the message but before it can send the acknowledgment, the message can be processed more than once at the consumer. Also, it can take an arbitrarily long time to process a message, and acknowledgments can be delayed.

Storage First Brokers and Transient Brokers

Message queues have been around for a long time, dating back to many years before the data revolution. These traditional message brokers were designed around transient messages where producers and consumers were online mostly at the same time and produced/consumed messages at an equal rate. Popular message brokers such as RabbitMQ[11] and Apache ActiveMQ[12] were all developed around this assumption. These brokers are neither designed to handle large amounts of data produced in a short period of time nor serve them to applications over a long period by storing them.

Owing to the large volumes of data involved in big data applications, storage first brokers were created. The first notable broker of this category was the Apache Kafka[13] broker. These store data in the disk before they are delivered to the clients. They use techniques to divide the queues into partitions so that data can be distributed across nodes. Transient brokers and storage first brokers are suitable for different applications and environments. Situations in which storage first brokers are best suitable include the following:

- Large amounts of data are produced in a small time window in which the consumers cannot process this data.

---

[11]https://www.rabbitmq.com/
[12]https://activemq.apache.org/
[13]https://kafka.apache.org/

- Consumers can be offline while large amounts of data are produced, leading to them being stored at the brokers.

- The data needs to be kept at the broker for longer periods to stream to different applications at separate times.

These are situations in which transient message brokers are best:

- Low-latency message transfer at the brokers.

- Dynamic routing rules at the message broker.

Both transient and storage first brokers are used in data processing systems depending on the use cases. But for handling large workloads, we would most likely need a storage first broker.

Summary

There is a vast amount of research and literature available in different databases, distributed file systems, and data formats. Data processing systems are tightly coupled to this data layer to read and write data. We discussed the low-level data storage systems, various data formats, NoSQL databases, and message brokers.

References

1. G. A. Gibson and R. Van Meter, "Network attached storage architecture," *Communications of the ACM,* vol. 43, no. 11, pp. 37–45, 2000.

2. M. Factor, K. Meth, D. Naor, O. Rodeh, and J. Satran, "Object storage: The future building block for storage systems," in *2005 IEEE International Symposium on Mass Storage Systems and Technology,* 2005: IEEE, pp. 119–123.

3. D. Box *et al.,* "Simple object access protocol (SOAP) 1.1," ed, 2000.

4. E. Christensen, F. Curbera, G. Meredith, and S. Weerawarana, "Web services description language (WSDL) 1.1," ed: Citeseer, 2001.

5. J. Clark, "Xsl transformations (xslt)," *World Wide Web Consortium (W3C). URL http://www.w3.org/TR/xslt,* vol. 103, 1999.

6. J. Clark and S. DeRose, "XML path language (XPath)," ed, 1999.

7. NOSQL Link Archive. "LIST OF NOSQL DATABASES." http://nosql-database.org/ (accessed June 5, 2010).

8. F. Chang *et al,* "Bigtable: A Distributed Storage System for Structured Data," presented at the OSDI, Seattle, WA, USA, 2006.

9. N. Francis *et al.*, "Cypher: An evolving query language for property graphs," in *Proceedings of the 2018 International Conference on Management of Data*, 2018, pp. 1433–1445.

10. M. A. Rodriguez, "The gremlin graph traversal machine and language (invited talk)," in *Proceedings of the 15th Symposium on Database Programming Languages*, 2015, pp. 1–10.

11. E. Brewer, "A certain freedom: thoughts on the CAP theorem," in *Proceedings of the 29th ACM SIGACT-SIGOPS symposium on Principles of distributed computing*, 2010, pp. 335–335.

12. M. Kleppmann, "A Critique of the CAP Theorem," *arXiv preprint arXiv:1509.05393*, 2015.

13. D. Abadi, "Consistency tradeoffs in modern distributed database system design: CAP is only part of the story," *Computer*, vol. 45, no. 2, pp. 37–42, 2012.

Computing Resources

Complex data analytics applications require multiple machines to work together in a reasonable amount of time. An application processing a large dataset needs to keep as much data as possible in the main memory of computers, but there are limits to a single machine, such as the amount of random access memory, hard disk space, and CPU power. As such, it is necessary to use many machines to execute applications when working on large datasets.

Nowadays even the tiniest home computer has multiple CPU cores, many gigabytes of memory, fast disks, and graphic processing units (GPUs). The simplest of programs use threads to utilize multiple CPU cores and thereby enhance the performance. In modern data centers, you will find powerful computers with many CPU cores, multiple GPUs, fast memory, and many disks.

Large computations need dedicated computing resources while they are executing. If critical resources such as a CPU core are shared between applications, they can see large performance reductions that are hard to investigate. To use the hardware resources efficiently for data analytics applications, we need deep knowledge about the inner workings of these resources and how they interact with each other.

Imagine we are starting with a data analytics project and bought a set of machines to store and process the data. The most probable first step would be to set up a distributed file system in the machines. Then it is time to develop and deploy the first programs to store the data and ideally get some insight. In the beginning, there are only a few applications, and they can be run one after another without interfering. All the machines are available all the time to execute the program as needed. As time goes on, people develop more applications that work on this data.

Now we need to coordinate between different developers to avoid executing the applications overlapping each other. If by accident two applications start to execute on the same resource such as a CPU, it can lead to an unexpected degradation in performance. Pinpointing the issue in a large set of machines can be difficult, as one overlapping computer may be causing a performance degradation for an entire application. To find the problem we may have to monitor the application in all the machines or send emails to all our co-workers asking whether they are also using the resources at the same time. Reasonably speaking, there is little chance of success pinpointing the problem in either case. And even if we do, we cannot guarantee it will not happen again in the future.

This has been an issue from the very beginning of cluster computing dating back to the 1980s. Eventually, computer scientists developed resource management software to efficiently allocate limited resources among applications. There are many forms of resource management software found in all types of large systems from clouds to high-performance computing systems. This software allocates computing resources to users or applications according to policies defined by organizations managing the resources and the application requirements. For example, when we request few virtual machines from a public cloud provider, a resource manager allocates them for a user. Application-level provisioners can be used after the resources are allocated or reserved for specific purposes. Apache Yarn is one example of an application-level resource manager for big data applications.

Data analytics frameworks hide the details of requesting computing resources and running applications on them. Application developers rarely need to consider the details of resource managers when designing. At the time of deployment, users can specify computing requirements of the application to the data analytics frameworks, which in turn communicate with the resource managers to satisfy those requests. Resource managers then make the scheduling decision of where to run the application by considering a range of factors such as computing nodes, racks, networks, CPUs, memory, disks, etc. Although most application developers are not concerned with the provisioning of resources for their applications, they should know about the type of computing environment in which the applications are deployed. There are many optimizations possible that can increase the efficiency of large-scale data applications by carefully considering the type of computing resources they use.

A Demonstration

As a test case, let's consider an application for detecting objects in images. Say we have a set of images and a few computers, and we want to develop an application that will efficiently identify objects in them, for instance, a car or a person. A simple application written using OpenCV, TensorFlow, and Python will satisfy this requirement. The most basic method is to run the resulting algorithm on a single computer as a sequential program that can go through images one by one in an input folder and label the objects in each.

The following is a simple Python program to detect objects in images using TensorFlow, Keras, OpenCV, and ImageAI libraries. This program assumes an images directory with images to examine and outputs the labeled images into an output directory.

```python
from imageai.Detection import ObjectDetection
import os

cpath = os.getcwd()

det = ObjectDetection()
det.setModelTypeAsRetinaNet()
det.setModelPath(os.path.join(cpath, "resnet50_coco_best_v2.0.1.h5"))
det.loadModel()

if not os.path.exists(os.path.join(cpath, "out")):
    os.makedirs(os.path.join(cpath, "out"))

for f in os.listdir(os.path.join(os.path.join(cpath, "images"))):
    img_path = os.path.join(cpath, "images", f)
    out_path = os.path.join(cpath, "output", f)
    detections = det.detectObjectsFromImage(input_image=img_path,
                                            output_image_path=out_path)

    for eachObject in detections:
        print(eachObject["name"], " : ", eachObject["percentage_probability"])
```

The program can be executed simply by typing the following command:

```
$ python3 detect.py
```

If the computer that runs the algorithm has multiple CPU cores and enough memory (which will be the case even for low-end computers nowadays), we can start multiple instances of the program at once to speed up the object detection process. We then divide the images into multiple folders and start program instances manually pointing to these folders.

So far everything looks good for a lone machine. Now it is time to think about how to use the rest of our resources. The manual method comes to mind first, where we can duplicate the single machine approach across multiple instances. This will work on a small scale. But when the number of machines increases, this approach becomes much harder, to the point where a human can't keep up. This is where a script can help to automate the process. The script can log into each machine using a secure shell (SSH) connection and start the processes. The files must be in the local hard drives of each machine or placed in a distributed file system accessible to all.

```
ssh machineIP `cd program_folder && source venv/bin/activate && python
detect.py` &
```

Multiple such commands for each machine can start and run our image detection program. Once the programs begin, scripts can check them for failures. If such a situation occurs without a mechanism to notify the user, the program may not produce the expected results.

This simple but important example assumes many things that can prove far more complicated in practice. For instance, most clusters are shared among users and applications. Some clusters do not allow users to install packages, and only administrators can install the required software. Even though our example is basic, we need to note that distributed programs and resource managers demand a more feature-rich version of what we have done so far.

Computer Clusters

Before the invention of the public cloud, clusters of physical machines were the only option to run distributed applications. Academic scholars used the supercomputing infrastructures provided by government agencies and universities. Companies had their clusters of machines to execute their applications, and most of the large computations were simulations. Some examples include physics simulations, biomedical simulations, and gene sequencing. These applications solve sets of mathematical equations by applying different optimization techniques. They start with relatively small amounts of data and can compute for days to produce answers even in large clusters. To run large applications, an organization needed to have an up-front investment of significant money and resources in the infrastructure.

With public clouds, large-scale computing is becoming a commodity where anyone can access a reasonably sized cluster in a matter of minutes to execute their applications. The previous model of dedicated physical machines is still used by government agencies and universities, as cloud performance for extreme-scale applications remains inadequate. Whether we are using public clouds or dedicated physical machine clusters, there are two broad situations in terms of application resource utilization. These can occur in either cloud environments or physical cluster environments.

In the case of a public cloud, we can allocate a set of machines to keep running a data cluster. This cluster can be used among many applications developed to work on this data. In such a case, it becomes a resource-sharing cluster. We can request a set of virtual machines every time we need to run an application. In this setting, it is a dedicated resource environment for the application.

The same applies to a physical machine cluster as well. We can purchase multiple machines to run a set of dedicated applications or share the physical cluster among many users, thus creating a resource-sharing environment. The latter is the mode used by supercomputers and large academic clusters. Organizations with requirements to host their own infrastructures can adopt either of these approaches depending on their applications.

There is a third option available for executing data analytics applications: cloud-based managed analytics engines. AWS EMR clusters and Google Cloud's cloud dataflow are examples of such managed clusters. Users are hidden from most of the details of the distributed environment, and only an application programming interface is exposed. These services use either dedicated clusters or resource-sharing clusters to meet the client's needs. However, in terms of understanding the underlying workings of data applications, this option is not relevant to our discussion.

Anatomy of a Computer Cluster

By definition, a computer cluster is a set of machines connected to each other by a network working together to perform tasks as if they are a single powerful machine. A computer in a cluster is often termed a *node*. Most clusters have a few machines dedicated to executing management-related tasks that are called *head nodes* or *management nodes*. The compute nodes do the actual computations. All nodes execute their own operating systems with their own hardware such as CPUs, memory, and disks. Often the management nodes and compute nodes have different machine configurations. Depending on the type of storage used, there can be dedicated machines for storing data, as shown in Figure 3-1, or storage can be built into the compute nodes, as shown in Figure 3-2. Usually, a dedicated network is used within the nodes of the cluster.

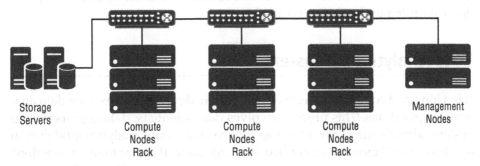

Figure 3-1: Cluster with separate storage

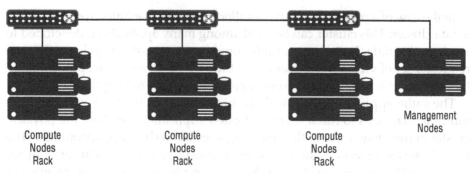

Figure 3-2: Cluster with compute and storage nodes

When assembling a cluster of machines in a public cloud, the storage can derive from a storage service offered by the cloud provider. The network can be shared among other machines not present in the cluster depending on the setting. In general, the topology of the networking and the location of the VMs are not visible to the user. Figure 3-3 shows a VM cluster setup with a storage service.

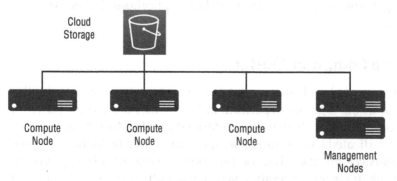

Figure 3-3: Cloud-based cluster using a storage service

SSH is the tool used to connect and execute commands in a cluster of machines. A user initially logs into a management node using an SSH connection. From there they can access the other nodes of the cluster. Depending on the access policies applied to the user, access can be restricted to other nodes. An application submitted to the cluster is called a *job*.

Data Analytics in Clusters

It is a long and complex undertaking to design, develop, and execute data analytics applications. This process involves data scientists, data engineers, and system administrators working together to create data analytics models that are then tested before being applied at a large scale. It is rare to see stand-alone data analytics applications without the support of distributed computing frameworks because of the complexities in developing them at a large scale. These frameworks provide APIs to program the applications and tools to execute and manage them. Once the applications are designed, they are further developed and tested in a local small-scale computer, such as a laptop, before being moved to larger environments like clusters and afterward into production clusters for even further testing.

Data frameworks supply different options for running applications depending on the nature of the resource-sharing environment. The dedicated cluster environment is the easiest to handle as it is not shared among many applications or users. We can think of a laptop as a dedicated resource environment for testing and development. Most frameworks provide a mechanism to run their applications in such a local environment. This mechanism is extended to run on a dedicated cluster as well. Table 3-1 shows some prominent data analytics frameworks along with options available to execute their applications on both shared and dedicated clusters.

Table 3-1: Data Analytics Frameworks and Resource Scheduling

FRAMEWORK	DEDICATED CLUSTERS	SHARED CLUSTERS
Apache Spark	Runs with a main program and set of worker processes on worker nodes. These main program and worker nodes manage the Spark applications.	Yarn, Mesos, Kubernetes
Apache Flink	Starts a set of processes called *manager* and *workers*. These manage the applications.	Yarn, Kubernetes
Apache Hadoop	Yarn is the default mode; can run in master, worker as in Spark or Flink.	Yarn
OpenMPI	Stand-alone jobs using SSH to launch.	Sun Grid Engine (SGE), and the open-source Grid Engine (support first introduced in Open MPI v1.2)
		PBS Pro, Torque, and Open PBS
		LoadLeveler scheduler
		Slurm
		LSF
		Yod (Cray XT-3 and XT-4)

Dedicated Clusters

At this point, we have seen systems adopting two approaches to start and manage applications. In the first one, every application is considered as stand-alone without any connection to other applications. The other method involves applications sharing resources in a dedicated environment using common processes. With this approach, applications for a particular framework have dedicated access, but alternative applications using the same framework can share the resources. Let's see how this approach is used in both classic parallel frameworks and big data frameworks.

Classic Parallel Systems

In classic parallel systems, an application is always thought of as a stand-alone entity. Here we see an example application and how it is run with four-way parallelism, first on a single node and then on two nodes. To run this program, we can install OpenMPI first:

```
$ sudo apt install libopenmpi-dev
```

Now we can use the following code written in C to run a test case. This program simply prints a message from each parallel process. Every process has a unique ID to distinguish itself from other processes.

```
#include <mpi.h>
#include <stdio.h>
int main(int argc, char** argv) {
    // Initialize the MPI environment
BatchTLink    MPI_Init(NULL, NULL);
    // Get the number of processes
    int world_size;
    MPI_Comm_size(MPI_COMM_WORLD, &world_size);
    // Get the rank of the process
    int world_rank;
    MPI_Comm_rank(MPI_COMM_WORLD, &world_rank);
    // Print off a hello world message
    printf("Hello world from process id %d out of %d processors\n",
world_rank, world_size);
    // Finalize the MPI environment.
    MPI_Finalize();
}
```

To compile the program we can use the following command assuming our program name is task.c.

```
$ mpicc.openmpi -o task task.c
```

Once compiled, the program can be run using the mpirun command:

```
$ mpirun -np 4 ./task
```

It will give the following output:

```
$ Hello world from process id 1 out of 4 processors
$ Hello world from process id 0 out of 4 processors
$ Hello world from process id 2 out of 4 processors
$ Hello world from process id 3 out of 4 processors
```

To run this example on two nodes, we need to install OpenMPI on both nodes and have `task.c` compiled and executable available on the same path for each. After meeting these requirements, we can use a file called `hostfile` to give the IPs/hostnames of the machines we are going to run on. Also, password-less SSH must be enabled on these hosts for the program to work across machines. The following is how a host file will look:

```
$ cat nodes
example.com.1 slots=2
example.com.2 slots=2
```

The first part of each line is the IP/hostname of the node. The slots config indicates how many processors we can start on the given node; in our case we set it to 2. This number depends on the number of CPUs available and how we use the CPUs in each process.

```
mpirun -np 4 --hostfile nodes ./task
```

It will again give the same output but will run on two machines instead of a single machine.

Big Data Systems

Big data frameworks are taking a mixed approach for dedicated environments nowadays. Some provide stand-alone applications, while others offer mechanisms for sharing applications in a dedicated environment. Apache Spark is one of the most widely used big data systems, so we will select it as an example.

Apache Spark cluster utilizes a master program and a set of worker programs. The master is run on a management node, while the workers run on the compute nodes. Once these programs are started, we can submit applications to the cluster. The master and workers manage the resources in the cluster to run multiple Spark applications within a dedicated environment. Figure 3-4 shows this architecture; arrows indicate communications between various components.

Spark applications have a central driver program that orchestrates the distributed execution of the application. This program needs to be run on a separate node in the cluster. It can be a compute node or another dedicated node.

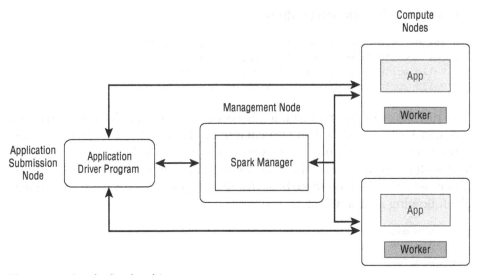

Figure 3-4: Apache Spark architecture

Here is a small hands-on guide detailing how to start a cluster and run an example program with Apache Spark:

```
## download and extract a spark distribution, here we have selected 2.4.5
version
$ wget http://apache.mirrors.hoobly.com/spark/spark-2.4.5/spark-2.4.5-
bin-hadoop2.7.tgz
$ tar -xvf spark-2.4.5-bin-hadoop2.7.tgz
## go into the spark extracted directory
$ cd spark-2.4.5-bin-hadoop2.7
## we need to change the slaves file to include the ip addresses of our hosts
$ cp conf/slaves.template conf/slaves
$ cat conf/slaves
localhost
# start the cluster
$ ./sbin/start-all.sh
# now execute an example program distributed with spark
$ ./bin/spark-submit --class org.apache.spark.examples.SparkPi --master
spark://localhost:7077 examples/jars/spark-examples_2.11-2.4.5.jar 100
```

It will give a long output, and there will be a line at the end similar to the following:

```
$ Pi is roughly 3.1416823141682313
```

In the case of Spark, we started a set of servers on our machines and ran an example program on it. By adding compute node IP addresses to the conf/slaves file, we can deploy Spark on multiple machines. Spark must be installed on the same file location on all the machines, and password-less SSH needs to be enabled between them as in the OpenMPI example. If we do not specify a master URL separately, it will start the master program on the node where we ran the cluster start commands.

Shared Clusters

As one might expect, resource-sharing environments are more complicated to work with than dedicated environments. To manage and allocate resources fairly among different applications, a central resource scheduler is used. Some popular resource schedulers are Kubernetes, Apache Yarn, Slurm, and Torque. Kubernetes is a resource scheduler for containerized application deployment such as Docker. Apache Yarn is an application-level resource allocator for Hadoop applications. Slurm and Torque are user-level resource allocators for high-performance clusters including large supercomputers. Table 3-2 shows popular resource managers, their use cases, allocation types, and units.

Table 3-2: Different Resource Managers

RESOURCE SCHEDULER	USE CASES	ALLOCATION TYPE	ALLOCATION UNIT
Kubernetes[1]	Enterprise applications and services, data analytics applications	Allocate a set of resources for applications	Containers
Slurm[2]	High-performance clusters, supercomputers	User-based allocation of resources	Physical hardware allocation, containers
Yarn[3]	Hadoop ecosystem-based applications	Application-level allocation	Physical hardware or virtual machine environments, containers

The same examples can be executed on a cluster environment with some tweaks to the configurations and submit commands.

OpenMPI on a Slurm Cluster

To run the OpenMPI-based application on a Slurm cluster, the following commands can be used:

```
# Allocate a Slurm job with 4 nodes
$ salloc -N 4
# Now run an Open MPI job on all the nodes allocated by Slurm
$ mpirun ./task
```

---

[1]https://kubernetes.io/
[2]https://slurm.schedmd.com/documentation.html
[3]https://hadoop.apache.org/docs/current/hadoop-yarn/hadoop-yarn-site/YARN.html

Note that we are missing the number of processes argument and the hostfile. OpenMPI knows it runs in a Slurm environment and infers these parameters from it. There are other ways to submit OpenMPI applications in a Slurm environment, such as using the batch command.

```
$ cat my_script.sh
#!/bin/sh
mpirun ./task
$ sbatch -N 4 my_script.sh
$ srun: jobid 1234 submitted
```

Spark on a Yarn Cluster

The same Spark application can be executed on a Yarn cluster with minor modifications to the configurations and submit command. Note the master is specified as yarn, and the deploy mode is specified as cluster.

```
$ ./bin/spark-submit --class org.apache.spark.examples.SparkPi --master
yarn --deploy-mode cluster examples/jars/spark-examples_2.11-2.4.5.jar 100
```

Distributed Application Life Cycle

Even though there are many types of hosting systems, including clouds, bare-metal clusters, and supercomputers, a distributed data application always follows a remarkably similar life cycle. The framework may choose different strategies to acquire and manage the resources depending on whether it is a resource sharing or dedicated resource environment. In a dedicated environment, distributed computing frameworks manage the resources and applications, whereas in shared environments the frameworks need to communicate with the resource managers to acquire and manage the required computing resources.

Life Cycle Steps

As we have seen in previous examples, it all starts at the command line with instructions to submit the application to the cluster. Sometimes frameworks provide UIs to submit applications. Once the command to submit an application is executed, the steps shown in Figure 3-5 are taken to distribute the application to the compute nodes. Following the application setup, a discovery step is used to figure out the details of various distributed parts of the application. The frameworks perform additional steps such as monitoring while the application executes.

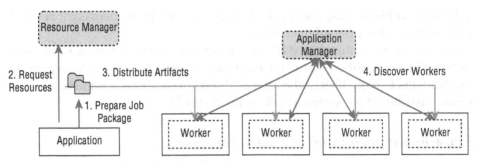

Figure 3-5: Life cycle of distributed applications

Step 1: Preparation of the Job Package

The framework prepares the job package to be distributed among the allocated machines. This step can execute additional validation steps to check whether the program is in an acceptable state to be submitted. In big data applications, the integrity of the dataflow graph is verified at this stage, and the availability of resources such as file paths can be checked.

The job package needs to be placed on different nodes to be executed. Various frameworks have specialized requirements in which the job needs to be formatted to run in these workers. For example, they may have a given folder structure with the executable in one folder, the dependencies of the application in another, and configurations in yet another. The job needs to be prepared according to a predefined format so that it can be placed on these workers to execute.

Step 2: Resource Acquisition

The program first requests resources from the cluster to execute. If the resources are not available at the time, the program is submitted to a queue where it waits until they are available. If the cluster cannot meet the requirements of the application, the application will be rejected. For example, should we request 1,024 CPU cores for an application when the cluster only has 512 CPU cores, that request cannot be satisfied and will fail.

There can be many policies set by administrators on the requirements of applications that can cause a rejection. In some resource managers, the application can request a time period for it to run. Since some clusters have limits on the number of hours an application can run, should the application exceed these limits it may not be granted resources.

Step 3: Distributing the Application (Job) Artifacts

At this point, the framework distributes the application artifacts to the allocated resources and starts executing the entry points of the program. In classic parallel systems, there is a distributed file system setup among the nodes. With a distributed file system, a separate distribution step is not necessary because files are accessible from all the nodes.

In cloud systems, this shared file system approach is uncommon, so the artifacts need to be distributed to all the machines. Some resource managers provide mechanisms to copy files to the allocated resources. Certain frameworks can utilize distributed file systems such as HDFS for file copying.

Step 4: Bootstrapping the Distributed Environment

In general, the locations (IP addresses) of the various parts of the program are unclear at the beginning of the program submission. Important information such as TCP ports used for communication between workers is similarly unknown. Given these conditions, bootstrapping a distributed application is a complex and time-consuming task, especially on a large scale.

To bootstrap, an application needs a process that has a known address (IP and port). This known point can be a central service such as a ZooKeeper, the submitting client, or a master program. Once the workers are spawned, they contact this known point to send their own information and discover information about other workers. This is a laborious operation when a very large number of parallel workers are involved (more than 10,000), and specialized hardware and algorithms can reduce the time required.

The processes started at the compute nodes are termed *worker processes*. These workers execute the actual program specified by the user and report their status to a master process for the particular job.

Step 5: Monitoring

An application needs to be monitored for faults and performance while it is running. Without monitoring, some parts of applications can fail without other parts knowing about it. Resource managers provide functions to keep track of applications. Application frameworks implement their own mechanisms for monitoring applications as well:

- **Detecting failures**—The program is monitored while it is executing to determine failures, performance issues, and progress. If a problem occurs, a recovery mechanism can be triggered to restart the program from a known previous state called a *checkpoint*. It is hard to detect failures in distributed environments. One of the most common methods is to rely on heartbeat messages sent from workers in a timely fashion. If a heartbeat is not received during a configured period of time, the worker is thought to be failed. The problem is that a worker can become slow and may not send the heartbeat message when needed, and the program can classify it as a failure when in reality it is not. Monitoring is a complicated aspect of keeping applications up and running.

- **Collecting logs**—Another common form of monitoring that occurs is collecting logs for determining the progress of the application. When hundreds of machines are involved in an application, they all can generate logs, and it is impossible to log into each of these machines to check for logs. In most distributed applications, logs are either saved in a distributed file system or sent to a common location to be monitored.

- **Resource consumption**—Cluster resource consumption can be monitored to see whether applications go over certain limits such as disk usage or memory usage and whether they encounter performance issues.

Step 6: Termination

After all the distributed computations complete, the application is stopped, the resources are deallocated, and the results are returned. When multiple machines and workers execute a distributed parallel application, there is no guarantee that every worker will stop at the same time. Distributed applications wait until all the workers are completed and then deallocate from the resource managers.

Computing Resources

Most of the computing power of the world is concentrated in data centers. These data centers provide the infrastructure and host the computing nodes to create public clouds, enterprise data warehouses, or high-performance clusters.

Data Centers

We are living in an age where massive data centers with thousands of computers exist in different parts of the globe crunching data nonstop. They work round-the-clock producing valuable insights and solving scientific problems, executing many exaflops of computations daily and crunching petabytes of data, consuming about 3 percent of the total energy used worldwide. These massive data centers host traditional high-performance computing infrastructures, including supercomputers and public clouds. The location of a data center is critical to users and cloud providers. Without geographically close data centers, some applications cannot perform in different regions due to network performance degradation across long distances.

A data center has many components, ranging from networking, actual computers and racks, power distribution, cooling systems, backup power systems, and large-scale storage devices. Operating a data center efficiently and securely while minimizing any outages is a daunting task. Depending on the availability and other features of a data center, they are categorized into four tiers. Table 3.3 describes the different tiers and the expected availability of data centers.

Table 3-3: Data Center Tiers

TIER	DESCRIPTION	AVAILABILITY
1	Single power and cooling sources and few (or none) redundant and backup components	99.671 percent (28.8 hours annual downtime)
2	Single power and cooling sources and some redundant and backup components	99.741 percent (22 hours annual downtime)
3	Multiple power sources and cooling systems	99.982 percent (1.6 hours annual downtime)
4	Completely fault tolerant; every component has redundancies	99.995 percent (26.3 minutes annual downtime)

Data center energy efficiency is an active research area, and even small improvements can reduce the environmental effects and save millions of dollars annually. A data center hosts computer clusters from a multitude of organizations. The individual organizations manage their computers and networking while the data center provides the overall infrastructure to host them, including connectivity to the outside world. Most data centers are built near the companies or the users they serve.

Power is one of the main expenses of running a data center. The availability of cheap power sources, especially green energy, is a big factor in choosing data center sites. Furthermore, places with low risk for natural disasters are chosen because it is costly to build systems that can withstand catastrophic events such as earthquakes or tsunamis. Cold climates can also reduce the cost of cooling, which is a big part of the overall power consumption for data centers. Table 3-4 shows some of the biggest data centers in the world and their power consumption.

Table 3-4: Massive Data Centers of the World

DATA CENTER	LOCATION	SIZE	POWER	STANDARD
The Citadel[4]	Tahoe Reno, USA	7.2 million square feet	650 MW	Tier 4
Range International Information Group[5]	Langfang, China	6.3 million square feet	150 MW	Tier 4
Switch SuperNAP[6]	Las Vegas, Nevada	3.5 million square feet	180 MW	Tier 4
DFT Data Center[7]	Ashburn, Virginia	1.1 million square feet	111 MW	Tier 4

---

[4] https://www.switch.com/tahoe-reno/
[5] http://worldstopdatacenters.com/4-range-international-information-hub/
[6] https://www.switch.com/las-vegas/
[7] https://www.digitalrealty.com/data-centers/northern-virginia

Even though most of the online services we use every day are powered by data centers around the world, as users we rarely notice their existence. Application developers are also unaware of the physical locations of these data centers or how they operate. Nevertheless, they play a vital role in large-scale data analytics.

Physical Machines

Before clouds and VMs became mainstream, physical machines were the only choice for running applications. Now we need to rely on physical machines only rarely thanks to the ever-increasing popularity of public clouds, virtual machines, and containers. Physical machines are still used in HPC clusters due to performance reasons. Some high-performance applications need access to the physical hardware to perform optimally and cannot scale to hundreds of thousands of cores in virtual environments. Small-scale in-house clusters usually expose physical machines to the applications due to the complexity of maintaining private clouds.

The biggest advantage of physical machines is direct access to the hardware. This allows applications to access high-speed networking hardware, storage devices, CPU, and GPU features otherwise not available through virtualization layers. This allows applications written with special hardware features to achieve optimal performance. For mainstream computing, these features are not relevant as the cost of developing and maintaining such applications outweighs the benefits.

Network

The computer network is the backbone of a data center. It connects computers and carries data among them so applications can distribute functionality among many machines. Networks can carry data between data centers, within a data center, or simply within a rack of computers. Most data centers provide dedicated high-bandwidth connections to other data centers and designated areas. For example, the Citadel in Tahoe Reno provides 10Gbps network connections with 4 ms latency between Silicon Valley.

Within a data center, there can be many types of networks utilized by different clusters created by various companies. The machines are organized into shelves we call *computer racks*. A rack typically consists of many computers connected using a dedicated network switch. The network between racks is shared by multiple machines. Because of this, the networking speed is much higher in a rack than between machines of different racks.

Numerous networks are available nowadays, but the most notable currently deployed is Ethernet. In most cases, Ethernet runs at around 10Gbps, and there is hardware available that can deliver up to 100Gbps speeds. Specialty networks have been designed to run inside data centers such as InfiniBand, Intel Omni-path, and uGini. These networks provide ultra-low latencies and generally higher bandwidths compared to Ethernet. They are mostly used in high-performance computing clusters including large supercomputers and are considered a vital component in scaling applications to thousands of nodes and hundreds of thousands of cores. Because of their efficiency, more and more clusters in data centers are using such features to accelerate networking performance. Table 3-5 shows some of the fastest supercomputers in the world, their number of cores, and the network they use along with their performance.

Table 3-5: Top 5 Supercomputers in the World

SUPER COMPUTER	LOCATION	CPU CORES AND GPUS	PEAK FLOPS	INTERCONNECT
Fugaku[8]	RIKEN Center for Computational Science Japan	7,630,848 cores	537 petaflops	Tofu interconnect D
Summit[9]	Oak Ridge National Laboratory USA	4608 Nodes, 2 CPUs per node. Each CPU has 22 Cores, 6 NVIDIA Volta GPUs per node.	200 petaflops	Mellanox EDR InfiniBand, 100Gbps
Sierra – IBM[10]	Lawrence Livermore National Laboratory USA	4320 Nodes, 2 CPUs per node. Each CPU has 22 Cores, 4 NVIDIA Volta GPUs per node.	125 petaflops	Mellanox EDR InfiniBand, 100Gbps
Sunway TaihuLight – NCRPC	National Supercomputing Center in Wuxi, China	10.65 million cores	125 petaflops	Sunway
Tianhe - 2A – NUDT	National Supercomputing Center in Guangzhou, China	4.98 million cores	100 petaflops	TH Express-2

---

[8] https://www.fujitsu.com/global/about/innovation/fugaku/
[9] https://www.olcf.ornl.gov/summit/
[10] https://hpc.llnl.gov/hardware/platforms/sierra

Virtual Machines

The virtual machine (VM) was invented to facilitate application isolation and the sharing of hardware resources. Virtualization is the driving technology behind cloud computing, which is now the most dominant supplier of computation to the world. When utilizing a cloud computing environment, we will most probably work with virtual machines.

A virtual machine is a complete operating system environment either created on top of hardware directly or atop another operating system, as shown in Figure 3-6. The virtual machines we start on our laptops are running on our laptop OS. In production environments, they will be directly running on hardware using virtualization layers. The virtual machine is called a *guest*, and the actual machine that runs the VM is called the *host*.

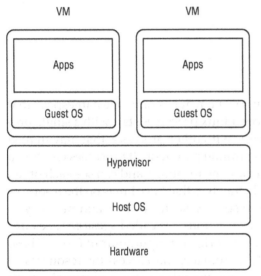

Figure 3-6: Virtual machine architecture

Containers

Containers operate in a lightweight virtual environment within the Linux operating system. Figure 3-7 shows a high-level architecture of containers where they run as a thin layer on top of the host operating system. Containers are lightweight compared to VMs because they do not run their own operating system kernel. This lightweight virtual environment is created mainly using Linux kernel cgroups functionality and namespaces functionality. Control groups are used to limit and measure the resources such as CPU or memory of a set of processes. Namespaces can be used for limiting the visibility that a group of processes has in the rest of the system.

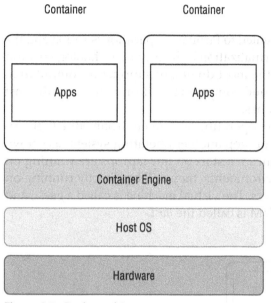

Figure 3-7: Docker architecture

By default, when we log into a Linux system, it has only one namespace that includes all the processes and resources. Linux processes start with a single process called `init`, and this process begins with other processes that may in turn start even more. As such, `init` is the common parent of all processes creating a single hierarchy or tree, all of which share the resources and can see each other.

With cgroups we can create process hierarchies that have limits on the resources they have available. We can allocate resources such as CPUs and memory to these process groups. The resource abstractions are called *subsystems*, examples of which include CPU, memory, network, and input/output (I/O). These subsystems control how the processes within a cgroup access the resources.

Namespace functionality facilitates deployment of process hierarchies with isolated mount points, process IDs, and networks. With namespace functionality, processes will see only the mount points created for them or the process IDs of the group. When enough of these limits and isolations are applied, we can create a totally isolated environment that does not interact with other processes of the system. This is the approach taken by container technologies such as Docker [1] and LXC.

Processor, Random Access Memory, and Cache

The CPU is the heart of a computer. For decades, a processing chip had only a single CPU core. Now single CPU core processors are almost nonexistent, and modern computers are equipped with chips that have multiple CPU cores. These are called multicore processors. A CPU core can execute a single thread (task) of the program at a time, and when many cores are available, it can execute tasks simultaneously. This allows programs to run in parallel within a single machine. Older computers with a single CPU provided the illusion of multitasking by rapidly switching between different threads of execution. With multicore processors, many threads of executions can truly occur on their own. A CPU core needs access to important structures such as the cache and memory to execute a program. In the days when chips contained only one core, caches and memory buses were all exclusive to that lone CPU. In modern multicore processors, some of these features are shared among multiple cores, while others are exclusive to each.

Apart from the CPU, random access memory (RAM) or main memory is the most important resource for data-intensive applications because of the amount of data being processed. RAM is expensive compared to other forms of storage such as disks. A single machine can have many memory modules that are connected to the CPU through memory buses. Imagine a processor with multiple cores and a single large memory connected to the processor with a single bus. Since every core requires access to the memory, they all need to share the same memory bus, which can lead to slower than average memory access speeds. Modern processors have multiple buses connecting numerous memory modules to increase the memory access times and bandwidth.

Accessing the main memory is a costly task for a CPU core because the memory bus is shared and because of the high number of CPU cycles required even with exclusive access. To reduce this access time, a much faster memory called a *cache* is used between the CPU core and the main memory.

Cache

It takes multiple CPU clock cycles to read an item from the main memory and load it to a CPU register. As a result, CPUs are equipped with caches, which are faster memory modules placed closer to the cores. The purpose of the cache is to reduce the average cost (clock cycles) required to access data from the main memory. These caches prefetch the most likely memory regions the CPU may use in future instructions. The CPU core can only access the memory in its cache, and when a memory request is made, it is first loaded into the cache and then served to the CPU core. If an item is not found in a cache, the CPU needs many clock cycles to fetch it from the main memory compared to loading it from the cache.

Modern computers have three caches called L1, L2, and L3, with L1 being closest to the CPU core. Figure 3-8 shows a cache hierarchy seen in modern processors. There are separate L1 caches for instructions to execute and find data. The fastest caches are the L1 instruction cache and L1 data cache. They are usually built near the CPU core in the same chip. These caches are equipped with fast memory and are expensive to build and hence limited in capacity. Next, there is the L2 cache, which is bigger than the L1 cache, and each core has one. Finally, there is an even larger cache called L3, which is shared among the cores of the chip.

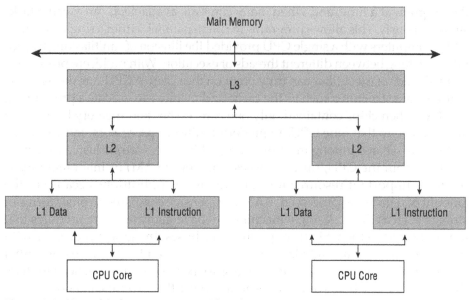

Figure 3-8: Hierarchical memory access with caches

We will look at the importance of cache for data-intensive application in later chapters.

Multiple Processors in a Computer

A computer can be built with numerous multicore processors in a single motherboard, most often referred to as *multiple-socket computers*. This allows more computing power to be packed into one node. When multiple CPUs are present, sharing memory I/O devices among different tasks running in them grows complicated. Certain architectures define how the resources are accessed in these configurations where a chip has multiple cores and there are several chips in a single machine. These are two popular architectures:

- Nonuniform memory access (NUMA)
- Uniform memory access (UMA)

It is important to understand these architectures to gain the best out of data-intensive applications. If programs are executed without considering these factors, serious performance degradation can occur.

Nonuniform Memory Access

NUMA is widely used in modern computers with multiple processors. In a NUMA computer, all the available memory is not uniformly (latency) accessible from a single core. The main memory is connected to the CPU cores using data buses. Each chip of a multiprocessor NUMA computer has its own memory buses to connect with memory modules. This means some memory is local to certain cores. The main memory, along with the cores and devices that are connected closely, are called a NUMA node. Different processor architectures may have one or multiple NUMA nodes per processor. Figure 3-9 shows a two-CPU configuration with two NUMA nodes.

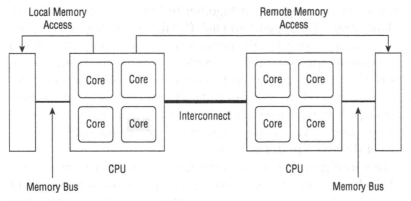

Figure 3-9: NUMA memory access

When a CPU core tries to access memory that is located in another NUMA node, the access can be slower than its local memory access. To utilize the memory efficiently, the locality of the memory must be considered by the programs. Note that NUMA only affects the performance of an application, and no matter how the memory is allocated, its correctness will not be impacted.

NUMA memory locality is preserved by the operating system (OS) to some extent. When a process runs on a NUMA node, the OS will allocate memory for that process on its local memory. If there is no space in the NUMA local memory, the memory will be allocated in another NUMA node, slowing down the performance. Applications are scheduled on different cores and sockets by the OS throughout its lifetime. If an application is scheduled on one NUMA node and later scheduled on another node due to memory requirements, the program's performance can lag. Operating systems provide mechanisms to attach processes to NUMA nodes to prevent such performance issues.

Resource managers offer mechanisms to preserve NUMA locality while allocating resources to applications. For high-performance applications, such configurations need to be taken into account to achieve the best performance possible.

Uniform Memory Access

Uniform memory access remains uncommon and is available in only a few system architectures. Intel Xeon Phi is one such example. In a UMA system, the cores and processes access the main memory equally.

Hard Disk

Disks allow for much cheaper permanent storage of applications. There are mechanical hard disks, solid-state drives (SSDs), and NVMe SSDs available, with mechanical hard disks being the cheapest and NVMe SSDs being the priciest. Mechanical disks are also slower compared to SSDs, while NVMe provides the best performance.

Multiple hard disks can be grouped together to form a single logical disk using Redundant Array of Independent Disk (RAID) technologies to ensure fault tolerance and increased read/write performance. Depending on the RAID configuration, different aspects such as I/O performance or fault tolerance can be given priority. Computers configured to analyze large volumes of data are equipped with many hard disks and multiple I/O controllers to fully utilize the disks. Most organizations have data that need to be archived for potential future applications. Tape drives can offer economical storage for archiving such data, at the cost of slow read performances.

When data sizes are bigger than available memory, data applications need to use the hard disks for storing temporary data of computations. It is important to configure fast disks for such operations to perform optimally. Also, when multiple processes (threads) of a data analytics application access the same hard disk, it can reduce the performance. Hard disks are optimized for sequential I/O operations, so the applications should try to avoid random I/O operations as much as possible.

GPUs

Most of us are familiar with graphic processing units thanks to video gaming. Originally GPUs were created to relieve the CPU from the burden of creating images for the monitor to display. With the gaming industry's ever-increasing demand for realistic environments inside games, more and more computing power was added to GPUs. Unlike CPUs, GPUs are equipped with hundreds of cores and thousands of hardware threads that can manipulate large chunks of data simultaneously. Eventually scientists realized the GPU's potential to do large computations efficiently for dense matrix multiplications. Dense matrix multiplication is important for training deep neural networks. Now GPUs power numerous deep learning workloads, and large data analytics tasks are executed on them regularly.

Mapping Resources to Applications

In most frameworks, applications can request specific resource requirements. Usually these are the memory and CPUs. For example, an application can say it has 12 computing tasks (Map tasks) and each of them requires 8GB of memory and 1 CPU core to execute. The framework transfers these application-specific requirements to cluster managers when executing the application.

For data analytics application tasks, it is important to adhere to stricter resource mapping like NUMA boundaries to execute efficiently. Many frameworks allow finer-grained control over how the application processes are mapped to the resources. A user can request a parallel process to bind to a single CPU throughout its execution. By binding to a CPU core, an application can avoid unnecessary OS scheduling overheads and cache misses. Linux OS uses mechanisms to map specific resources to specific processes in order to achieve this level of control. When using cluster resource managers and frameworks, the users do not need to go to the Linux details and can instead apply these policies through various configurations.

Cluster Resource Managers

Efficient management of cluster resources is a topic all its own. Most mature cluster resource managers today offer equal functionality and performance. For the purpose of this textbook, we will not go into detail on how cluster resource managers are implemented but instead focus on their overall architecture and mechanics so that we can discuss them in the context of data analytics applications. Numerous such systems are available and at a glance their architecture and functionality are virtually identical. The details of their implementation can vary, but for the purposes of a data analytics application, they provide similar functionality with a common architecture. Because of this, by studying a few of them we can generalize the knowledge related to all. From a distributed application's perspective, a cluster resource manager performs three important tasks:

- Allocate resources for an application and give access to them. These resources can be any combination of containers, nodes, VMs, CPUs, memory, cache, GPUs, disk, or network.

- Job scheduling to determine which jobs run first (in case there are many jobs competing for resources) as well as determine the resources on which to run the jobs.

- Provide mechanisms to start and monitor distributed applications on these resources (life cycle management of the applications).

A resource provisioner has a set of server processes for managing cluster resources as well as interfacing with the users. To manage the actual compute nodes, daemon processes are started on each of them. The management servers and the processes run on the compute nodes communicate with one another. Additionally, the status of each process is monitored and reported to the management nodes. From the user side, there is a set of queues to submit applications, normally called *job queues*. These are used for prioritizing the jobs submitted by various users. An authentication mechanism can be used to distinguish and apply different capabilities to the users such as limits on the resources they can access.

Kubernetes

Kubernetes is a resource manager specifically designed to work with containers. When set up on a cluster of computers, it can spawn and manage applications running on containers. These applications can be anything, ranging from data analytics to microservices to databases. Kubernetes provides the infrastructure to spawn containers, set up auxiliary functions such as networking, and set up distributed storage for the spawned containers to work together. Some of the most important functions of Kubernetes include the following:

- Spawning and managing containers
- Providing storage to the containers
- Handling networking among the containers
- Handling node failures by launching new containers
- Dynamic scaling of containers for applications

Kubernetes supports the container technologies Docker, containerd, and CRI-O. Docker is the first container technology and made containers famous. CRI-O is a lightweight container technology developed for Kubernetes, and containerd is a simplified container technology with an emphasis on robustness and portability.

Kubernetes Architecture

Figure 3-10 shows the Kubernetes architecture. It has a set of servers that manages the cluster. These are installed on a dedicated server that does not get involved in executing the applications. There is also a set of worker nodes that run the actual container-based applications.

Management Servers

These are the features of management servers:

- **API Server**—This is a REST-based service that provides endpoints for clients to interact with the Kubernetes clusters. Client APIs are available in many different languages.
- **etcd cluster**—Kubernetes uses the etcd cluster to store the cluster state and metadata. Kubernetes uses a distributed coordinator called etcd that can synchronize various distributed activities among the worker processes.

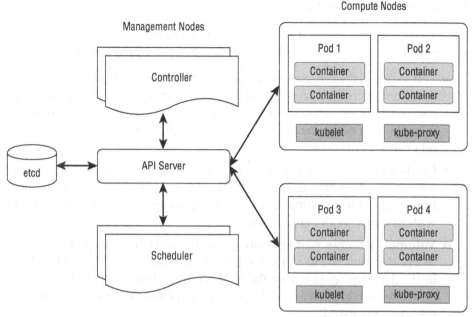

Figure 3-10: Kubernetes architecture

- **Controllers**—Kubernetes runs many controllers to keep the cluster at a desirable state. The controller watches the state of the cluster and tries to bring it to the desired state specified by the user. The Deployment controller and Job controller are two built-in controllers available.

- **Scheduler**—Choose the compute resources to run the pods of an application.

Kubectl

This is a command-line tool provided by Kubernetes to interact with the cluster. The users connect to the Kubernetes API server to launch applications through the client API or using this command-line tool.

Worker Nodes

Each worker node runs kubelet process and the kube-proxy process. A worker node can be a virtual machine or physical node in a cluster.

- **kubelet**—This process manages the node and the pods that runs in that node. It accepts requests to start pods and monitors the existing pods for failures. It also reports to the controllers about the health of the node and the pods.

- **kube-proxy**—Handles individual subnetting within a node and exposes the services to external entities.

Kubernetes Application Concepts

There are many application specific features in Kubernetes. We will briefly look at some of the most relevant features for data intensive applications.

- **Pod**—This is the basic allocation unit in Kubernetes. A pod can run multiple containers, and an application can have multiple pods. It also encapsulates resources such as storage and network. A pod is a virtual environment with its own namespace and cgroups. So, pods are isolated from each other in a single node.

- **Containers**—Inside a pod we can run multiple containers. These containers can share the resources allocated to the pod. We run our applications inside the containers. A container packages the application along with its software dependencies.

- **Volume**—Volumes represent storage and are attached to a pod. A volume of a pod is attached to all the containers running inside that pod and can be used to share data within them. There are ephemeral volumes that are destroyed when pods exist. The persistent volumes retain data even if the pods are destroyed.

The original design goal of Kubernetes was to support more general forms of distributed applications such as web services. Container launching is still a time-consuming task compared to just launching processes in distributed nodes. With the support of major data processing platforms, Kubernetes is becoming a preferred destination for data analytics applications.

Data-Intensive Applications on Kubernetes

Now let us briefly examine how a data-intensive application will execute in a Kubernetes cluster without going into the details of any specific data-intensive framework. Because we are considering a distributed application, it will need multiple pods. Few of the pods will be dedicated to the management processes of our application, and the rest will run the computation in parallel. Most probably we will run one container per each pod. We are going to run each application in isolation without any connection to others in the Kubernetes cluster.

Container

Our container will be prepackaged with the framework software. We will need to transfer the job package to the container instances at runtime.

Worker Nodes

There are many controllers available in Kubernetes to create a set of pods that does the work in parallel. In a data-intensive application, these pods can run the worker processes that does the computations.

- **Deployment**—A configuration that describes the desired state of an application. Deployment controllers are used for updating pods and ReplicaSets.

- **ReplicaSet**—A ReplicaSet maintains a set of replica pods for long-running tasks. We can deploy a ReplicaSet as a deployment. Kubernetes will guarantee the availability of a specific number of pods at runtime.

- **Job**—A job consists of one or more pods that does some work and terminates. We can define how many pods to complete for a job to be successful. If this is not specified, each pod in the job will work independently and terminate.

- **StatefulSets**—This controller manages a set of replica pods for long-running tasks with added functionality such as stable unique network identifiers, stable persistent storage, and ordered graceful deployments and scaling.

Because of the added functionality, let's assume we are going to use a StatefulSet for our worker nodes. We will mount an ephemeral volume for workers to keep the temporary data.

Management Process

This process is responsible for coordinating the worker nodes. For example, it can tear down the application when it is completed and provide functions to handle failed worker processes. We can use a StatefulSet to start the management process because it provides a unique IP for other workers to connect.

Workflow

When a user submits a job package to run, we will first start the management process as a StatefulSet. After it is started, we can start the StatefulSet for worker processes by giving the IP address of the management process. Before the worker processes start, they need to wait for a copy of the job package to the containers. We can use the Kubernetes functions to copy the job package from client to the containers.

Once the pods are started, the workers will connect to the management processes. They will do a discovery step to find the addresses of other processes with the help of the management process. Once they know the IP addresses of others, they can establish network connections.

At this point, worker processes can start running the parallel application. Once they are done with executing the code, they can send a message to management process, which will terminate the pods by asking the Kubernetes.

There are many choices for executing a data-intensive application on top of Kubernetes at each step we described. What we described here is a great simplification of an actual system, but the core steps will be similar.

Slurm

Slurm [2] is a widely used resource manager in high-performance clusters, including the largest supercomputers. Slurm works by allocating physical resources to an application. These can be anything, from compute nodes to CPUs or CPU cores, memory, disks, and GPUs. Slurm has a similar architecture to Kubernetes with a set of servers for managing the cluster and daemon processes to run on the cluster nodes. As shown in Figure 3-11, `slurmctld` is the main process that manages the cluster, and `slurmdbd` is for keeping the state of the cluster persistent to a database. The `slurmd` daemons run on the compute nodes managing the resources and the processes spawned on them.

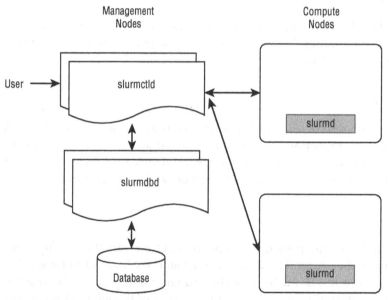

Figure 3-11: Slurm architecture

Slurm provides an API and a set of command-line utilities wrapping these APIs to interact with it. Command-line utilities are the preferred choice for most users to interact with Slurm. Slurm supports allocations both in batch and interactive modes. In interactive mode, once resources are allocated, users can SSH to them and execute any processes they might need. In the batch mode, a distributed application is submitted up front and run by Slurm. Due to human involvement, interactive mode does not use the resources very efficiently. Many production clusters only allow batch submissions in the main compute nodes and permit interactive jobs on just a small number of nodes for debugging purposes.

Slurm has different built-in job scheduling algorithms. There are API points to define custom algorithms as well. By default, Slurm uses a first-come, first-serve job scheduling algorithm. Other algorithms such as Gang scheduling and backfill scheduling are available as well.

Yarn

Yarn was the first resource scheduler designed to work with big data systems. It originally derives from the Hadoop project. Initially Hadoop was developed with resource management, job scheduling, and a map-reduce application framework all as a single system. Because of this, Hadoop did not have a mechanism to work with external resource managers. When Hadoop was installed on a cluster, that cluster could only be used to run Hadoop applications. This was not an acceptable solution for many clusters where there were other types of applications that needed to share the same resources.

Yarn decoupled the resource management and job scheduling from map-reduce applications and evolved as a resource scheduler on its own for big data applications. MapReduce became another application that uses Yarn to allocate resources. As one might expect, Yarn has a similar architecture to Kubernetes and Slurm where there is a central server called ResourceManager and a set of daemon processes called NodeManagers that run on the worker nodes.

An application in Yarn consists of an application manager and a set of containers that runs the worker processes. A data analytics framework wanting to work in a Yarn environment should write the application manager code to acquire resources and manage the workers of its applications. Figure 3-12 shows this architecture with two application managers running in the cluster.

Similar to Slurm, Yarn has a queuing system to prioritize jobs and various scheduling objectives can be applied to the applications. One of the most popular considerations in Yarn applications is the data locality. Yarn also implements various job scheduling algorithms [3] such as fair scheduling and capacity scheduling to work in different settings.

Job Scheduling

The goal of a job scheduling system is to allocate resources to users or applications in the most efficient way possible. In a cloud environment, the objective may be to minimize the cost while maximizing performance. In a research

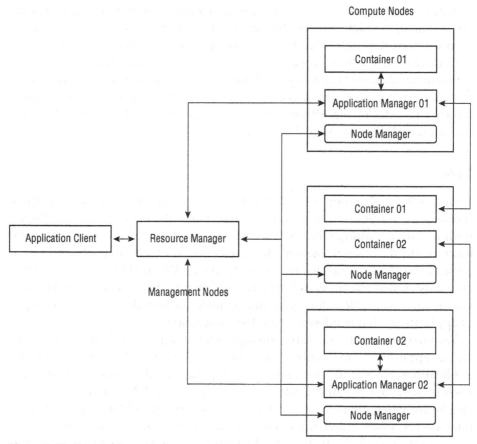

Figure 3-12: Yarn architecture

cluster, one might aim to keep the cluster fully utilized all the time. This presents unique challenges for the algorithms created to schedule the workloads on such clusters. Most application developers do not need to fully understand the details, and as such they are sometimes not visible to them. For example, when we request a set of VMs from a public cloud provider to run our application, the cloud provider considers many factors before deciding what physical nodes to use for creating the VMs.

A job scheduling system takes a set of jobs as input and outputs a job schedule, which indicates the order of the jobs as well as the specific resources for each job. It is often a challenge to find the best schedule in a reasonably complex system with many jobs competing for resources. Most algorithms make assumptions and lower the requirements to tackle the problem in a finite period as there is no point in devoting a large amount of time to finding the best schedule while your resources are idling.

A scheduling system consists of three parts: a scheduling policy, objective functions, and scheduling algorithms [4]. The scheduling policy states high-level rules to which the system must adhere. The objective function is used to determine a particular job schedule's effectiveness. The algorithms incorporate the policies and objective functions to create the schedule.

Scheduling Policy

A scheduling policy dictates high-level requirements such as what type of resources are accessible to which users and priority of different applications. Say, for instance, we take a data analytics cluster that runs jobs each day to determine critical information for an organization. This cluster is also shared with data scientists who are doing experiments on their newest machine learning models. The organization can define a policy saying the critical jobs need to run no matter what state the cluster is in. When this policy is implemented, an experimental job run by a data scientist may be halted to run a higher priority job, or it may have to wait until the higher-priority jobs complete.

So, a scheduling policy contains a set of rules that specifies what actions need to be taken in case there are more resource requests than available.

Objective Functions

An object function determines whether a resource schedule is good or bad. Objective functions are created according to the policies specified by the organization. A cluster can run many jobs at any given time. These applications demand various resource requirements (number of processors, nodes) and execution times. At any given time, the free resources of a cluster can be scattered across many racks of nodes. Furthermore, some applications can benefit from special hardware support and placement of the worker processes. These requirements can be specified with the job scheduling algorithms to make better decisions about where to place applications. We can look at few common objective functions used in resource schedulers.

Throughput and Latency

Throughput and latency of the system are two main metrics used to determine the quality of a scheduling system. Throughput is measured as the number of jobs completed within a given period. Latency can be taken as the time it takes to complete jobs.

Priorities

Algorithms can take the priorities of applications into account when scheduling. Usually, priorities are configured with different job queues. Jobs submitted to queues with higher priorities are served first. For example, when used with Gang scheduling, the higher-priority jobs will get more execution time compared to the lower-priority ones.

Lowering Distance Among the Processes

A scheduling algorithm can try to lower the distance between various parts of an application in terms of networking to improve its performance. Slurm uses the Hilbert space-filling curve [5] to order nodes to achieve good locality in 3D space. The Hilbert curve fitting method transforms a multidimensional task allocation problem into a one-dimensional space, assigning related tasks to locations with higher levels of proximity. Lowering the networking distance can greatly increase the efficiency of network I/O-intensive programs.

Data Locality

Data locality–aware scheduling is common in big data schedulers like Yarn. It applies to clusters with computing and storage cohabited in the same nodes. A prime example is an HDFS cluster. A scheduler tries to minimize the distance between the data and the computing as much as possible. If all the cluster nodes are available, this means placing the application on the same nodes where the data is present. If the scheduler cannot run the application on the nearest nodes, it can instead place them on the same racks as the data.

When many jobs are running on a cluster, it is impossible to completely guarantee data locality. Data can be spread across more nodes than the number requested by the application, or the application may ask for more nodes than the nodes with the data. Other applications might also be executing on the nodes with the data.

Data locality was much more important in the early days of big data computing when the network was vastly slower than reading from the hard disk. By contrast, nowadays networks can be many times faster. In cloud systems, data is stored in services such as S3. As such, data locality is not as important as it was before.

Completion Deadline

Some jobs need to run within a given deadline to be effective. The resource scheduler needs an approximate time of completion from the user to achieve this. Usually, we know the time to run an application with a set of given parameters and resources from prior experience of running it. Resource schedulers do not try to allocate more resources (increase parallelism) on their own to finish a job quickly as it can decrease performance in some applications.

Algorithms

The goal of a scheduling algorithm is to select which jobs to run when the demand is higher than the available resources. The algorithm should select the jobs such that it creates a good schedule according to the objective functions defined. If we can run every job immediately because there are resources available, we do not need to use these algorithms.

There are many scheduling algorithms available in the literature. In practical systems, these algorithms are adapted to support various objective functions according to the applications they support.

First in First Out

First in First Out (FIFO) is the most basic scheduler available in almost all systems. As the name suggests, jobs are executed in the order they are submitted. It is simple to understand and works with systems that have relatively less work compared to the resources available, although it can lead to idle resources and low throughput. We will see an example later with the backfill scheduling algorithm.

Gang Scheduling

Gang scheduling is a technique used for running multiple applications on the same resources simultaneously by time sharing between them. In this case, applications are oversubscribed to the resources, and they must take turns executing like in OS threads. To achieve gang scheduling, the resources required by all applications running on a single resource must be less than its capacity. An example is a temporary hard disk space used by applications. If the requirement of all the applications running simultaneously is bigger than the capacity of the hard disk, gang scheduling will fail. Another such resource is the RAM used by the applications.

Gang scheduling allows a scheduler to improve responsiveness and utilization by permitting more jobs to begin executions faster. Shorter jobs can finish without waiting in queues for longer jobs to terminate, increasing the responsiveness of the overall cluster.

List Scheduling

This is a classic and simple scheduling technique where it runs the next job that fits the available resources. Because of its simplicity, it can be implemented efficiently and even provides good schedules in practical systems.

Backfill Scheduling

The backfilling [6] algorithm tries to execute jobs that are ahead in the job queue in case it cannot execute the head of the queue due to resources not being available. When it picks a job that is down in the queue, it tries not to postpone the job at the head of the queue. This requires knowledge of the job execution times for each job.

Figure 3-13 shows the difference between FIFO and backfill scheduling. Imagine we have two resources (r) and four jobs. Jobs 1 to 4 take resources and time pairs of Job1 - {r = 1, t = 2}, Job2 - {r = 1, t = 4}, Job 3 - {r = 2, t = 3}, Job 4 - {r = 1, t = 2}. These are submitted in the order of 1 to 4. If we strictly follow the FIFO schedule, Job 4 needs to wait until Job 3 is completed. With backfill scheduling, we can start Job 4 after Job 1 completes. Note that the Job 3 start time does not change because of this.

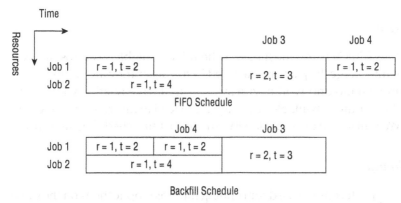

Figure 3-13: Backfill scheduling and FIFO scheduling

Summary

We discussed the various resources that are available for executing data-intensive applications and how they are managed in cluster environments. Depending on the frameworks, there can be many configuration parameters available to fine-tune the resources to map application requirements. Programming and deploying data analytics applications while being aware of the computing resources can greatly increase efficiency and reduce cost.

References

1. D. Merkel, "Docker: lightweight linux containers for consistent development and deployment," *Linux journal*, vol. 2014, no. 239, p. 2, 2014.

2. A. B. Yoo, M. A. Jette, and M. Grondona, "Slurm: Simple linux utility for resource management," in *Workshop on job scheduling strategies for parallel processing*, 2003: Springer, pp. 44-60.

3. J. V. Gautam, H. B. Prajapati, V. K. Dabhi, and S. Chaudhary, "A survey on job scheduling algorithms in big data processing," in *2015 IEEE International Conference on Electrical, Computer and Communication Technologies (ICECCT)*, 2015: IEEE, pp. 1-11.

4. J. Krallmann, U. Schwiegelshohn, and R. Yahyapour, "On the design and evaluation of job scheduling algorithms," in *Workshop on Job Scheduling Strategies for Parallel Processing*, 1999: Springer, pp. 17-42.

5. J. A. Pascual, J. A. Lozano, and J. Miguel-Alonso, "Analyzing the performance of allocation strategies based on space-filling curves," in *Job Scheduling Strategies for Parallel Processing*, 2015: Springer, pp. 232-251.

6. A. K. Wong and A. M. Goscinski, "Evaluating the easy-backfill job scheduling of static workloads on clusters," in *2007 IEEE International Conference on Cluster Computing*, 2007: IEEE, pp. 64-73.

Data Structures

Every program that does meaningful work deals with data structures. Whether it is a large-scale distributed application or a serial program running in the cluster, we can find data structures everywhere. The simplest data types we use are primitive types such as integers and doubles. Computers are designed to work on such fundamental data by loading them into special hardware units inside CPUs called *registers* wherein they make decisions and perform arithmetic operations.

Utilizing simple primitive types in computing is an efficient and well-documented endeavor these days. Compilers supply excellent support to optimize operations involving them. But a complex program cannot rely solely on just simple types to meet its data needs. To represent complex data, composite types are created from their less complicated brethren. Examples of such are present in any programming language. In C we program with structs, while in Java or C++, we program classes to create composite types.

An array is another composite data structure widely used in computing. An array has multiple values of the same type in a contiguous space in memory. The individual value of an array can be accessed using an index and can be of multiple dimensions, making it extremely efficient.

When we deal with substantial amounts of data, we need to use data structures that can hold them as composite forms. It all boils down to how efficient a data structure is in terms of access speed and storage. Different application classes have found certain data structures to be best suited for their use cases.

Application frameworks designed to work on these application classes naturally choose the most productive data representations. For example, big data frameworks prefer table data structures to store the data, while deep learning frameworks tend to use tensors.

Virtual Memory

Before diving into the details of data representations, let's quickly have a refresher about the memory organization of a program. The physical random-access memory of a program is shared by the operating system kernel and multiple programs executing at the same time. If a program directly uses physical memory addresses, it will have to deal with all the other programs and the operating system. This makes it harder to allocate contiguous memory spaces, as well as move the programs. Furthermore, parts of the programs need to be swapped between memory and disk to free memory for executing other programs. To handle these requirements, all modern computer architectures use virtual memory.

With virtual memory, a program sees a continuous virtual address space for allocating objects. The operating system maps the virtual address space of a program into physical memory as needed. Every memory access needs to translate from this virtual address space to physical addresses, which can be a costly operation. To speed up the mapping process, modern computers use a special hardware unit called a *memory management unit* (MMU).

A program's memory consists of several large sections. As a programmer, you will be dealing with the heap memory and stack memory regions. Figure 4-1 shows how the Linux operating system divides the virtual memory into sections. In modern 64-bit computers, the possible virtual address space is 2 to the power 64, which is exceptionally large. Due to hardware limitations, computers cannot support this much memory for a program.

The heap is the space where we can dynamically allocate memory. For example, when our program starts running, we are going to read a file into memory, which requires a large buffer in memory. The size of the buffer is not known at the time we write the program, so we will allocate a buffer at runtime using the malloc (Unix) function. Stack space is allocated for keeping the call stack of functions. This space is managed by the compiler according to the program we wrote. For instance, when we program `int value = 10` inside a Java function, the variable value is created on the stack.

When looking at Figure 4-1, one thing immediately stands out: the amount of memory we can use is limited by the space between stack and static data. But we need to keep in mind that this is an exceptionally large space for a 64-bit program. The theoretical addressable memory of a 64-bit computer is about 16 exabytes.

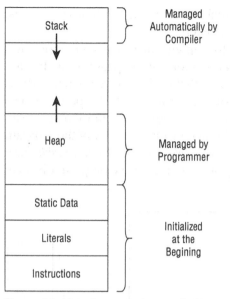

Figure 4-1: Virtual memory layout of a Linux program

The limits on memory allocation can be seen with the command `ulimit` on Linux systems. In Linux, the default limit for a user is called a *soft limit*, and the maximum the user can increase it is the hard limit. In the following system running Ubuntu 18.04, the stack is set to 8 kilobytes, but we can increase it to `unlimited`. The virtual memory is unlimited by default.

Here is the stack size soft limit and hard limit:

```
$ ulimit -S -s
8192
$ ulimit -H -s
unlimited
```

Here is the virtual memory soft limit:

```
$ ulimit -S -v
unlimited
```

Paging and TLB

Paging is a technology developed on top of the virtual memory systems to facilitate efficient use of memory while keeping part of the programs in the hard disk. This was important in the old days when computers had smaller main memory. With the larger memory available in modern machines, allocating some parts of programs in the disk is no longer as important. The clusters that run data analytics programs rarely run other competing programs in them.

Because of this, the whole memory is available to the data analytics programs, so swapping out is not common in those clusters.

Paging is used by the operating system to map virtual addresses into physical addresses in modern systems. The virtual memory of the program is divided into smaller units called *pages* that are 4KB or 8KB in size. Since virtual address space is exceptionally large, we need not keep track of all the pages. These pages are mapped to physical memory regions of equal size known as *frames*. Operating systems monitor not only the allocated virtual memory of the program but also the mapping to the physical memory. We call this the *page table* for a program. Figure 4-2 shows this mapping of virtual memory pages to physical memory frames.

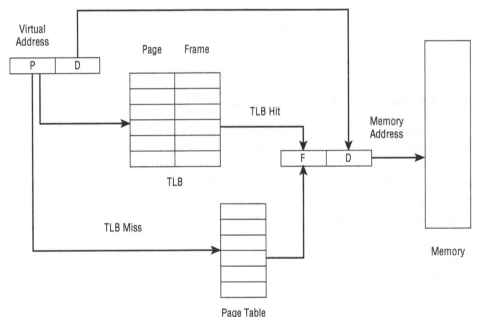

Figure 4-2: Mapping of virtual memory to physical memory

Imagine a program presenting a virtual address to a CPU to fetch some data to a register. We first need to translate this virtual address to an actual physical address before we can ask the memory subsystem to retrieve the data. To do so, the OS must go through the list of virtual pages mapped to physical frames. Page tables can be huge for programs using large memory. For example, a page table of a 16GB memory program will have 4 million entries assuming a 4KB page size. If this lookup happens for every memory reference, it will be a drastic performance hit, as the OS may need to go through hundreds of thousands of entries.

To reduce this burden, modern systems have a page mapping cache called the *translation lookaside buffer* (TLB). TLB is implemented in hardware and is much quicker compared to rifling through the page table one at a time. A CPU looking to translate a virtual address to a physical address goes to the TLB first to see if there is a hit. If the item is in the TLB, the lookup is performed swiftly. Otherwise, the OS must cycle through the page table, which can take a significant amount of CPU time. TLB is a scarce resource with limited slots. If a program accesses a large memory space randomly, it will create a lot of TLB misses, thus hindering the performance. Figure 4-3 shows this address translation using the TLB and page table.

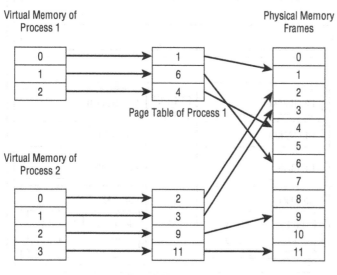

Figure 4-3: Translating virtual address to physical address

Cache

The CPU cache is one of the most important resources a program has available to enhance its processing speed. In modern CPUs, the main memory is always accessed through the cache. Data is fetched from main memory to cache in chunks called *cache lines*. Accessing cache is many times faster than accessing the main memory.

When we access a 4-byte integer value in the memory, the CPU first looks at its caches. If the value is not found in the caches, it checks to see if the memory page with this address is in the main memory. If not, it is loaded from the disk to the main memory. A cache line (64 bits) of memory having the referenced memory is loaded to the cache, after which the program accesses the 4-byte integer. When we retrieve the next 4 bytes, they will be in the cache and can be returned at once. If we request 4 bytes that are 300MB away, the CPU may need to fetch it from the main memory.

From this description, if the memory referenced is not in the cache, it can take a long time to fetch it. This is called a *cache miss*. If an application can keep the working dataset in the cache, it significantly enhances the performance. Figure 4-4 shows the cache structure of an Intel Xeon W-2145 CPU where there are eight cores each with its own L1 instruction cache, L1 data cache, and L2 cache. The L3 cache is shared among the cores.

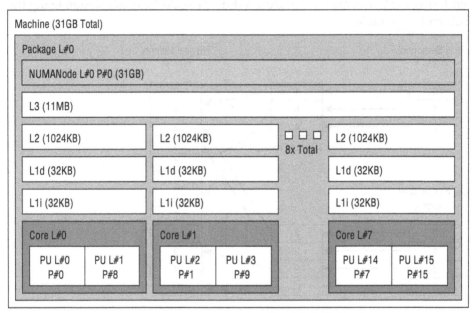

Figure 4-4: Cache structure of an 8-core Intel CPU with L1, L2, and L3 caches

The Need for Data Structures

Main memory costs are rapidly decreasing, and it is not uncommon for computers to have a large main memory, sometimes beyond 256GB. These modern machines can store a huge amount of data in memory and process them. Even though we call the main memory of a computer random access memory, the access patterns of memory can make a significant difference in performance. When the amount of memory used by a program becomes larger, the difference in terms of computing time increases as a result.

Cache and Memory Layout

We can illustrate the importance of cache and the memory layout with an example. The following program accesses a large array of data with three different patterns. This array consists of a class called Record, which has an integer field and a double field. First, we create the array as a contiguous memory containing

Record objects. Then we access each Record object sequentially starting from the beginning.

```cpp
class Record {
public:
  Record() {}
  Record(int id, double value) : id(id), value(value) {}
  int id;
  double value;
};

double array_access(Record* records, int length) {
  double sum = 0.0;
  for (int i = 0; i < length; i++) {
    sum += records[i].value;
  }
  return sum / length;
}

double array_indirect_access(Record** records, int length) {
  double sum = 0.0;
  for (int i = 0; i < length; i++) {
    sum += records[i]->value;
  }
  return sum / length;
}


void shuffle_array(Record **arr, int n) {
  unsigned seed = 0;
  std::shuffle(arr, arr + n, std::default_random_engine(seed));
}
```

Next, we allocate the record objects in the heap separately and keep a pointer to these heap objects in the array. Every time we access a value we must index into the array, which points to another memory location. To read the actual value, we must fetch this memory location. Thus, we need two memory accesses. This is important depending on the programming language being used; for example, Java only allows indirect access to objects stored in an array. Note that since we are allocating the record objects in the memory one after another, they will most likely be placed in a contiguous region of memory by the memory allocation call.

Lastly, we are going to shuffle the pointers in our array so that the record accesses become random. Table 4-1 shows the time taken for all three types with 100 million records, and Table 4-2 shows the time with 200 million records. A machine with Intel Xeon W-2145 CPU at 3.70GHz and 32GB main memory is used. The time displayed is for accessing the array 10 times.

Table 4-1: Time for Accessing 100 Million Records in Three Methods

METHOD	TIME FOR ACCESSION 100 MILLION RECORDS	TIME/ARRAY ACCESS TIME
Sequential access	1076ms	1
Indirect access	2490ms	2.3
Random indirect access	15279ms	14.2

Table 4-2: Time for Accessing 200 Million Records in Three Methods

METHOD	WHEN WE INCREASE THE SIZE OF RECORDS OR ACCESSES THE RECORDS RANDOMLY, IT WILL LEAD TO MORE TLB MISSES CAUSING THE LARGE DEGRADATION IN PERFORMANCE	TIME/ARRAY ACCESS TIME
Sequential access	2209ms	1
Indirect access	5018ms	2.3
Random indirect access	48638ms	22

As we can see from this exercise, how we store objects in the heap and the access patterns used can have a significant impact on the performance. Incidentally, when the array size is bigger, the random-access performance suffers.

Cache is the chief reason behind the performance differences between the three experiments we conducted. When we access an array (contiguous space in memory) sequentially from low index to high, the CPU can prefetch the data to the cache, which is very efficient. In the second experiment, we have an indirection. Even though that is the case, the data is still allocated in a contiguous space as is the array with the pointers, leading to effective use of the cache. In the third example, since the memory accesses are random, there will be more cache misses. When we increase the size of records and access the data randomly, it will lead to more TLB misses causing the large degradation in performance.

Memory Fragmentation

Memory fragmentation occurs when the memory is reserved in noncontiguous blocks with small free regions in between. When this happens, the free memory between these allocations becomes harder to use for new allocations due to the amount of memory in the free spaces being smaller than the required amount. At this point, the system has free memory, but it cannot be used. This situation can lead to out-of-memory errors or a slowdown of the system.

One solution to avoid memory fragmentation is to use larger memory allocations and put the small objects into them. Such fixes waste memory but can still speed up the applications. Different memory allocators other than malloc, such as jemalloc [1], have adopted efficient methods of allocating memory to reduce fragmentation. We cannot directly control the memory fragmentation in languages such as Java, but in general, avoiding large numbers of small objects helps a great deal when doing garbage collection.

Data Transfer

In-memory data representation has a significant impact on network communication of data messages. For network communication to take place, the data needs to be in a continuous buffer space in the memory. When dealing with throughput-sensitive applications, it is not efficient to send many small messages through the network. We need to collect small messages and build large enough buffers before sending them to use the network fully. Both factors directly depend on how the data is represented in memory.

Data Transfer Between Frameworks

Data transfer between different frameworks versus data transfer within a framework has distinct variations. Data transfer within a framework can use internal protocols. When transferring between different frameworks, data must be in a generic format that other framework can understand. To ease this process, we usually accompany data with metadata such as schema types, versions of the software, and layout information. The most famous protocol for transferring data between systems is HTTP with JSON payloads.

We cannot use language-level objects for transferring data between frameworks that are written with different programming languages. A Java object serialized into a byte array will be unrecognizable to a Python program. You can still send it, but the Python program may not be able to make much sense out of the bytes.

Every factor we have discussed so far suggests it is essential to keep our data in continuous regions of main memory. This improves cache use and reduces memory fragmentation. Just as important is that when data is in continuous buffers of memory, they can be sent through the network with minimal overhead.

Cross-Language Data Transfer

Nowadays cross-language data transfer is becoming increasingly important due to data processing systems being developed in a combination of languages. Most notably the deep learning frameworks are created with C/C++ kernels and Python/Java user APIs. Some Python-based data processing systems are adopting the same approach. If the memory layout of data is program language–independent, they can be transferred with less overhead among different language runtimes.

Object and Text Data

When data processing was still in its infancy, most frameworks focused on object data structures and text data. This is a loose representation of data where the frameworks offer flexibility to the user to program with any object type they choose. This was one of the reasons behind the success of early data frameworks. Say we have an enormous collection of files having JSON objects, with each object holding information about a person. To read these JSON objects, we can use a library to map them into a class. Let's call this class `Person`. In our example, each JSON object may have many details that we are not interested in, so we only map the required information from the JSON to the object.

```
Class Person {
    Private String name,
    Private short age,
    Private int phone;
    Private int zipCode;
}
```

We can put each `Person` object into a data structure such as a list. Now we can go through the list to process and extract the data. For example, if we want to filter out people who are under the age of 30 from this list, we can easily write a `for` loop to carry out this goal. Now note the number of memory references we must go through at a minimum to access the age of each person. Another major structure we use is text. Text data is represented as strings inside frameworks. Even though strings can be considered as an array of characters, we decided text deserved its own description given its importance.

Object and text data structures are mostly used when processing raw datasets. Application programming interfaces (APIs) in frameworks such as Spark and Flink use Java objects to stand for the data and process them. The Spark RDD API is based on Java objects as is Flink's DataSet API. These APIs only expose the user to the Java objects and hide the details such as going through a list of objects manually to filter them. When substantial amounts of objects are present in memory, it can create issues in memory-managed languages such as Java and Python.

Serialization

A distributed program dealing with higher-level objects in languages such as Java and Python needs to convert them into the byte format before sending them over the wire. There are various forms of serialization technologies available to achieve this. For instance, Java has built-in serialization technologies to convert objects into byte arrays. There are third-party libraries that can do the job better than the built-in capabilities of languages. In the Java world, Kryo[1] is a widely used object serialization technology.

Objects of same class are not of fixed length when serialized, and there is no way of knowing or enforcing a fixed length to objects if we use generic serialization techniques. Because of this, when objects are transferred their length needs to go with the data as well.

Object serialization and deserialization are tasks that require a significant amount of CPU power. Often this becomes a bottleneck for applications dealing with substantial amounts of small objects. Transferring individual small objects through the network is an inefficient task. The senders and receivers need to work on multiple objects grouped together into network buffers to increase network efficiency. All these tasks demand added CPU time.

Vectors and Matrices

Vectors and matrices are two common mathematical objects in computations. A vector of dimension n is an ordered collection of n elements. A matrix is a collection of numbers arranged into a fixed set of rows and columns. A vector can be thought of as a single-row matrix. Both these data types are represented using arrays inside applications.

Arrays are contiguous spaces in memory holding multiple values of the same data type. They can be single-dimensional or multidimensional. Array traversal is extremely efficient compared to other compatible data types such as linked lists. We can simply calculate the memory address of an array element by using the base address of the address and the byte size of an element. If our array is an integer array with each element having 4 bytes, the memory address of ith element will be *base address* $+ i \times 4$.

To access a value in a linked list, we would have to navigate through the links of the list. If the element we need is the 1,000th element, that would mean going through the earlier 999 links between nodes: a time-consuming affair. Linked lists are more efficient in cases where there are frequent additions and deletions in random places. If the application permits, it is always a desirable choice to use arrays over other structures. Figure 4-5 shows this advantage.

Deep learning and machine learning algorithms employ vectors and matrices extensively for computations. The following sections describe how they are stored in memory.

---

[1]https://github.com/EsotericSoftware/kryo

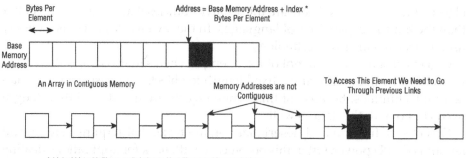

A Linked List with Elements Pointing to Next Elements Memory Address

Figure 4-5: Array memory layout versus list memory layout

1D Vectors

We can use arrays to store one-dimensional vectors easily, as it is a natural fit. Assume we have an integer vector we want to put into an array.

```
V = {1, 2, 3, 4, 5, 6, 7, 8, 9, 10}
```

This vector consists of integers from 1 to 10. We can hold an integer with 4 bytes of memory. Since this array has 10 elements, it needs 40 bytes of contiguous memory. To create this array, the OS will allocate a 40-byte contiguous memory chunk in virtual memory. Note that this chunk of memory will not necessarily be on a contiguous physical memory as the data can be in multiple pages that map to multiple frames in memory. Allocating into multiple pages is unlikely to occur for our 40-byte array, but for larger arrays, especially with sizes greater than page size, this is true. Arrays are accessed using indexes. Say we create the previous array in C language:

```
int V[10] = {1, 2, 3, 4, 5, 6, 7, 8, 9, 10};
```

Now we can access an individual element by using the index. For example, to access the ith element, we can use the syntax $V[i]$.

Matrices

A matrix is a two-dimensional representation of numbers and has associated operations such as sum, multiplication, and transpose. It can be thought of as a rectangular array of numbers arranged in rows and columns. We can access an individual value of a matrix using the row index and column index. The number of rows and columns in the matrix forms its dimensionality. Figure 4-6 shows a matrix of four rows and three columns. We call such an example a 4×3 matrix. The right side of the figure shows how we address each value in the matrix using the two indexes. Note this is a zero-based index. The first value of the index is the row index, and the second number is the column index. For example, in our matrix, the corresponding value at cell [1, 2] is 2.

1	3	3
4	4	2
0	2	1
3	6	8

0,0	0,1	0,2
1,0	1,1	1,2
2,0	2,1	2,2
3,0	3,1	3,2

4 × 3 Matrix with Values   Indexes of 4 × 3 Matrix

Figure 4-6: Matrix and indexes

Matrices are represented in-memory using arrays. If the matrix is of dimensions $r \times c$, we need an array of size $r \times c$ to store it in the memory. The matrix representation is quite versatile and is a favorite in scientific applications. While matrices are rich in expressiveness, care must be taken to yield the best performance when implementing them on different computer architectures.

For example, memory access can be significantly faster due to caching if sequential memory addresses are accessed. In some cases, the computations need to access a matrix by going through each row sequentially. Or a calculation may need to access the matrices by columns. To ensure efficiency, a matrix can be stored in either column-major or row-major format. Such representations allow the cache to be used effectively for various computations.

Row-Major and Column-Major Formats

Row major and column major are by far the most popular matrix representations. In row-major format, the first row is placed in contiguous memory, then the next row, and so on. Figure 4-7 shows how a 4×3 matrix is placed in memory using the row-major format. The cells show their matrix indices.

With the column-major format, values of a column are stored contiguously in memory. Figure 4-8 displays the memory layout of the same matrix stored in the column-major format.

As we discussed earlier, these representations are trying to put the data into memory to match the access pattern of an application. If an application randomly accesses values of a matrix, both representations will work equally. But most numerical computations have specific access patterns that benefit from these representations.

To see the effect of these two formats, we will create a simple program that accesses a matrix. This program takes two matrices and multiplies each element of the first matrix by the same index in the second. We are then going to replace

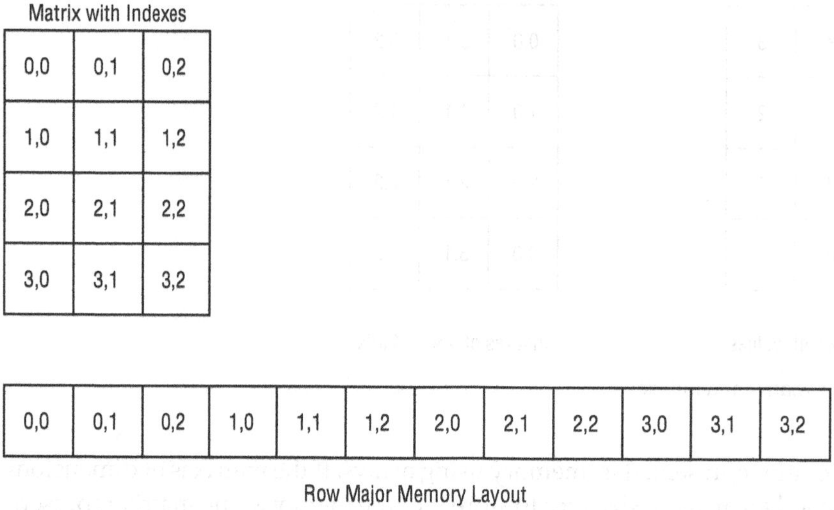

Matrix with Indexes

0,0	0,1	0,2
1,0	1,1	1,2
2,0	2,1	2,2
3,0	3,1	3,2

0,0	0,1	0,2	1,0	1,1	1,2	2,0	2,1	2,2	3,0	3,1	3,2

Row Major Memory Layout

Figure 4-7: Row major representation of a matrix

Matrix with Indexes

0,0	0,1	0,2
1,0	1,1	1,2
2,0	2,1	2,2
3,0	3,1	3,2

0,0	1,0	2,0	3,0	0,1	1,1	2,1	3,1	0,2	1,2	2,2	3,2

Column Major Memory Layout

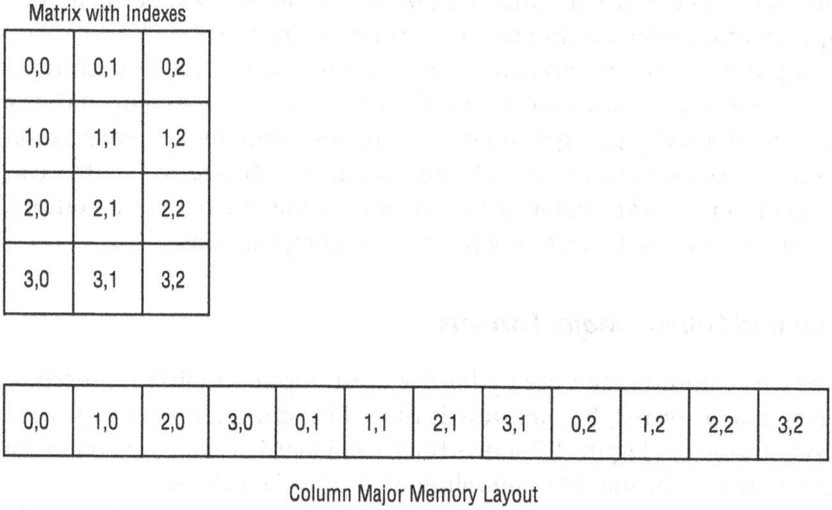

Figure 4-8: Column major representation of a matrix

the first matrix with these multiplied values. The matrices are generated as row major, and we will access them row-wise and column-wise to perform the same calculation.

C++ Program for Accessing a Row-Major Matrix Using Column-Wise and Row-Wise Access

```cpp
class Matrix {
public:
  int64_t* buffer{};
  int32_t rows = 0;
  int32_t cols = 0;
};
```

```
void MulMatrixByCol(const Matrix& y, const Matrix& x) {
  // going through column index
  for (size_t col = 0; col < y.cols; ++col) {
    // going through row index
    for (size_t row = 0; row < y.rows; ++row) {
      // here we are not accessing consecutive memory addresses,
      // consecutive memory address accesses jumps by y.cols
      y.buffer[row * y.cols + col] += x.buffer[row * x.cols + col];
    }
  }
}

void MulMatrixByRow(const Matrix& y, const Matrix& x) {
  // going through row index
  for (size_t row = 0; row < y.rows; ++row) {
    // going through column index
    for (size_t col = 0; col < y.cols; ++col) {
      // we access consecutive memory addresses
      y.buffer[row * y.cols + col] *= x.buffer[row * x.cols + col];
    }
  }
}

void GenerateMatrix(Matrix& m, int rows, int cols) {
  int64_t val = 0;
  m.buffer = new int64_t[rows * cols];
  m.rows = rows;
  m.cols = cols;
  for (size_t row = 0; row < m.rows; ++row) {
    for (size_t col = 0; col < m.cols; ++col) {
      m.buffer[row * m.cols + col] = val++;
    }
  }
}

int main() {
  Matrix m, n;
  int rows = 10240;
  int cols = 10240;
  GenerateMatrix(m, rows, cols);
  GenerateMatrix(n, rows, cols);
  auto t1 = std::chrono::high_resolution_clock::now();
  MulMatrixByCol(m, n);
  std::cout << "By column access time : "
      << std::chrono::duration_cast<std::chrono::milliseconds>(
      std::chrono::high_resolution_clock::now() - t1).count()
      << std::endl;

  Matrix q, r;
  GenerateMatrix(q, rows, cols);
```

```
GenerateMatrix(r, rows, cols);
t1 = std::chrono::high_resolution_clock::now();
MulMatrixByRow(q, r);
std::cout << "By row access time : "
      << std::chrono::duration_cast<std::chrono::milliseconds>(
        std::chrono::high_resolution_clock::now() - t1).count()
      << std::endl;
return 0;
}
```

Figure 4-9 shows the times for distinct matrices using column access and row access of a row-major matrix. The difference is more than 10 times in this instance between row-wise access and column-wise access. If we did the same experiment for a column-major matrix, the results would flip.

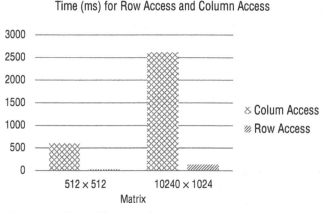

Figure 4-9: Time difference of access patterns

Any array allocated by a low-level programming language such as C/C++ can be viewed as a byte buffer. Since arrays are just byte buffers in memory, they are flexible in defining data transferring APIs. The only downside to arrays is the difficulty in managing complex object types. Since arrays are just byte buffers, it is possible to put any object into them, but it requires a bit of extra work by the programmer.

There are many abstractions created on top of arrays to handle large datasets. NumPy is one such popular package among data scientists to store arrays and matrices inside the Python language.

N-Dimensional Arrays/Tensors

Tensors can be thought of as a generalization of algebraic objects like scalars, vectors, and matrices. Tensor operations [2] have become the basis of machine learning and AI in recent times. Leading frameworks such as TensorFlow[2] and PyTorch[3] are based on the tensor data model. Despite the multidimensional representation, tensors are stored as contiguous arrays in memory. Reshape operations that alter the index to element mapping can rearrange the view of a tensor without changing its byte layout. Figure 4-10 is the memory representation of a 3D tensor in a contiguous memory buffer.

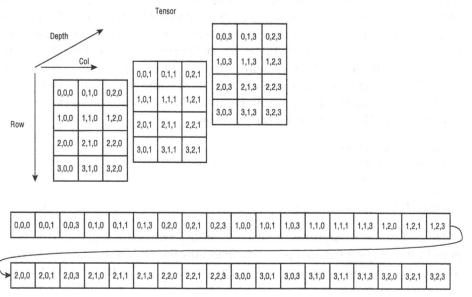

Figure 4-10: Memory representation of 3D tensor

NumPy

Python does not have a native array data type. Instead, it uses list type for arrays. Depending on the list implementation, Python requires more memory to keep track of the elements. Also, list access is not efficient compared to arrays due to indirection. NumPy[4] [3] fills this gap, supplying a native array implementation. It can store n-dimensional arrays as well.

NumPy is popular for scientific computations with Python and is considered the driving force behind the success of that coding language in the scientific community. Unlike a regular array in a programming language, NumPy has operations associated with it. These include areas such as mathematical, logical, shape manipulation, sorting, I/O, discrete Fourier transforms, basic linear

---

[2]https://www.tensorflow.org/
[3]https://pytorch.org/
[4]https://numpy.org/

algebra, basic statistical operations, random simulation operations, and many more. The core NumPy and all the operations it supports are implemented in C with native performance. The Python API around the C code does not do any heavy computations. This design makes NumPy arrays efficient for practical applications compared to a native Python implementation.

NumPy has many APIs and functions that would require another book to fully describe. Instead, we will look at how NumPy uses a contiguous memory buffer to store various array-based data types and operations. From the ground up, NumPy is designed to be a Python library and not an interoperable data format between systems. As such, the internal implementation of the data structure as an array can be changed without affecting the user APIs. But over the years, NumPy has become a stable library, and some projects use its internal representations to directly manipulate buffers for efficiency reasons.

First, we will look at how we can create an array using NumPy.

```
import numpy as np
# one dimensional array of 12 elements going from 0 to 11
>>> a = np.arange(6)
>>> a
array([ 0,  1,  2,  3,  4,  5])
```

This array is a contiguous region in memory with six integer values. Now NumPy has a concept of a shape that defines how the array is indexed. If we want to index the previous array as a 3×4 matrix, we can reshape the array as follows:

```
>>> a = a.reshape(3, 2)
array([[ 0,  1],
       [ 2,  3],
       [ 4,  5]])
```

By default, NumPy uses the row major representation to keep the array in contiguous memory. The previous reshaping merely set the size of the rows and column variables for the matrix. Hence, NumPy requires no heavy operations such as memory copying to create this 2D structure from a 1D array. Now we can access array elements using the following syntax:

```
>>> a[1,1]
3
```

If we try to reshape the previous array to a 3×5 matrix, it will give an error, as expected. We only have 6 elements in this array, and it cannot be a matrix with 15 elements.

```
a = a.reshape(3,5)
Traceback (most recent call last):
  File "<stdin>", line 1, in <module>
ValueError: cannot reshape array of size 12 into shape (3,5)
```

Once we have our arrays configured, we can apply operations to them. Assume we want to multiply the array by 3:

```
>>> a *= 3
>>> a
array([[ 0,  3],
       [ 6,  9],
       [12, 15]])
```

Or we want to add another array to a:

```
>>> b = np.arange(10, 22).reshape(3, 2)
>>> c = a + b
>>> c
array([[10, 14],
       [18, 22],
       [26, 30]])
```

Some operations change the in-memory buffers of NumPy, while others create new copies. The previous multiplication is an in-place operation.

Memory Representation

NumPy can store matrices in both row-major and column-major formats. It uses identifier c for row-major format and F for column-major format. This is owing to a historical reason. Fortran and c are the most popular languages for writing mathematical codes; Fortran uses the column-major format for 2D arrays, while c prefers row-major format. As a result, NumPy has chosen c for row major and F for column major. Going back to our examples, let's create the same matrix in both formats.

```
>>> row_matrix = np.array([[1,2,3], [4,6,7]], order='C')
>>> col_matrix = np.array([[1,2,3], [4,6,7]], order='F')
>>> print(row_matrix.flags)
  C_CONTIGUOUS : True
  F_CONTIGUOUS : False
  OWNDATA : True
  WRITEABLE : True
  ALIGNED : True
  WRITEBACKIFCOPY : False
  UPDATEIFCOPY : False

>>> print(col_matrix.flags)
  C_CONTIGUOUS : False
  F_CONTIGUOUS : True
  OWNDATA : True
  WRITEABLE : True
  ALIGNED : True
  WRITEBACKIFCOPY : False
  UPDATEIFCOPY : False
```

The flags associated with the NumPy arrays show whether they are stored in column (F) or row (C) formats. We can now navigate the data associated with each array according to the order in which they are stored.

```
>>> print(row_matrix.ravel(order='K'))
[1 2 3 4 6 7]
>>> print(col_matrix.ravel(order='K'))
[1 4 2 6 3 7]
```

The `ravel` method returns the contiguous array holding the values. The parameter `order=K` says it to return the contiguous array as it is stored in memory. As expected, the column matrix and row matrix are stored differently.

K-means with NumPy

Let's return to our K-means example from Chapter 1 and learn how to implement it using NumPy. We will look at a serial version of the program to understand how K-means can help to create an algorithm such as NumPy.

```python
import numpy as np
import matplotlib.pyplot as plt


k = 3
iterations = 20


np.random.seed(0)
# we are going to generate 300 points with 2 attributes around 3 centers
X = np.concatenate((np.random.randn(100, 2) + np.array([1,1]),
                    np.random.randn(100, 2) + np.array([20,20]),
                    np.random.randn(100, 2) + np.array([10,10])), axis = 0)
# choose k random points from X
centroids = X[np.random.randint(X.shape[0], size=k)]


# Initialize the vectors in which we will store the
classes = np.zeros(X.shape[0], dtype=np.float32)
distances = np.zeros([X.shape[0], k], dtype=np.float32)
# Loop for the maximum number of iterations
for i in range(iterations):
    # calculate the distances
    for j in range(k):
        distances[:, j] = np.linalg.norm(X - centroids[j], axis=1)

    # each member is assigned to the nearest class
    classes = np.argmin(distances, axis=1)

    # use the new centers to replace the old
    for c in range(k):
        centroids[c] = np.mean(X[classes == c], 0)
```

In this code we first generate a set of points with two attributes (2D) around three centers. This is the data we use for the K-means algorithm. Then we generate three centers randomly and use two arrays called `classes` and `distances` to keep track of the intermediate data. Then we have a loop that runs 20 iterations. In this loop, we calculate the distance of each point to the center. After the distance calculation, we assign points to the nearest center. New centers are calculated as the average of the points assigned to the centers.

Sparse Matrices

Another noticeable consideration is the representation of dense versus sparse matrices in memory. Sparse matrices are defined as matrices where most elements are zero [4]. Storing these as regular dense matrices wastes both memory and CPU cycles during computations. As an alternative, there are efficient layouts such as compressed sparse column (CSC), compressed sparse row (CSR), and doubly compressed sparse column (DCSC) for sparse matrices.

Figure 4-11 illustrates an example sparse matrix represented in the usual dense matrix format. In addition to the obvious drain on memory, using such a matrix in a regular general matrix multiply (GEMM)–like operation will unnecessarily waste computing power due to multiplication by zero. The CSR representation of the same matrix in Figure 4-12 is a suitable alternative if the matrix is accessed by row order. It introduces three contiguous arrays: one holding nonzero entries (labeled Non-Zero Value), another storing column indexes of those entries (labeled Column Index), and the third storing the starting array index of Column Index corresponding to a row. For example, if we want to retrieve the value 1.9 at (2,4), we look at Row Pointer indexes 2 and 3. This gives us the index range of the Column Index array that we should scan to find column 4. More specifically, we get the right-open interval (3,5). In this interval we find column 4 at index 4 (just a coincidence!) in the Column Index. The corresponding nonzero value is thus found at index 4 of the Non-Zero Value array.

	C_0	C_1	C_2	C_3	C_4	C_5
R_0	0.3	0.0	0.0	0.0	4.2	0.0
R_1	0.0	0.0	0.0	0.0	0.0	3.4
R_2	0.0	0.0	3.1	0.0	1.9	0.0
R_3	0.0	8.7	0.0	0.0	0.0	0.6

Figure 4-11: Dense representation of a sparse matrix

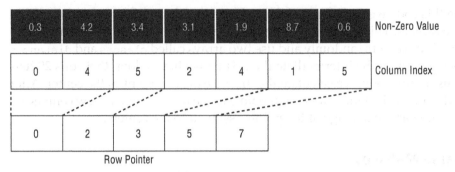

Figure 4-12: CSR representation of the sparse matrix

The CSC representation is like CSR except it has Column Pointer and Row Index arrays rather than Row Pointer and Column Index arrays. CSC is faster than CSR if the matrix is accessed as columns. We can improve these representations further when the matrix has entire rows and columns of zeros.

Sparse matrices are mostly used in numerical computations for simulations. Machine learning and deep learning systems tend to work on dense matrices. As such, we will not go into details on sparse matrices and present them here only to complete our discussion.

Table

Array structures are meant to hold homogeneous values. We cannot hold strings and integers in the same array unless we treat them as some type of generic data types such as a Java object or C void pointer. To load data that is heterogeneous and structured into memory, we can use a table abstraction. Going back to our earlier example, after we process the JSON objects and filter the people, we are going to save our data in a CSV file. The CSV file has the attributes shown in Table 4-3.

Table 4-3: CSV File with Attributes

NAME	AGE	PHONE	ZIP
John Doe	29	3218323456	32532
Annie Smith	28	2318323321	31331
------	------	------	------

This CSV file has information about thousands of people. Unlike the JSON file where we had hierarchies of information, this is a more structured data that looks like a table. We meet a lot of applications in practice dealing with such structured data that can be represented as a table.

We can read this CSV file into a table structure in the memory. Unlike in a regular RDBMS, we are not allowing multiple clients to concurrently do ACID operations on the CSV files based on the table structure. Instead, we can use the table as a read-only view of the CSV. If we are going to change the table in memory, we must write a new CSV with the modified data. Viewing data as tables gives us another important advantage. Once we model a dataset as a table, we can use SQL to write queries. SQL is such a popular and usable tool that SQL interfaces to datasets are the go-to method in the data processing field.

Table Formats

As in our JSON example, data are present in formats that are unsuitable for table structures. We need to do some preprocessing before we can transform them into a table format. Later we can use this table data to execute queries efficiently. A table has a set of columns, each with a name and a type. These columns are filled with data. As described here, a table can be thought of as a collection of columns or rows. As in our earlier object approach, we can create the table as a list of Person objects. But there are more efficient ways to store table data.

Column data format and the row data format are the two common forms of table representations in memory. Row data formats are better for transaction processing. Column-based formats are great for read-only data with analytical workloads. Let's look at these two formats in detail.

Column Data Format

A column data format stores the table by arranging columns in contiguous memory. Say our Person table had 1,000 entries. Name is a string column, Age is a short column, Phone is a string column, and ZipCode is an integer column. When we arrange this table in column format, it will have four contiguous buffers (arrays) each with 1,000 values, as shown in Table 4-4.

Table 4-4: Column Arrays

COLUMN	REPRESENTATION
Name	Array of strings
Age	Array of integers
Phone	Array of strings
ZipCode	Array of integers

The biggest advantage of this approach is that we can access data in a column quickly through an array lookup. Even though we say columns are stored as arrays (contiguous buffers), there is nothing that restricts us from storing them as lists. As we discussed earlier, lists are significantly slower compared to arrays for sequential as well as random access. But if our columns need frequent deletions and additions at random places, lists may be preferable.

Assume we are using an array to hold the columns. At the minimum, we will need to keep track of empty/null values in our tables. To keep null values, a separate array can be used. This array has special markers for the indexes where null values are present. For data types with a fixed-length memory, location of a data value can be calculated as index × data byte length. To store variable-length data such as bytes or strings, we need to keep track of the end of each record by using another array or inserting lengths into the array.

Row Data Format

When we think about data in a table, we always think in terms of rows. In our example, a single person is recorded in a row. A row has a complete record of data, so it is only natural to store table data as a set of rows. Keeping a list of `Person` objects is the crudest form of row data format. We can be more sophisticated than this to keep data in a contiguous space in memory. As in the column case, we use byte arrays to place the values into a contiguous array and deploy auxiliary arrays to keep track of null values and data offsets.

Apache Arrow

Apache Arrow[5] is a column data format for storing data with heterogenous attributes in a table. Its layout specification defines how distinct types of data are arranged in the memory. Arrow considers a dataset as a set of columns. Each column has a data type and a name. A data type can be primitive or composite, such as a struct and union.

One of Arrow's main goals is to supply a unified memory layout so that the same data can be understood from different runtimes written in various languages. This is especially important when programs use multiple languages within the same process. A good example is a Python library using C++ code to enhance performance, which is common in Python data processing frameworks. As we saw with NumPy, the Arrow data structure is created inside the C++ code. The Arrow structure can be accessed from Python without copying the complete structure from C++ to Python memory space. This is a huge advantage in designing easy-to-use Python APIs around high-performance code written in C++.

---

[5]https://arrow.apache.org/

Another advantage comes when transferring data between different frameworks. Say we have Java runtime processing data and feeding this data to a deep learning framework. These two frameworks are running on separate computer resources. Apache Arrow format can transfer data between the frameworks without the need to alter formats between them, preserving valuable CPU time.

Next, we will examine the Arrow data structures and how they can be used for data processing. Arrow data format only defines the memory structure of a data column. How these columns are combined to create table structures is up to the implementations. Also, the specification does not define how the metadata for the tables and columns are represented and instead leaves that to the implementations.

Arrow Data Format

An Arrow table is a collection of columns of the same row count. Each column has a data type and a name assigned to it. Since the Arrow specification does not talk about tables, it only asserts how data in every column is set in memory. Each column is viewed as an array (vector) of a data type. Depending on the data type, an array may require multiple buffers in memory to store the data. A buffer is continuously spaced in-memory reserved by a heap allocation function such as malloc.

Primitive Types

Primitive types include our familiar data types of integers and floating-point numbers. Arrow is platform-independent, and all the primitive types have bit width and signedness specified. For example, Arrow has primitive data types such as int32 (int in Java), int64 (long in Java), float32 (float in Java), and float64 (double in Java). Their bit width is fixed, and so we call them fixed-width types. A fixed-width type has a validity buffer and the actual data. The validity buffer holds information about null values.

We will now examine how the following int32 array is presented in memory by Arrow. In it, we have four values and zero null values. The length and the null count comprise the metadata about this array. The two buffers are padded up to 64 bytes to allow cache alignment of the buffers.

```
Array - [1, 5, 1], Metadata - Length 4, Null count 0
```

Validity Buffer

BYTES	0	1-63
VALUE	00001111	0 (padding)

Data Buffer

BYTES	0-3	4-7	8-11	12-63
VALUE	1	5	1	unspecified

Here is an array with a NULL value. Here, bytes 4–7 are not specified, and the validity buffer is changed.

```
Array - [1, NULL, 1], Metadata - Length 4, Null count 1
```

Validity Buffer

BYTES	0	1-63
VALUE	00001101	0 (padding)

Data Buffer

BYTES	0-3	4-7	8-11	12-63
VALUE	1	unspecified	1	unspecified

Variable-Length Data

Arrow considers variable-length data as byte arrays. String (text) is displayed as variable-length byte data. To have variable-length data, Arrow needs an added buffer to hold the offsets of values in the data buffer. This offset buffer has the beginning index of the corresponding item. Assume the following string data is a buffer:

```
Array = ["One", "Tw"]
```

Validity Buffer

BYTES	0	1-63
VALUE	00000011	0 (padding)

Offset Buffer

BYTES	0-3	4-7	8-63
VALUE	0	4	unspecified

Data Buffer

BYTES	0	1	2	3	4	5	6	9-63
INT VALUE	111	110	101	0	116	119	0	unspecified

At this point, we have only discussed two data types. Here is the complete list of different types supported by Arrow.

- **Primitive**—A sequence of values each having the same byte or bit width.
- **Binary** (fixed size and variable size)—A sequence of byte values each having a fixed or variable byte length.
- **List** (fixed size and variable size)—A nested layout where each value has the same number of elements taken from a child data type, for example, a list of integers.
- **Struct**—A nested layout consisting of a collection of named child fields, each having the same length but distinct types.
- **Sparse and dense union**—A nested layout storing a sequence of values, each of which can have a type chosen from a collection of child array types.
- **Null**—A sequence of all null values.

Arrow Serialization

Unlike in our object representation, we can directly use the contiguous spaces in memory for the data transfer. When combined with networks that can directly copy user space data to the network, these transfers become extremely efficient. Arrow has its own library called Arrow Flight for transferring data between systems.

Arrow Example

Let's look at a simple Arrow example to read a CSV file done in Python, which is the language of choice for many data scientists. Implementations of Arrow specification are available in many other languages, and this data can be transferred to programs running in them through the Arrow APIs.

```
>>> from pyarrow import csv
>>> table = csv.read_csv('persons.csv')
>>> df = table.to_pandas()
>>> df
     Name   Age        Phone    Zip
0    John    33   2313213312  34560
1   Smith    20   2314563312  56622
2    Lyla    49   2313789312  23561
3     Nia    42   4245513312  34362
4    John    33   2313213312  34560
5   Henry    22   1233343312  54560
>>>
```

Pandas DataFrame

Pandas DataFrame[6] [5] is a popular in-memory data table abstraction in Python. NumPy and Arrow are two data structures written in high-performance C/C++ languages. By contrast, Pandas is written in Python. Regardless, data scientists use it every day to load and process structured data. Pandas is mostly applied in the preprocessing and post-processing stages of machine learning applications. For example, we can load a CSV file using Pandas, clean it, and transform the data to a format suitable for a machine learning algorithm. Pandas does not use its own compact data structure as in Arrow to store the data in memory. Instead, it relies on Python data structures and NumPy.

Pandas has two main data structures called `Series` and `DataFrame`. A series is a one-dimensional array and can hold any data type. The most important data structure in Pandas is the `DataFrame`, which is a table with some operators attached to it. Since Pandas represents data as a table, it is natural to support relational algebra operators on it. It implements the fundamental relational algebra operators as shown in Table 4-5 and supports many other operators that are not in relational databases as well. Altogether, there are more than 200 operators built on top of Pandas DataFrame.

Table 4-5: Fundamental Relational Algebra Operations of Pandas DataFrame

OPERATION	DESCRIPTION
Selection	Select rows
Projection	Select columns
Union	Set union of two DataFrames
Difference	Set difference of two DataFrames
Join	Combine two DataFrames using a condition
Distinct	Remove duplicate rows
GroupBy	Group rows based on selected column values
Sort	Lexicographical ordering of rows

Here we have a simple program to clean a CSV file by removing any duplicates:

```
import pandas as pd

# making data frame from csv file
data = pd.read_csv("persons.csv")
print(data)
```

---

[6]https://pandas.pydata.org/pandas-docs/stable/index.html

```
# remove duplicate values
data.drop_duplicates(subset ="Name",
                        keep = False, inplace = True)
print(data)
```

Here is a `persons.csv` file along with the output of the program:

```
     Name    Age      Phone     Zip
0    John     33   2313213312   34560
1   Smith     20   2314563312   56622
2    Lyla     49   2313789312   23561
3     Nia     42   4245513312   34362
4    John     33   2313213312   34560
5   Henry     22   1233343312   54560
```

Here is the output:

```
     Name    Age      Phone     Zip
1   Smith     20   2314563312   56622
2    Lyla     49   2313789312   23561
3     Nia     42   4245513312   34362
5   Henry     22   1233343312   54560
```

A Pandas DataFrame can have an index associated with it. This index allows efficient searching of values in the table as well as supporting operators such as joins. Here is an example of an equijoin operator with indexes:

```
import numpy as np
import pandas as pd

df1 = pd.DataFrame({'lkey': ['first', 'second', 'third', 'fourth'],
                    'value': [11, 22, 33, 44]})
df2 = pd.DataFrame({'rkey': ['second', 'fifth', 'second', 'first'],
                    'value': [222, 555, 222, 111]})
print(df1)
print(df2)

joined = df1.merge(df2, left_on='lkey', right_on='rkey')
print(joined)
```

Here is the output of the program:

```
     lkey    value
0    first     11
1   second     22
2    third     33
3   fourth     44
     rkey    value
0   second    222
1    fifth    555
```

```
2    second      222
3     first  .   111
       lkey   value_x    rkey  value_y
0     first        11   first      111
1    second        22  second      222
2    second        22  second      222
```

Column vs. Row Tables

Either a row representation or a column representation can be efficient depending on the specific queries on tables. For numerical computations with matrices, the row major or column major representations can lead to large performance differences. Because of this, frameworks working with matrices support both formats. These frameworks allow users to load data into one format and convert it to the other at runtime.

Most data processing frameworks use either a row or a column representation of a table. In these frameworks, the details are hidden from the user. Because of this, once a framework is chosen, it is harder to change the way tables are represented. Most large data applications query the data to extract information. These applications do not change the data. As a result, most of the user-facing queries are read-only in data analytics systems. For such queries, column data formats are a better fit [6].

Summary

In this chapter, we looked at the importance of in-memory data structures for data processing. Numerical computations in machine learning/deep learning algorithms and data processing algorithms can benefit immensely by loading data into memory to optimize access and storage. The general rule of in-memory data is to match the data layout with the access patterns of data. If the accessed data is stored consecutively in memory and the access pattern also matches, we achieve the best performance. This is not possible in all cases as some applications need random access.

References

1. D. Durner, V. Leis, and T. Neumann, "On the impact of memory allocation on high-performance query processing," in *Proceedings of the 15th International Workshop on Data Management on New Hardware*, 2019, pp. 1-3.

2. Y. Ji, Q. Wang, X. Li, and J. Liu, "A survey on tensor techniques and applications in machine learning," *IEEE Access*, vol. 7, pp. 162950-162990, 2019.

3. S. Van Der Walt, S. C. Colbert, and G. Varoquaux, "The NumPy array: a structure for efficient numerical computation," *Computing in science & engineering*, vol. 13, no. 2, pp. 22-30, 2011.

4. Z. Zhang, Y. Xu, J. Yang, X. Li, and D. Zhang, "A survey of sparse representation: algorithms and applications," *IEEE access*, vol. 3, pp. 490-530, 2015.

5. W. McKinney, "pandas: a foundational Python library for data analysis and statistics," *Python for High Performance and Scientific Computing*, vol. 14, no. 9, pp. 1-9, 2011.

6. D. J. Abadi, S. R. Madden, and N. Hachem, "Column-stores vs. row-stores: how different are they really?," in *Proceedings of the 2008 ACM SIGMOD international conference on Management of data*, 2008, pp. 967-980.

Programming Models

Programming a parallel data-intensive application is a complex undertaking. Data-intensive frameworks provide programming abstractions to make it easy to develop applications at scale. The programming models and data structures used by frameworks have a large impact on their performance and generality. Here, we will look at a few popular programming models and APIs for data-intensive applications.

Introduction

A parallel computing model provides an easy-to-use abstraction needed to express an algorithm and its composition for solving problems using many computers [1]. The effectiveness of a model is defined by how generally applicable it is to express problems in the application domain and the efficiency of the programs developed using it.

Algorithms are expressed using abstract concepts such as vectors, matrices, graphs, tables, and tensors, along with the operations around them. These abstract concepts are represented in computers using data structures such as arrays, lists, trees, and hash maps, and we can implement various operations around the like.

A parallel programming API is a combination of a computing model, data structures, and operations. In other words, the data structures and operations make a domain-specific parallel programming API using a parallel programming model. More operations and data structures supported by an API means it will be able to solve a variety of problems easily. Also, if the data structures are generic enough to support many problems, the programming API can become more applicable overall.

Parallel Programming Models

We can view parallel programming models according to how they decompose a problem into parallel tasks and how the parallel processes are programmed to interact with each other.

Parallel Process Interaction

Parallel programming models can be broadly classified as providing implicit and explicit parallelism. In an explicit parallel model, the user is aware of the parallel environment and programs accordingly. In an implicit model, the user is not aware of the parallel nature of the program, and there is a compiler or runtime that converts user code into a parallel program.

The most popular explicit parallel model is the single process multiple data (SPMD) style of programming supported by the message passing for synchronizing state. Implicit parallel models are popular in data-intensive applications and are implemented according to a partitioned distributed data model used in frameworks like Spark and Flink. Such distributed data APIs come under the general umbrella of partitioned global address space (PGAS) models.

Problem Decomposition

Another way to look at programming models is to understand how they decompose a problem into a set of parallel tasks. We have the options of task-parallel and data-parallel programming models. In a data-parallel programming model, the same program runs on different parts of the data and can be thought of as SPMD or PGAS programs. Batch data-intensive programs use this method.

Task-parallel programming models consist of tasks doing different computations simultaneously. They can be considered multiple processes, multiple data (MPMD) programs. Streaming applications are one such example.

Data Structures

In Chapter 4, we studied popular data structures and their memory layouts. Data-intensive frameworks are designed around these data structures and the operations that surround them. An operation can be local or distributed. The local operations work on data in a single process, while distributed operations handle data in multiple processes.

The frameworks provide built-in operations, as well as the ability to define custom code and thereby allow a user to specify logic unique to an application. The programming interfaces for operations differ according to the programming model and the execution adopted by a framework, but the semantics of operations are the same in the framework. Table 5-1 shows the popular choices of data structures and programming models for data-intensive applications.

Table 5-1: Applications, Data Structures, and Programming Models

APPLICATION CLASS	DATA STRUCTURES	PROGRAM MODEL
Batch ETL	Tables, arrays	Data parallel, implicit parallel
Streaming	Tables, objects	Task parallel, implicit parallel
Machine learning	Arrays, graphs, tables	Data parallel, implicit or explicit parallel
Deep learning	Tensors, arrays	Task parallel, implicit parallel, data parallel

Batch ETL applications mostly use tables, while streaming applications are designed around messaging and tables, and machine learning (ML)/deep learning applications use matrices/tensors. Implicit parallel programming models are popular in data-intensive frameworks, and only the most demanding applications are programmed with explicit models.

Data Structures and Operations

Tensors, matrices, tables, and graphs are the most widely used data structures in data-intensive applications. An operation takes as input one or more of these data structures and produces one or more data structures. A local operation does not require network communication. Distributed operations specify the semantics of these operations when the data is present in multiple computers/processes and requires network communications. We need both distributed operations and in-process operations (local) to write applications that work with many computers.

Data Types

Let us start with the basic data types and then move on to the composite (complex) data types created from them. Not every data type is supported by every system, and usually there are mechanisms to define custom data types. Table 5-2 shows common primitive data types, while Table 5-3 highlights common complex data types.

Table 5-2: Common Primitive Types Supported by Data Systems

DATA TYPE	BIT WIDTH	DESCRIPTION
UInt8	8	8-bit unsigned integer
UInt16	16	16-bit unsigned integer
UInt32	32	32-bit unsigned integer
UInt64	64	64-bit unsigned integer
Int8	8	8-bit signed integer
Int16	16	16-bit signed integer
Int32	32	32-bit signed integer
Int64	64	64-bit signed integer
Float64	64	Double-precision floating-point number
Float32	32	Single-precision floating-point number
Byte	8	A single byte

The primitive data types are stored in contiguous memory using a predetermined bit width. Different programming languages and hardware architectures have various names for the same primitive type with equal bit width. For example, in C++ an integer bit width is dependent on the platform. In Java, the integer variable is 32 bits regardless of the platform. To avoid such variances, we used the C++ notation to identify the data type with the bit width.

Table 5-3: Common Complex Types Supported by Data Systems

DATA TYPE	DESCRIPTION
Array	An array of basic data type
String	Text
Big integer	Large integers
Map/hash table	Key, value pairs
Object/class/struct	Complex types
Table	Data arranged into rows and columns
Tensor/matrix	Multidimensional array
Graph	Vertices and edges

As discussed in Chapter 4, we can use various memory layouts to store complex data types in memory.

Local Operations

Every data structure has operations associated with it originating from the abstract concept they represent, such as vectors or matrices. An integer data type falls in the realm of arithmetic operations such as summation, multiplication, and division. Similarly, complex types have associated operations as well. One of the simplest operations on an array is to retrieve a value using an index. If we consider two numeric arrays of equal size to represent two vectors, we can define arithmetic operations such as summation for them.

In an abstract sense, an operation can take many inputs and produce a range of outputs. The input can be of diverse types. For example, we can do a summation over a float and an integer. Input and output types do not have to match either. An operation can be implemented by the user or be provided by the system. Summation over numeric values is an operation provided by every computer. More complex operations such as summation over two arrays need user code.

Distributed Operations

An operation that works on data distributed in many processes is known as a *distributed operation*. These are key to data-intensive applications at scale. The semantics of a local operation and a distributed operation can vary depending on the type. Figure 5-1 displays a distributed operation happening among n processes. This operation takes two datasets as input and produces one dataset.

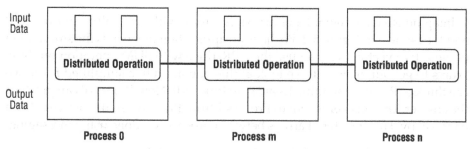

Figure 5-1: Distributed operation

A distributed operation considers data distributed in all the processes when calculating, so it needs to send data among processes using network communications. Since the operation works on data in multiple processes, it will output data in those processes as well.

Array

Arrays are the foundational data structures of scientific computing, machine learning, and deep learning applications. This is because numerical calculations use arrays to stand for vectors, matrices, and tensors. An array consists of a set of elements of the same data type, and each element can be addressed by an index.

A single value array of a type is equivalent to a variable of that type. As such, arrays can stand for all primitive types. The common distributed operations around arrays can be found in the Message Passing Interface (MPI) specification. Table 5-4 describes some of the common operations. In the following chapters, we will go through these operations in detail and examine how they are implemented.

Table 5-4: Distributed Operations on Arrays

OPERATION	DESCRIPTION
Broadcast	Broadcasts an array from one process to many other processes.
Gather/AllGather	Collects arrays from different processes and creates a larger array in a single process or many processes.
Scatter/AllToAll	Redistributes parts of an array to different processes.
Reduce/AllReduce	Element-wise reduction of arrays. Popular operations include SUM, MIN, MAX, PROD.

Imagine we have two integer arrays (vectors) with two values in process 0 and 1, as shown in Figure 5-2. We have an application that needs the summation of these two vectors. We can use the AllReduce with SUM operation on these arrays to get our answer. If we look at this operation in a simplified form, we can think of Process 1 sending its array to Process 0. Now Process 0 can produce the answer. This answer is sent to Process 1 from Process 0 so that Process 1 can have a copy. This transfer of arrays between processes is done using messaging.

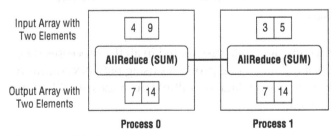

Figure 5-2: AllReduce on arrays on two processes

Tensor

The recent explosion of machine learning and deep learning systems has made tensors prominent. TensorFlow and PyTorch are two popular frameworks built around the tensor application programming interface (API). While the mathematical definition of tensors may sound complicated for all programming purposes on these frameworks, one may think of a tensor as a multidimensional array along with defined operations.

Internally, tensors are implemented as lightweight data structures that keep a pointer to the actual storage and other metadata such as size and shape. Tensor data itself is stored in a contiguous buffer. This form of implementation allows multiple tensors to share the same data but supply different views of it.

Tensor frameworks support many different operations on tensors. We will look at a few essential functions in this chapter, both local and distributed. Also, for the sake of brevity, we will refer to only PyTorch tensors for code examples, though TensorFlow and Numpy have similar APIs.

Indexing

As tensors are multidimensional in nature, we need a way to access elements of a given dimension. The tensor API for this is like regular array indexing, as shown next. Here, we create a one-dimensional tensor with five elements and access its second element. Also, we create a two-dimensional 4×3 tensor and access the first element of its second row. Note how the returned values are also tensors even though they are just one element long.

```
import torch

a = torch.rand(5,)
print(a)
# tensor([0.7341, 0.5129, 0.0473, 0.4183, 0.4692])
print(a[2])
# tensor(0.0473)

b = torch.rand(4, 3)
print(b)
# tensor([[0.7461, 0.8151, 0.4354],
#         [0.2528, 0.2452, 0.1515],
#         [0.5252, 0.7654, 0.0050],
#         [0.7997, 0.5275, 0.4667]])
print(b[2, 1])
# tensor(0.7654)
```

Slicing

Like indexing, slicing allows us to refer to part of the tensor. For example, to get a tensor view of row 2 of b, one could do b[2, :]. Slicing along a dimension takes the form of start:end:step, and omitting all these as shown previously means omitting everything along that dimension.

Broadcasting

When tensors have different dimensions, certain operations may not be performed without first getting both to the same dimensions. Broadcasting is an automatic operation that happens according to some convention in such operations. A simple example would be multiplying tensor a = [1, 2, 3] with tensor b = [4]. As b is a single-element tensor, broadcasting will happen before multiplication, such that b would look like a tensor [4, 4, 4]. The rules of broadcasting are a topic on their own, especially with multidimensional tensors, so we refer you to Numpy's or PyTorch's documentation on the topic.

Other than these primitive tensor operations, there are many element-wise examples such as addition, subtraction, and division. There are also matrix operations, including matrix multiplication, transpose, and inverse. Moreover, as tensors are suitably generic, custom operations are defined over them using existing primitives.

Table

Tables are popular in ETL applications. A table is an ordered arrangement of data into rows and columns. There are many names used for rows and columns in such instances. For instance, a row is sometimes called a *tuple*, *record*, or *vector*. A column is referred to as an *attribute*, *field*, *parameter*, or *property*. There are frameworks that work with key-value pairs, and these can be thought of as a table with two columns, one for key and one for value. Columns of a table can have different data types, but a single column can have values of only a single data type.

APIs around tables are often called DataFrame APIs. The natural operations around a table are defined in relational algebra. Relational algebra is built around five basic operations, as listed in Table 5-5.

We can use these five to build a rich set of operations around tables for data processing. Many other operations are possible in order to make programming around tables easier. Table 5-6 lists some prominent examples.

If tables of the same schema are present in multiple computers, we can think of it as a distributed table with partitions. There are many techniques we can use to partition a table, including row-based partitioning and column-based partitioning. Data processing systems work with row-based partitioning.

Table 5-5: Basic Relational Algebra Operations

OPERATOR	DESCRIPTION
Select	Filters out some records based on the & value of one or more columns
Project	Creates a different view of the table by dropping some of the columns
Union	Applicable on two tables having similar schemas to keep all the records from both tables and remove duplicates
Cartesian Product	Applicable on two tables having similar schemas to keep only the records that are present in both tables
Difference	Retains all the records of the first table, while removing the matching records present in the second table

Table 5-6: Auxiliary Operations on Tables

OPERATOR	DESCRIPTION
Intersect	Applicable on two tables having similar schemas to keep only the records that are present in both tables.
Join	Combines two tables based on the values of columns. Includes variations Left, Right, Full, and Inner joins.
Order By	Sorts the records of the table based on a specified column.
Aggregate	Performs a calculation on a set of values (records) and outputs a single value (record). Aggregations include summation and multiplication.
GroupBy	Groups the data using the given columns; GroupBy is usually followed by aggregate operations.

On top of a partitioned table, we can apply all the previous operations. The data is partitioned, so the results of operations will be partitioned as well. For example, if we try to do a distributed sort on the tables shown in Figure 5-3 using the Year column, it can produce the tables shown in Figure 5-4. Note that we have sorted the tables in ascending order with the lowest values going to Process 0. If we did sorts only on individual partitions, which is a local operation, the results would be completely different.

The resulting table in Process 0 has records from the original tables in Processes 0 and 1. So, the sort operation needs to transfer records from Process 1 to Process 0 and vice versa. This is called a *shuffle operation* on tables, which we will look at in more detail in Chapter 6.

Table-Partition-0		
ID	Year	Value
1	1984	.90
2	1975	.90
3	2001	.82
4	1984	.009

Table-Partition-1		
ID	Year	Value
5	1956	.96
6	1968	.92
7	2002	.82

Figure 5-3: Table partitioned in two processes

Table-Partition-0		
ID	Year	Value
5	1956	.96
6	1968	.92
2	1975	.90

Table-Partition-1		
ID	Year	Value
1	1984	.90
4	1984	.009
3	2001	.82
7	2002	.82

Figure 5-4: Tables after a distributed sort on Year column

Graph Data

Graph is a fundamental data representation common to a variety of problem domains. Technically, a graph is defined as $G = (V, E)$, a collection of vertices V and edges E. Graphs are used to model complex interactions or relationships between entities. For example, a map could be represented as a graph, where cities are the vertices and roads connecting them are edges. This is one of the most common applications of graphs. Pages on the web represent a graph through hyperlinks. The spread of a disease such as influenza can be modeled using a human interaction graph, where humans are vertices and those who come into contact with them are linked through edges. A social network is a graph representing humans and related people. Sensors used in ocean research could construct a dynamic graph. The applications of graphs like this are endless, thus establishing the footing for graph data structures.

Unlike primitives, arrays, and tensors, graphs do not have a fixed representation in programming languages and frameworks. In fact, a graph can be represented in several ways. Adjacency matrix and adjacency list are two common methods.

For the graph in Figure 5-5, the first matrix form shows the adjacency matrix representation. It is a square matrix, and each nonzero entry represents an edge between the two vertices corresponding to the row and column indexes. The adjacency list representation is compact and shows only the vertices connected by a given vertex.

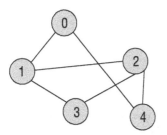

0 →	1,	4	
1 →	0,	2,	3
2 →	1,	3,	4
3 →	1,	2	
4 →	0,	2	

	1			1
1		1	1	
	1		1	1
	1	1		
1		1		

Figure 5-5: Graph representation

A third representation of a graph is to keep an edge list such as $G = \{(0,1),(0,4),(1,2),(1,3),(2,3),(2,4)\}$. Here, we are showing an undirected graph, meaning the edge $(0,1)$ is the same as $(1,0)$. A fourth type is the incidence matrix.[1] This is also a matrix representation, where each row represents a vertex and each column an edge. Nonzero entries indicate that an edge in a column is incident on the corresponding vertex.

Given a graph, a few primitive operations include adding/deleting a vertex or edge, retrieving the degree of a vertex, setting the value of a vertex or an edge, testing if a given vertex is a neighbor of another vertex, and extracting a subgraph of choice. Beyond these, the number of algorithms one could run on graphs is practically unlimited. Triangle counting, spanning trees, breadth-first search, depth-first search, topological sort, strongly connected components, and shortest path are a few well-known examples. There is also a collection of graph algorithms that are considered hard, such as graph partitioning, graph isomorphism, Steiner tree, vertex coloring, and the famous traveling salesman problem. It should be noted that the implementation of these algorithms relies on the primitive operations mentioned earlier.

Capturing relationships in a graph as shown in Figure 5-6 allows us to present an SQL-like query on top of it. For example, the figure captures the relationship between people and the movies they have seen. This allows one to query, for example, "select the friends of Alice who have seen the movie Aliens."

---

[1]https://mathworld.wolfram.com/IncidenceMatrix.html

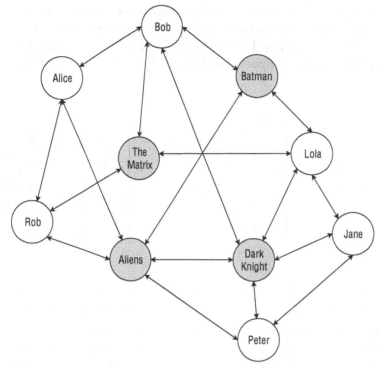

Figure 5-6: Graph relationships

Message Passing Model

Message passing between parallel processes is one of the fundamental requirements for executing programs on multiple computers. It allows parallel processes to exchange data so they can divide work and synchronize state when needed. Any programming model or framework that works at scale on multiple computers uses a messaging implementation.

Since message passing provides only the bare minimum requirements of a parallel application, it allows the user to program the application in any way or shape they want. The user is free to use any data type and call both local and distributed operations on the data. In this model, the user handles the following:

▪ Decomposition of the data into parallel tasks

▪ Use of threads and scheduling of computations

▪ Use messaging to synchronize the data

When programming at the message passing level, users are aware of the parallel nature of the program. Only batch applications are developed with the message passing model in practice because it is hard to use it for streaming applications.

Model

The message passing model assumes there are N parallel processes, each possessing a unique identifier that positions them with respect to other processes. For example, processes can have identifiers from $0,\ldots,N$, and they allow a process to have a relative positioning compared to others.

The N processes execute the same program but work on different partitions of the data and are hence categorized as SPMD. The programs at runtime can choose their own data by using the identifier. For example, if we are going to process a large table by creating N partitions and our program consists of N parallel processes, the 0th process can choose Partition 0, the second process can choose Partition 1, and so on.

Every process is responsible for loading the data assigned to it by the algorithm, processing it, and performing data synchronizations using the communication primitives. Multiple processes can participate in distributed operations on data, which are implemented on top of messaging. A message can have any data type we previously discussed, such as objects, a byte buffer, an array, a table, or a basic type.

Message Passing Frameworks

There are several messaging implementations available for distributed communication between parallel processes. A few of them are listed in Table 5-7.

Table 5-7: Message Passing Implementations

IMPLEMENTATION	DESCRIPTION
MPI and implementations	Most widely used messaging standard for scientific computing. Used in deep learning and data processing frameworks.
Gloo[2]	Implementation of several collective operations. Used in deep learning training applications.
NCCL[3]	Distributed operations on NVIDIA GPUs.
UCX[4]	Messaging API for point-to-point and collectives hiding details of hardware. MPI implementations uses UCX underneath.

Message Passing Interface

MPI is a standard [2] that defines a set of operations required by a library for implementing a message passing model–based application. Since it is a standard,

---

[2]https://github.com/facebookincubator/gloo
[3]https://developer.nvidia.com/nccl
[4]https://www.openucx.org/

it comes with datatypes, methods, and limits on what a message passing application can do. The specification supplies a set of methods for sending messages between two processes, and another set for distributed operations called *collectives*.

MPI was designed from a scientific background. As such, the base methods it supplies are based on array data structures. One can build custom operations on data structures on top of the point-to-point operations of MPI. Distributed operations in MPI are called *collectives*, some of which are described in Table 5-4.

The most common method of using MPI is to take a program and run multiple instances of it in parallel. The program instances are supplied with a unique identifier at runtime called *rank* to distinguish them from each other. The IDs start from 0 and go up to (*n*-1) in a parallel application that has *n* processes. These identifiers are used for sending and receiving messages between processes as well as decomposing parallel programs into parts.

Now, let us look at how we can invoke AllReduce operations, as we saw in Figure 5-2.[5] In this program, we first initialize the MPI environment. We will see similar statements in all the frameworks. Then we get the number of parallel processes and the rank of our process. If the rank is 0, we create an array with values [4, 9], and if the rank is 1, we create an array with values [3, 5]. Every process invokes the AllReduce operation with its local array, and we get the sum of the two arrays when the operation completes.

```
#include <mpi.h>
#include <stdio.h>
int main(int argc, char **argv){
  int rank, p;
  int sum[2] = {0}, val[2] = {0};
  MPI_Init(&argc, &argv);
  MPI_Comm_size(MPI_COMM_WORLD, &p);
  MPI_Comm_rank(MPI_COMM_WORLD, &rank);

  if (rank == 0) {
    val[0] = 4;
    val[1] = 9;
  }
  if (rank == 1) {
    val[0] = 3;
    val[1] = 5;
  }
  MPI_Allreduce( \
    val, sum, 2, MPI_INT, MPI_SUM, MPI_COMM_WORLD);
  printf("Rank %d sum=[%d, %d]\n", rank, sum[0], sum[1]);
  MPI_Finalize();
  return 0;
}
```

---

[5]https://www.open-mpi.org/doc/v4.1/man3/MPI_Allreduce.3.php

To compile this program, we can use the following commands. Then we use the mpirun command to run two parallel instances of the program. Each process will print its own sum array that holds the same values.

```
mpicc all_reduce.c
mpirun -np 2 ./a.out
Rank 0 sum=[7, 14]
Rank 1 sum=[7, 14]
```

Bulk Synchronous Parallel

Bulk synchronous parallel (BSP) is known for its simplicity. It is a restricted version of the message passing model where tasks participate in global communications that synchronize them (distributed operations, collectives). A BSP program is broken down into a set of super steps. At each super step, every task does computation, communication, and synchronization.

- **Task**—Can compute accessing the local memory.
- **Messaging**—Tasks can communicate using messaging.
- **Synchronization**—The tasks synchronize with each other.

Figure 5-7 shows the execution of super steps. The tasks can be processes or threads as in a hybrid memory model or distributed mode. Global synchronization is achieved through messaging. BSP is not limited to MPI and can be seen in other frameworks such as Spark, Hadoop, and Flink.

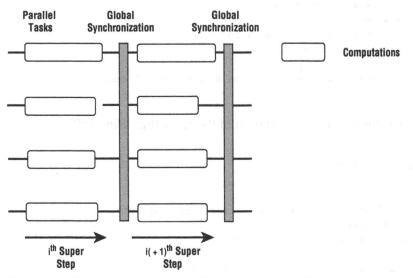

Figure 5-7: BSP program with computations and communications

Now, let us look at how to implement the K-means algorithm using BSP-style programming with MPI.

K-Means

To illustrate use of the message passing API, let us try to implement the K-means algorithm using MPI. The algorithm is listed next in a pseudocode format. First it partitions the points into multiple parallel processes and keeps the same number of centroids in each process. For instance, if there are 1 million data points and 10 parallel processes, each process will get 100,000 data points. All the processes start with the same random centers and update their local centers at each iteration. At the end of the iteration, the information from local centers is combined to create a set of global centers.

This is done using an MPI_Allreduce operation, which can combine a set of arrays using an operation like summation. In this case, we keep the centers array in each process. This has the sum of all the points assigned to a centroid. By combining all these arrays, we can create a global sum of points for all centers. Then we divide this by the global number of points assigned to every vector to create the new global centers. One iteration of the algorithm is a super step in the BSP model where there is a calculation and global synchronization of data.

```
W number of parallel processes
P point partition
C initial centers
C1 = C
for i = 1 to iterations do
  Ci+1= 0 // next set of centers
  For p=in P do
    Calculate the nearest center I for p in Ci
    Add p to the i center in Ci+1
  end for
  All reduce sum on Ci+1 and take the average (no of assigned points)
end for
```

Now, let us study an implementation of the algorithm using MPI:

```cpp
struct Coord {
  double features[4];
};

void initializeCenters(const std::vector<Coord> &points,
    double *centers,
    int num_centers, int num_features) {
  if (rank == 0) {
    for (int i = 0; i < num_centers; i++) {
      int ran = rand() % points.size();
      auto point = points[ran];
```

```
      for (int j = 0; j < num_features; j++) {
        centers[i * num_features + j] = point.features[j];
      }
    }
  }
  // we pick the initial centers at process 0 and send it to all
  MPI_Bcast(centers,    // the arrays
            num_centers * num_features, // num elements
            MPI_DOUBLE,     // data type
            0,         // root process
            MPI_COMM_WORLD);
}

// caclulate the distance from point to the center
double calculate_distance(const Coord &c, double *center,
                          int num_features) {
  double sum = 0;
  for (int i = 0; i < num_features; i++) {
    double dis = c.features[i] - center[i];
    sum += dis * dis;
  }
  return std::sqrt(sum);
}

void add_point(double *new_center, const Coord &c,
               int num_features) {
  for (int i = 0; i < num_features; i++) {
    new_center[i] += c.features[i];
  }
}

void kmeans_algorithm(const std::vector<Coord> &points,
    int num_centers, int num_features, int rank,
    double **out_centers) {
  // we keep all the centers in a single array, array will have centers
in row format
  int center_elements = num_centers * num_features;
  // the global centers
  auto global_centers = new double[center_elements]();
  // the centers calculated locally
  auto local_centers = new double[center_elements]();
  // initialize the centers to random points
  initializeCenters(points, global_centers, num_centers, num_features,
rank);
  // keep track of points per center, initialize to zero
  int *point_counts = new int[num_centers]();
  // keep track of global points per center, initialize to zero
  int *point_counts_global = new int[num_centers];
  // we go for 10 iterations
  for (int i = 0; i < 10; i++) {
```

```cpp
    std::fill(point_counts, point_counts + num_centers, 0);
    std::fill(local_centers, local_centers + center_elements, 0);
    for (auto point : points) {
      double min_distance = std::numeric_limits<double>::max();
      int min_center_index = 0;
      for (int c = 0; c < num_centers; c++) {
        double distance = calculate_distance(point, global_centers + c *
num_features, num_features);
        if (distance < min_distance) {
          min_distance = distance;
          min_center_index = c;
        }
      }
      // add the point to new centers
      add_point(local_centers + min_center_index * num_features, point,
num_features);
      point_counts[min_center_index]++;
    }
    // get the global sum of centers
    MPI_Allreduce(local_centers,     // the sending array
                  global_centers,    // the array to get the sum
                  center_elements,   // num of elements in array
                  MPI_DOUBLE,        // the data type of the array
                  MPI_SUM,           // operation to perform
                  MPI_COMM_WORLD);   // every process participates in this call
    // get the global sum of centers per
    MPI_Allreduce(point_counts,
                  point_counts_global,
                  num_centers,
                  MPI_INT,
                  MPI_SUM,
                  MPI_COMM_WORLD);
    // normalize the centers by dividing
    for (int j = 0; j < center_elements; j++) {
      global_centers[j] = global_centers[j] / point_counts_global[j / num_
features];
      local_centers[j] = 0.0;
    }
  }
  *out_centers = global_centers;
  delete[] local_centers;
  delete[] point_counts;
  delete[] point_counts_global;
}

int main(int argc, char **argv) {
  MPI_Init(NULL, NULL);
  int rank;
  MPI_Comm_rank(MPI_COMM_WORLD, &rank);
  std::vector<Coord> points(100);
```

```
// read the points from the files according to rank
// -----------
double *centers;
kmeans_algorithm(points, 4, 4, rank, &centers);
delete[] centers;
MPI_Finalize();
return 0;
}
```

The MPI-based K-means implementation as shown here follows the distributed memory model we presented in Chapter 1. If we run n parallel processes, they all will execute the same program. One crucial point to note is how the code has been reduced to seeing the local view of computing over the global view we saw in both the serial and shared memory implementations. For example, each process starts with a fraction of the total number of points. The body of the algorithm only traverses this set of points in its `for` loop.

The global view of what needs to happen is with the programmer. This is realized through messages passed between processes at the correct synchronization points. Here, the number of points belonging to each center needs to be synchronized over all the processes. The `MPI_Allreduce` calls provide this synchronization. After the reduction, every process has the global knowledge of point allocation to centers, so they can update the new center values as shown in the last `for` loop.

Distributed Data Model

In the distributed data model, the user is given an abstract object that represents the data distributed across the cluster. The user applies operations to this global data that produces more distributed data objects. This is an implicit parallel programming model that has been present in various forms under the general umbrella of partitioned global address space (PGAS) programming model and is used by data-intensive frameworks extensively.

Eager Model

With an in-memory distributed data model, the operations can be executed immediately. We call this the eager model. Combined with SPMD-style user code, we can create powerful and efficient APIs for data-intensive applications.

In the following code, assume "A" represents a partitioned table in multiple computers. Now "B" and "C" are also partitioned tables.

```
DataFrame A = readFiles(SourceFunction source)
DataFrame B = A.filter(Function filter) // users supply the filter function
DataFrame C = B.sort()
C.save()
```

To write user code, we can convert the partitioned data to in-memory data structures and apply the user code, as shown here:

```
DataFrame A = readFiles(SourceFunction source)
DataFrame B = A.filter(Function Filter)
Table T = B.toTable();    // now T is an in-memory object we can work with
Integer i = T.column(0)[10] // to access 10th value in column 0
```

This code will run according to SPMD style, but the data structures and operations can reduce the burden of the programmer by providing a global data structure. The previous code uses the distributed memory model we discussed in Chapter 1 with no threads.

Dataflow Model

Data-intensive applications constantly work with datasets that do not fit into the available random access memory of computing clusters. To work with large datasets, we need to support streaming computations that utilize external storage. The previous API with eager execution is not suitable here, and we can illustrate this with the following example:

```
A = readFiles(SourceFunction source)  // We need to store A in the disk
B = A.filter(Function filter) // B is still large, so we need to store B
in the disk
C = B.sort()      // to sort B, we need to use disk and then store C in
disk
C.save()          // save C to disk
```

If we execute the previous program one call at a time, we need to store A, B, and C into the disk. We can avoid that by combining these steps into a graph and processing data in a streaming fashion bit by bit. Assume we need to process 200GB of data with the previous program and we can run two processes. Each process can load only 50GB of data in-memory. Figure 5-8 shows how we can execute this program in four steps.

We divide the 100GB file into two 50GB pieces and hand one piece at a time to the filter. Once the filter processes a piece, it sends it to the distributed sort operation. The sort operation will shuffle and sort this piece using external storage. Then the filter can process the next piece. Once the distributed sorting operation has all the data, it can do final processing and hand over the data piece by piece to the file save operation.

Even though we described the program as processing 50GB file parts, the frameworks can divide this data further into records, completely hiding the details of how much data it loads into memory at once. A record can represent data in a single line. Under the radar, it loads an adequate amount of data into the memory.

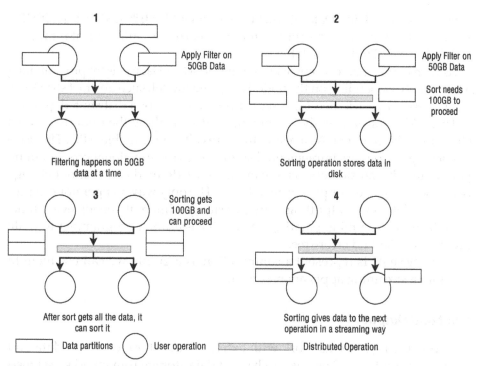

Figure 5-8: Large data processing occurring in a streaming fashion

The previous execution is on a graph data structure that combines the filter operation and the save operation using a communication link that does the distributed sorting. This is a more general form of representing a computation that allows users to specify a complete program as a set of functions and operations that form a task graph. In addition to the streaming execution and external storage-based computations, this model brings many more advantages:

- The framework can optimize the program.
- Any execution method can be used, i.e., threads, processes.
- Supports streaming computations.

The task graph-based execution is popular in data-intensive applications, and from here onward we will focus on this model. It is not necessary to use external memory for task graph-based programs. They can model in-memory computations equally well.

Data Frames, Datasets, and Tables

Popular data processing engines such as Spark, Flink, and Google Data Flow all enable a functional programming API through a dataflow API similar to what we described earlier. A large, distributed dataset is represented as a programming construct such as Flink Dataset and Spark Resilient Distributed Dataset (RDD). In Spark, the table-based programming construct is called a DataFrame or DataSet, and in Flink it is a Table.

As we have seen, the concept of DataFrame, RDD, or DataSet is for programming a task graph. Depending on the underlying data model, such abstract structures can represent a distributed table, a distributed tensor, or a distributed graph.

These APIs for data analytics sometimes do not allow the underlying data structure to be changed. As a result, they are called immutable APIs. The user-defined operations are implemented according to the functional programming paradigm with no side effects, meaning a user-defined code cannot change out-of-scope datasets or passed-in datasets. The only way an operator can produce new data is by outputting it, thus creating a different version every time. This clean programming paradigm makes it easier for a programmer to write programs faster and error-free.

Since these APIs represent a computation as a graph, we can use them to program a streaming application as well.

Input and Output

Data processing systems work with external data storage to read data and write the output data. There is a rich set of data storage frameworks designed to support various use cases as mentioned in Chapter 2. To make programming easier, data processing frameworks supply built-in input/output modules to work with. These I/O modules are optional components of frameworks, and often users end up writing modules to satisfy their specific requirements.

Input and output operations deal with many data formats such as CSV, text, JSON, Parquet, Avro, or Protocol buffers. It is up to the input functions to parse these data and convert them to the proper data structures expected by an application.

For example, a file-based data source can support reading from text, JSON, Parquet, or Avro formats. For an event source based on a message broker, data types may be text or JSON.

Task Graphs (Dataflow Graphs)

A parallel application can be broken down into a set of parallel tasks and the data dependencies between them. A task encapsulates a system-defined local operation on data or a user-defined application logic. Data dependency between tasks can be expressed as a communication operation. So, when a parallel computation is modeled as a task graph, a node represents a local operation, and a link represents a distributed operation. Sometimes we call this a Dataflow graph as well.

There are many possibilities to program a task graph and its functions. In most cases, the user writes a program that does not resemble a graph, and internally the frameworks converts it to a graph. We cannot convert an arbitrary program to a task graph, and it has to be written in a way that is compatible with the model.

Model

To be compatible with the task model, the program needs to be written as a set of functions that does not share data with other functions using the main memory. The only way a function can share information with another is through messaging facilitated by the links between them. The framework can make data available to a function through systems-specific implementations other than the links. For example, some systems allow the user to broadcast a value so that function instances can access it at runtime.

Since the computation is modeled as a directed graph, there are source nodes that do not have any incoming links and sink nodes without any outgoing links. There are also nodes that have both input and output links in the middle. A graph needs a source node, but other nodes are optional.

In this model, computations are data-driven (event-driven). The sources produce data, and this data activates the next connected computation. The middle nodes can produce more data, and so on, until they reach a sink node. For batch applications, the sources read from a data source like a file system or a database, and the sinks write to a file system or database.

The links carry data between graph nodes that can be within the same process or in different processes across machines. Links have unique identifiers so that we can differentiate the messages received. The generic graph model does not restrict where the nodes should be, but usually there are constraints applied to nodes that force them to be scheduled into computers depending on the framework and the application. Additionally, the functionality of links and the nodes depends on the data structures and the operations we build around them.

User Program to Task Graph

Figure 5-9 shows the general workflow of a task-based program. The user program is specified as a data transformation or SQL or other high-level data structure. This program is sent to an optimizer that creates an optimized graph to execute. A scheduler develops a physical plan to execute the graph in the computer resources.

The task model is generic and can be used in applications with varying data types, execution styles, and mappings to computer resources. Streaming task graphs continuously process data, while batch task graphs terminate, meaning the execution is different. The scheduling of tasks is also not the same in streaming and batch task graphs. We will look at the execution details in Chapter 7.

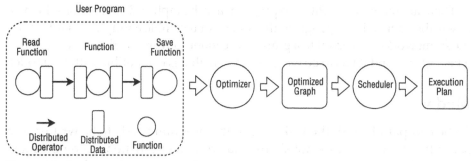

Figure 5-9: Program to execution graph

Some frameworks allow direct programming of the task graph, while others provide abstractions such as distributed data APIs that build a task graph.

Tasks and Functions

From the programmer's perspective, a task is a function specified in the program. From the perspective of a framework, a task is an execution unit and can execute one or more functions. At runtime, many instances of a function will be created depending on the parallelism of the program. Each function instance will have the following information provided to it by the framework:

- **Index (rank)**—Index to distinguish itself from other instances
- **Name**—Name of the function; can be an ID as well
- **Parallelism**—Number of instances running in parallel

Source Task

A source task is invoked by the framework to read data from external sources by way of a user function. The instances of a source task need to know which partitions to read. This information can be calculated at a central place, or source instances can figure out the partition on their own. The first option is the most popular in current systems. The source user function does the following:

- **Read a partition of data**—The function outputs the data by dividing the partition into smaller records.
- **Convert data from external representations into internal representations of the framework**—For example, the data can be a CSV file, and internally the framework may be using a table data structure to represent this data.

In Hadoop, for example, the source function is implemented as a class called `RecordReader`. The `InputFormatter` divides the data into multiple partitions so that sources can work on them.

Compute Task

A compute task gets records of a data partition as input and produces a new data partition as output. A compute task accepts a user-defined function. For example, `Filter`, `Write`, and `Window` are functions that can be implemented as user-level functions. A computing task can write data to disk as well by accepting a sink function.

Implicit vs. Explicit Parallel Models

We looked at an explicit parallel model with message passing and an implicit parallel model with distributed data APIs backed by task graphs. These models are the subject of much debate among users about which is better. The answer depends on the application, developers, and resources available. The implicit model has the following advantages:

- The framework hides the complexities of communication and distributed aspects.
- The framework handles the execution.
- It is easier to write the program without knowing the intricate details of parallel computing.
- The framework can easily incorporate external memory computations without user knowledge.
- The framework can compute an optimized plan by rearranging functions and removing or adding new functions. It does not apply to every API.

Disadvantages of implicit programming models include the following:

- Users know best about their programs, and some of the optimizations possible may not be visible or are hard to do with higher-level APIs.
- There is more overhead involved in the execution. The graph needs to be optimized, scheduled, and executed.

Remote Execution

Data processing systems such as Apache Spark and Dask provide a workflow model for executing programs. They allow users to create programs (jobs) that are developed using their API in a central place and submit them to a cluster to execute. But keep in mind, these are not full workflow systems as they do not support the execution of heterogeneous programs written in different languages. Let us call this remote execution to avoid any confusion with workflows.

In the early days of data computing, there was only Hadoop, which boasted just two operations (map and reduce). To express applications that required more steps than a single map and reduce, the programmers had to submit multiple jobs to the Hadoop cluster. The output of the Hadoop program was saved into the HDFS and used by the next program as input.

This was not an efficient model for implementing a complex program, as it required disk access. To remove the disk access in the middle, we can keep the data in memory between programs. This is the approach used in the remote job executing model adopted by Spark.

The application provides mechanisms to keep the data in memory for the next program to consume, and it is how Spark became the next version of Hadoop with a more efficient execution model. We cannot simply write independent jobs and expect them to communicate via memory. To achieve this, the programs need a shared data structure between them so that they know how to keep the data in-memory for the next program.

Components

Let us try to define some relevant terms:

- **Driver**—The program sends the computation to the cluster.
- **Job context**—This is the common data structure used by multiple jobs so that they know they are in a single overall program.
- **Computation**—A piece of an overall program that can be run as a single unit. The computation may have data dependencies on other computations. The computations are represented as a task graph.

In summary, a remote execution model for data-intensive applications performs as follows:

1. The driver can send multiple computations to the cluster. These computations can be submitted to run concurrently, or they may have data dependencies.

2. Each computation can define its resource requirements and data dependencies.

3. The results of a computation can be transferred to the driver so that it can examine them to make decisions.

4. The results of a computation can be persisted in the cluster for the next computation to use. Results can be saved in permanent storage or saved in memory.

The driver-based method is used only in batch applications, as streaming applications do not send multiple programs to execute with data dependencies between them. As in workflow systems, we can use the driver program to control the execution of programs in the cluster. For example, we can submit multiple jobs in a loop and stop submission if a certain condition becomes true.

Batch Dataflow

A batch task graph computation works on one or more input datasets and ends in a finite amount of time. After termination, we are left with only the output of the batch calculation.

- **Dataflow applications**—These computations are not iterative and are expressed as a directed graph. A computation may have several batch graphs executed one after another, taking input from the output of a previous graph.
- **Iterative applications**—These are used in machine learning and deep learning algorithms to find mathematical solutions. After completing a computation for an iteration, the output will become input to the next iteration.

Data Abstractions

Batch applications use all the data structures we described earlier such as tables, tensors, and graphs. Dataflow systems like Spark and Flink use table-based abstractions, while deep learning systems rely on tensor abstractions.

Table Abstraction

Table abstractions can be seen as keys, value pairs, or full table abstractions with many columns. For example, Apache Spark supports key-value pairs through RDD and full tables through its DataFrame APIs. The first thing we need to do with a table abstraction is to provide the schema information.

The tables can have many operations apart from the few basic ones we described earlier. Tools such as Spark and other data abstractions like Pandas offer hundreds of suitable operations. Table 5-8 lists some prominent operation categories.

Because of the implicit nature of APIs, it is not obvious whether some operations are distributed or not. From the operations we described in Table 5-5 and Table 5-6, select and project are the only operations that do not need communication among parallel processes. The rest of the operations use communications to redistribute the data. Shuffle is the most important operation in table-based APIs.

Matrix/Tensors

Tensors as implemented in PyTorch or TensorFlow support hundreds of mathematical operations that enable users to access values, transform tensors, and do calculations.

Table 5-8: Table Operations

OPERATIONS	DESCRIPTION
Searching	Searches tables based on various conditions
Indexes	Builds indexes for efficient searching and to use in other operations
Table modifications	Drops columns, drops rows, renames columns
Date/time	Functions for working with time fields including different date/time formats, comparison, and arithmetic functions
Math	Mathematical functions such as less than, greater than, and geometry
String	Functions for string manipulation such as length, substring, and converting to uppercase
Load/write	Reads different data formats, writes to different data formats

It is not common to develop matrix-based or tensor-based applications using external storage due to performance implications. Applications requiring such operations are run in clusters that have enough memory available to accommodate them, and in rare circumstances they are executed with external memory. For example, the PyTorch API is similar to the in-memory distributed data API we described earlier. When executing at scale, they use the distributed operation we showed for arrays in Table 5-4.

Functions

We write source, compute, and sink functions in a dataflow program. Now let us look at their semantics.

Source

A batch source is a function that produces data for the rest of the graph. The source must read a finite amount of data and then end. It can read from an external data source or even generate data.

A framework runs multiple instances of a source function at the runtime depending on the parallelism of the application. Each source function reads a partition of the dataset and inserts it into the rest of the graph. Because of the streaming execution, the source function should further divide the data into smaller chunks so that the computation can progress without overflowing the memory. If partitioning is not done correctly, it can lead to load imbalance and wasted resources.

Compute

A batch compute function reads input from incoming links and produces output to outgoing links. Here is the pseudocode for the compute function:

```
Function void compute(Record record)
```

If there are n records in a partition processed by the function, it will be invoked n times with each record. A compute function can take only one input because we are inserting input piece by piece according to this streaming execution. If two inputs are needed, we have to insert all combinations of the inputs to the function, which is not practical. We can illustrate this with an example. Table 5-9 shows records of Input-1 and Input-2.

Table 5-9: Input Records of Two Datasets

INPUT-1 RECORDS	INPUT-2 RECORDS
T-1-1	T-2-1
T-1-2	T-2-2

If compute function works only on in-memory data, we can just add Input-1 and Input-2 as complete datasets to the function. But since we are feeding the function in a streaming fashion, we cannot do that. If we are going to do so, we need to feed the cross product of the records of the two datasets to the function by default. There are a couple of options we can follow to get multiple inputs to a function.

- We can combine the required inputs into a single dataset. This combination should be done in a way that the function expects data. In our earlier example, if the function needs to access the entire Input-2 records for each Input-1 record (cross product), we must create a dataset that combines each Input-1 record with all the Input-2 records. Our combined input will have these records: (T-1-1, T-2-1), (T-1-1, T-2-2), (T-1-2, T-2-1), (T-1-2, T-2-2). Depending on the requirements of the function, we can create the combined input.

- If one dataset is small enough to fit in the memory, we can give it as in-memory data to the function. This allows the function to process the larger dataset in a streaming fashion with access to the second data.

The second option is an optimization provided by most frameworks. Option 1 is the most generic and works in any situation even if the datasets are larger than memory. But it needs to be used carefully to avoid exploding the size of the combined dataset.

Sink

A sink can save data to an external storage or memory. Saving data to memory is important for applications that reuse the data computed from one task graph in another. Once the data reach the sinks and they finish, the computation stops.

At the end of the computation, a parallel program will have multiple data partitions in different computers. The program outputs these partitions separately. In the case of file output, it will be a set of files with unique names. We can append the data partition identifier at the end of the file to make them unique and associate them with the tasks or partitions that produced them.

As with source functions, output functions need to transform data into different formats expected by the users. The most common output formats are Text, CSV, Parquet, JSON, and Avro files. To convert the data as such, more information may be needed.

Another aspect of data output is failure handling. Some frameworks supply checkpointing and rollback functions to allow writes to be rolled back in case of a failure.

An Example

Let us examine a simple ETL program to load a CSV file, apply a filter operation, and then do a groupBy count. For this we are going to use a CSV file with the fields ID, Name, and DOB.

```java
import org.apache.spark.api.java.function.FilterFunction;
import org.apache.spark.sql.Dataset;
import org.apache.spark.sql.Row;
import org.apache.spark.sql.SparkSession;
import org.apache.spark.sql.types.DataTypes;
import org.apache.spark.sql.types.StructType;

import java.sql.Date;
import java.text.ParseException;

public class QueryExecutor {
  public static void main(String[] args) throws ParseException {
    SparkSession spark = SparkSession
      .builder()
      .appName("Java Spark SQL basic example")
      .config("spark.some.config.option", "some-value")
      .getOrCreate();

    StructType schema = new StructType()
        .add("ID", DataTypes.IntegerType)
        .add("Name", DataTypes.StringType)
        .add("DOB", DataTypes.DateType);
    Dataset<Row> df = spark.read()
```

```
          .option("header","true")
          .schema(schema).option("dateFormat", "yyyy-MM-dd")
          .csv("path_to_csv_files");
    Dataset<Row> after2000 = df.filter(new FilterFunction<Row>() {
      @Override
      public boolean call(Row row) throws Exception {
        return row.getDate(2).after(Date.valueOf("2000-01-01"));
      }
    });
    Dataset<Row> dob = after2000.groupBy("DOB").count().cache();
    dob.write().csv("out.txt");
    dob.show();
  }
}
```

The first function reads a CSV file as a set of partitioned tables. Data is sent through a filter that reduces the total amount. The records are grouped according to the hash of the DOB attribute. After that step, we can count the number of people for each day (group). In the previous program, there are a few interesting observations to note:

- The user does not see a table structure in the program; instead, the APIs expose the rows of the table.

- The user does not see any communication operations. Rather, they see data transformations that are applied on a partitioned distributed table. The groupBy operation needs a communication operation to redistribute the data so that records with the same day end up in the same partition.

- The framework takes the responsibility of reading and writing files.

- Even if the data does not fit the memory, the user does not need to change the program to accommodate this.

Frameworks supporting distributed data abstractions provide similar APIs to the one we described in this program. Their operation names and semantics may vary, but at the end of the day, they all offer the same functions.

Caching State

Imagine we are working on a dataset and created a new set by applying a set of operations. Now, we need to use this data in a few other subsequent computations that happen one after another. To avoid doing calculations multiple times, we should keep the original data around. We can instruct the framework to explicitly cache a dataset to achieve this functionality. The example in Figure 5-10 reads a file and applies a filter to generate a dataset.

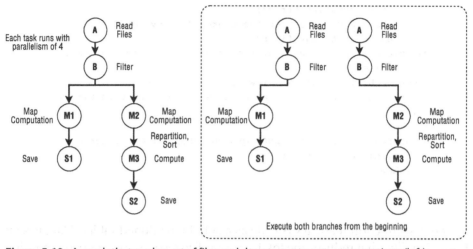

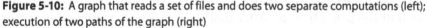

Figure 5-10: A graph that reads a set of files and does two separate computations (left); execution of two paths of the graph (right)

The output of the filter is then used in two separate computations as shown in the left and right branches. We need to first execute the read and filter, then perform the map computation of both branches, and so on. If we had four CPUs to execute this workflow, we still could not run both branches at the same time due to resource constraints. We must instead run one branch first and the second one afterward.

The left side of Figure 5-10 shows the trivial approach for running both branches separately. However, we are executing both read file and filter twice for executing the branches, which can be inefficient. Furthermore, if the filter is not deterministic, when two branches are run, it can produce inconsistent results.

To avoid this, we introduce the concept of caching. Caching allows us to save processed data either in memory or on disk for use by later computations. This way, the computations do not need to read the file again and can work through the cached data (see Figure 5-11).

With a message passing–based application, this will be equivalent to keeping the data in memory, which is natural for that model. Owing to the nature of the graph execution, we need to pay special attention to this concept.

Evaluation Strategy

There are two evaluation styles we see in distributed data processing systems called *lazy* and *eager* evaluation.

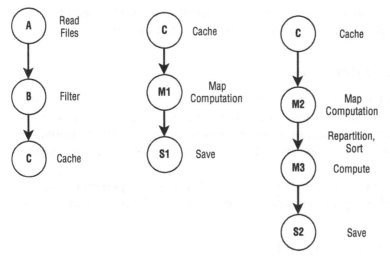

Figure 5-11: Execute and cache (left); execute left path (middle); execute right path (right)

Lazy Evaluation

Lazy evaluation is another name given to the notion of building the graph and executing it at a later point. Up to the lazy execution point, all we need to do is build the graph. At the execution point we create the graph, schedule it on the resources, and execute it. In some APIs, graph building is not obvious, so we are given special methods to invoke the graph execution.

Here is an example from Apache Spark where it builds a graph and executes at the end. Note that the graph is created and executed at the `write().csv()` call.

```
SparkSession spark = SparkSession
    .builder()
    .appName("Spark Example")
    .getOrCreate();

Dataset<Row> df = spark.read().csv("example.csv");
// building of the task graph through operations
RelationalGroupedDataset name = df.groupBy("DOB");
Dataset<Row> count = name.count();
// this will execute the graph and save
count.write().csv("age_count");
```

Eager Evaluation

In a system with eager evaluation, the user code is executed immediately. Systems such as PyTorch and TensorFlow support this model. The biggest advantage is the ability to debug and see the results immediately. In lazy evaluation systems, the user graph can be optimized by the system, and it may be hard to debug them. Eager evaluation can be inefficient when implemented as remote execution because each computation needs to be submitted to a cluster.

Iterative Computations

Iterative computations are common in machine learning algorithms. According to the data dependencies between the iterations of a loop, we need to follow different methods to run iterative computations in parallel. The computations inside a for loop can have loop-carried dependencies, or they can be independent of the loops.

In a loop-independent computation, there is no data dependency between the data created in a previous iteration of the loop and a new iteration. Here is such a loop:

```
for (int i = 1; i < n; i ++) {
    a[i] = computation_func(b[i]);
}
```

Now here is a loop with a dependency on values created in a previous loop:

```
for (int i = 1; i < n; i ++) {
    a[i] = computation_func(a[i - 1]);
}
```

There are three broad types of parallel loops depending on the type of dependency that exists between iterations.

DOALL Parallel

There is no data dependency between consecutive iterations. Parallel processes can run independent iterations by dividing the work. This is the simplest to implement and is usually supported by all parallel computing models. This form of parallelism can also be thought of as pleasingly or embarrassingly parallel, as introduced in Chapter 1.

DOACROSS Parallel

In this type of loop, there is a calculation that can run independently, and we run this part in parallel. There is another part that has loop-carried dependencies and needs synchronization.

The K-means algorithm we described earlier is a DOACROSS parallel algorithm where we do the distance calculation independently using the partitioned points and the centroids. Once every process calculates its centroids, they sum them up to make the global centers. These are fed back into the next iteration.

Pipeline Parallel

Pipeline parallelism is like an assembly line. A parallel computation is divided into tasks that depend on one another. Once a task finishes, it sends its result to the next in the pipeline. The pipeline is driven by the loop that feeds the data into it.

Task Graph Models for Iterative Computations

There are two approaches used in the task graph-based APIs for handling parallel loops. First is to create a graph that connects to itself to create a loop. There are frameworks such as Naiad [3] and Flink built on top of this model. The task graph needs more information sent through its edges to recognize the iterations they are at. Parallel loops can have dynamic termination conditions that depend on the data produced by the iterations. These types of conditions are harder to implement in this model. In addition, the complexities of nested parallel loops hinder the use of such models.

The second approach is to create a regular loop and execute the graph computation inside it [4]. In this model, we need to extract the output of the graph and feed it back again. In practice, there are two ways to achieve this, as shown in Figure 5-12. The first approach shown on the left side is to use a central driver to control the computation. For each iteration, the graph is created at a single server and given to the cluster to execute. The results of the execution are sent back to the driver in case they need to be examined to decide how the iteration should progress, for example, the termination conditions.

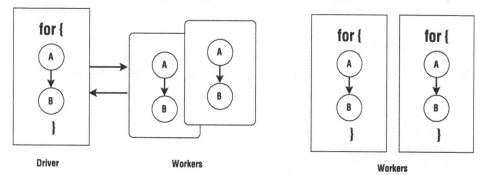

Figure 5-12: Loop outside the task graph. Central driver submits the graph in a loop (left); every worker does the `for` loop (right).

Instead of running the `for` loop and graph creation at a central driver, we can move the `for` loop to all the cluster workers, illustrated on the right side of Figure 5-12. This will result in everyone running the same code. As such, the overhead of sending the graph to the cluster every iteration and getting results back from the cluster are gone. This model has proven to be successful in scaling to thousands of cores running large-scale applications.

So far we have looked at how to execute the `for` loop. Figure 5-13 displays how DOACROSS and pipeline parallel programs will work across processes. If our algorithm is a DOACROSS parallel one, we can run the same task graph in every worker. We will need distributed data operations in the graph to synchronize the state across the parallel work. This type of parallelism is common in machine learning algorithms.

If we are working with a pipeline parallel algorithm, we will create a task graph with tasks doing different computations in different processes connected by communication links. Pipeline parallelism is popular with parallel deep learning training in systems such as Gpipe [5] and PipeDream [6].

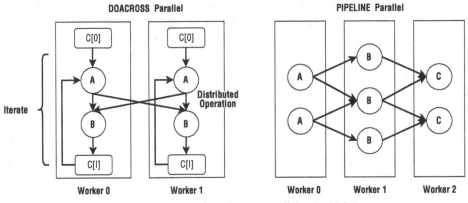

Figure 5-13: DOACROSS parallel tasks (left); PIPELINE parallel tasks (right)

K-Means Algorithm

Here is an example of the K-means algorithm implemented in Spark:

```python
import sys
import numpy as np
from pyspark.sql import SparkSession

def closestCenter(point, centers):
    centers = np.asarray(centers)
    return np.argmin(np.sum((centers - point)**2, axis=1))

if __name__ == "__main__":
    spark = SparkSession.builder.appName("KMeans").getOrCreate()
    K = int(sys.argv[2])
    lines = spark.read.text(sys.argv[1]).rdd.map(lambda l: l[0])
    points = lines.map(
            lambda line: np.array([float(x) for x in line.split(',')])).\
    cache()
```

```
centers = points.takeSample(False, K, 1)
for i in range(10):
    closest = points.map(
        lambda p: (closestCenter(p, centers), (p, 1))).cache()
    pointStats = closest.reduceByKey(
        lambda p1_c1, p2_c2: (p1_c1[0] + p2_c2[0], p1_c1[1] + p2_c2[1]))
    newPoints = pointStats.map(
        lambda st: (st[0], st[1][0] / st[1][1])).collect()
    for (iK, p) in newPoints:
        centers[iK] = p
print("Final centers: " + str(centers))
spark.stop()
```

Spark's execution model follows the separate driver and worker model found in Figure 5-16. In the code example provided for K-means, the main method runs in the driver. In this program we run a fixed set of iterations (10). During execution, it creates a distributed table of points in the form of an RDD. We cached the data because we are going to use it many times in the subsequent iterations. If we did not, every iteration will run the file read, as described earlier.

Next, it creates a set of initial centers by taking k points from this data. These centers are used within the main convergence loop that runs in the driver program. The first step in the loop is to find the closest center to each point. The resulting dataset has the structure [center index, (point, 1)]. The first value (key) is the center index to which the corresponding point is nearest. The value is a pair, where the first element is the point itself, and the second is number 1.

The next step is a reduceByKey, where we group the points with the same center index and do a summation over the points and 1. After this we have the [center index, (summation of points, number of points)]. Now, if we divide the summation of points by the number of points, we will get the new center point.

The second map operation inside the loop does this by taking the averages of the summed-up points for each center and giving the updated centers. Note the distributed operation is executed when collect() is called.

Up to this step, the points data was distributed, and the centers were broadcasted from the driver to all the workers. Then map operations happened in the distributed workers on respective data partitions. Next, another data transfer occurs from workers to the driver. That is the transfer of updated centers back to the loop executing in the driver. It is not visible in the code, but the framework handles it internally.

reduceByKey is a table operation, and we had to transform our data to include 1 with each point to create the sum. This a consequence of using a table data abstraction to perform array-based calculations.

Streaming Dataflow

Most data applications that collect data from sources in real life and process them continuously can be thought of as streaming applications. A streaming application works continuously on the data and produces outputs. In the context of stream processing, events are delivered as messages. A stream is a sequence of limitless tuples or events of the form $(a_1, a_2, \ldots, a_n, t)$ generated continuously in time. Here, a_i denotes an attribute, and t denotes the time. A good example is sensor data in the form of messages sent to a stream processing infrastructure. In a large-scale stream processing setting, billions of events pass through the systems.

We cannot process such large volumes of data using a single computer. To scale up the processing, the events are partitioned into multiple computers and processed in parallel. Sometimes such parallel processing elements need to exchange messages and redistribute the partitions to achieve the desired application outcomes.

Streaming engines or distributed stream processing frameworks (DSPF) [7, 8] are specifically designed to handle such large volumes of data. All the systems use the task graph model to program and execute streaming applications.

Distributed stream processing has an intricate relationship with message brokers. It is rare to see a distributed stream processing application connected directly to an event source. Instead, they are connected to message brokers. Sometimes message brokers provide certain functions we often see in distributed stream processing engines. Figure 5-14 shows the general architecture of distributed stream processing.

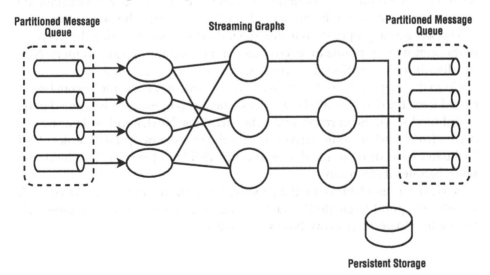

Figure 5-14: Distributed streaming architecture with message queues

A streaming graph is different from a batch graph because every task is contin-uously processing the incoming stream. Batch task graphs are executed in stages wherein we need to finish the earlier operation before continuing to the next one. This point is illustrated in Figure 5-15. As a result of this, the mapping of tasks to resources (scheduling) is different in streaming. Since we run multiple tasks that run numerous programs at the same time, it is an MPMD-style program.

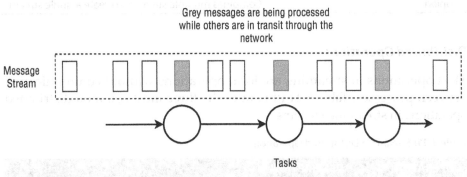

Figure 5-15: Streaming processing with all the tasks active at the same time

Data Abstractions

From the perspective of a stream processing application, it receives a set of records over time. These records can be thought of as rows of a table. Since streams of data are partitioned and processed in parallel, we can model a streaming com-putation with a distributed table abstraction.

Streams

A stream is a logical entity defined to identify a set of streaming data partitions. We use streams to program our applications without thinking about individual partitions and how they are processed at runtime.

As the streams are dynamic, we cannot divide them into perfect partitions as we do with batch data. Depending on the nature of the data sources, partitions may have more data at a given time. As such, the data is ingested into streaming applications first and then load-balanced within the applications dynamically.

Table 5-10 shows some common operations provided by frameworks to work on streams. Windowing is one of the most important operations in streaming systems.

Table 5-10: Streaming Operations

OPERATOR	DESCRIPTION
Filter	Filters tuples based on a function
Map/FlatMap	Computes functions on streams
Window	Creates a window
Union	Combines multiple streams to create a single stream

Distributed Operations

Most operations in streaming are local operations without communication between processes. Table 5-11 illustrates the three most common distributed operations in streaming systems.

Table 5-11: Streaming Distributed Operations

OPERATOR	DESCRIPTION
Partition (shuffle)	Redistributes an event stream based on a property of the data. If we use key-value pairs to represent a record, the key can be used to partition, but it is not a requirement, as any attribute or combination of attributes can be used to partition.
Broadcast	Creates multiple copies of an event stream and distributes those copies.
Gather	Gathers elements from multiple stream partitions.

Streaming Functions

User code is written as functions in streaming systems. In general, we can write source, compute, and sink functions.

Sources

Streaming sources connect to message brokers or file systems to read streaming data. By definition, they read data records and insert them into the rest of the task graph without stopping. At the brokers, the streams are divided into substreams that can be processed by multiple source instances. An example is Kafka's topics and partitions.

Some streaming applications need ordered processing of data coming from a source. If an application is in such a position, we cannot simply divide a stream (substream) among multiple source instances because it will lose the ordering.

Compute

A compute function takes one input record at a time, processes it, and can then output another record or multiple records to the downstream tasks. Since streaming systems work on in-memory data, we can have streaming functions that can take multiple input streams. Streaming compute functions need to keep track of the state variables to process the data streams. Such state can be kept in volatile memory within the function or in a distributed storage. Higher-level functions such as map, flat map, and window are some functions built using compute functions.

Sink

Streaming systems can write output to the message brokers or data storage systems. Most frameworks provide functions to write to existing systems in known formats, as we saw in batch systems.

An Example

Here is the classic word count example in Apache Flink with custom `source` and `flatMap` functions. In this example, the sink function is printing the values of the stream.

```
public static void main(String[] args) throws Exception {
  StreamExecutionEnvironment env =
      StreamExecutionEnvironment.getExecutionEnvironment();
  DataStream<Tuple2<String, Integer>> dataStream = env
      .addSource(new RandomSource())
      .flatMap(new Splitter())
      .keyBy(value -> value.f0)
      .window(TumblingProcessingTimeWindows.of(Time.seconds(5)))
      .sum(1);
  dataStream.print();
  env.execute("Window WordCount");
}

public static class RandomSource implements SourceFunction<String> {
  private final Random random = new Random();
  @Override
  public void run(SourceContext<String> sourceContext) throws Exception {
    byte[] tmp = new byte[5];
    random.nextBytes(tmp);
    sourceContext.collect(new String(tmp));
  }
  @Override
  public void cancel() {
```

```
        }
    }

    public static class Splitter implements
        FlatMapFunction<String, Tuple2<String, Integer>> {
        @Override
        public void flatMap(String sentence,
                        Collector<Tuple2<String, Integer>> out) throws
    Exception {
            for (String word : sentence.split(" ")) {
                out.collect(new Tuple2<String, Integer>(word, 1));
            }
        }
    }
}
```

Windowing

One of the most widely used features in streaming data processing is to group the messages into batches to process them. We call this grouping of messages *windowing*. To understand the need for windowing, let us take an example of an event stream that sends the number of people entering a building. Each event has a timestamp with the time the measurement was taken. Now, we can send this event stream through a streaming graph and start calculating the sum of the people who entered the building. The summation will be an increasing count through time. What we may be more interested in will be something like how many people entered the building during the last 15 minutes. To do this, we can create windows of 15-minute length and calculate the events within those windows. Figure 5-16 displays such a windowing strategy. In this mode, we can now get information about the last 15-minute window, and we need to wait 15 minutes to get the next update. These are called *tumbling windows*.

To reduce the update time, we can create many overlapping windows. Figure 5-17 has a window of 15 minutes with a step of 3 minutes. With this model, we can get an update of the last 15 minutes with a maximum time delay of 3 minutes. This is called *sliding windows*, as the current window is sliding through the event time, creating many windows.

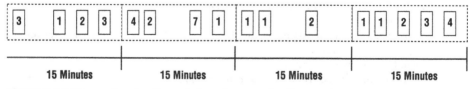

Figure 5-16: Nonoverlapping time windows for grouping the events

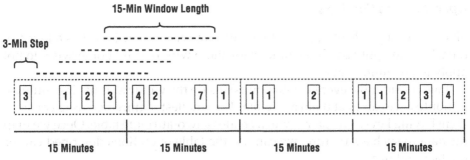

Figure 5-17: Overlapping time windows for grouping the events

Windowing Strategies

There are a few windowing strategies used by systems.

- **Sliding windows**—Overlapping groups. A window has a fixed length, and the starting time can overlap on another window. An event can belong to multiple windows.

- **Tumbling windows**—Nonoverlapping groups. Each event is in exactly one window.

- **Session**—Windows are defined based on the data. The data carries session identifiers, and windows are created based on them.

A streaming window has a starting point and a length. We can define windows based on count or time. Counting windows are straightforward. Most of the real use cases are based on time. We can use event time, ingestion time, or processing time to define windows.

- **Event time**—Time the actual event occurred. This can be a timestamp in the event.

- **Ingestion time**—Time the event entered the system. The system does not have to be the streaming engine and can be another part of the system such as a message broker.

- **Processing time**—Time the event is processed by the user code.

Event time is useful but harder to work with because events can arrive out of order or late. We might miss such events in a window and must take added measures to process them later when they arrive. Processing time and ingestion time are much easier to work with because they are generated by the system. Processing time is always guaranteed to increase for consecutive events in a stream.

Operations on Windows

Since we group sets of events into a window, we can consider it as a batch of data. We can apply batch operations for these windows that otherwise do not apply to streaming data.

If we consider the events (data points) inside the window as having multiple attributes, we can treat them as a table. The smallest requirement is to consider them having key-value pairs, which creates a two-attribute table. Once we map the data to such a structure, we can use the table operations described earlier on the windows.

Table 5-12 describes some of the operations on windows. Once a window is created, it is possible to apply any batch operation on it.

Table 5-12: Popular Operations on Windowed Data

OPERATOR	DESCRIPTION
Join	Joins data from two streams in a window
Aggregation	Aggregations on windows, including functions such as SUM, MIN, MAX, Mean
Map/process window	Processes the data in the window

Handling Late Events

Some events can come late and be dropped from the stream because no window is there to process them. We can allow a grace period for these events to arrive. Also, we can create separate streams from the late events to process them separately.

SQL

SQL is a popular approach for programming frameworks dealing with structured datasets. It is designed to work on table data structures, originating as it does from relational algebra. The data processing frameworks that offer SQL-based queries [9] map the data to a table structure or are based on a table data structure.

Sometimes the difference between a database and a data processing system that supports SQL is not clear. Let us look at some of the differences between data processing systems and databases:

■ A data processing system allocates resources for each application separately, fetches data to run the query, and executes the query. On the other hand, a database is a set of long-running processes that execute queries from many users within the cluster. Some databases can use external processing engines to run SQL queries on top of them as well.

- Databases work with data in disks and can change the data they work on. Once a data processing system reads a dataset, unless it overrides the original dataset with a new one, it does not change the original dataset.

Still, these lines can be quite blurry in real systems. Data processing frameworks are not full databases, and as such they support only a subset of SQL operations. SQL-based operations are built around a few key operations listed in Table 5-6 and many other auxiliary operations listed in Table 5-7.

Queries

The first requirement of an SQL-based abstraction is the schema for a dataset (table). The schema defines the names of the attributes and the data types of tables. A framework can be inferring schema from the data or can have a user-specified one. For example, a Parquet file has a schema associated with it that can be directly translated to a table schema. CSV files have attribute names, and programs can gather data types of the attributes by examining them.

Once the schema is defined, we can use SQL or a programming API to develop the queries. The framework translates these queries to the task graph and executes them. If the SQL language is used, we need an SQL parser for building a model using the query. An SQL query optimizer [10] can be used to create an optimized task graph and an execution plan before executing the queries.

Here is the same program we wrote earlier to count the people each day after 2000 with SQL syntax in Spark:

```
SparkSession spark = SparkSession
  .builder()
  .appName("Java Spark SQL basic example")
  .config("spark.some.config.option", "some-value")
  .getOrCreate();

StructType schema = new StructType()
  .add("ID", DataTypes.IntegerType)
  .add("Name", DataTypes.StringType)
  .add("DOB", DataTypes.DateType);
Dataset<Row> df = spark.read()
        .option("header","true")
        .schema(schema).option("dateFormat", "yyyy-MM-dd")
        .csv("path_to_csv_files");

df.createGlobalTempView("person");
spark.sql("SELECT DOB, COUNT(DOB) " +
  "FROM global_temp.person " +
  "where DOB >= '2000-01-01' " +
  "GROUP BY DOB").show();
```

Summary

A programming API for a data-intensive application is created around data abstractions and programming models. For example, the Apache Spark API is created around a table abstraction with a distributed data programming model.

In this chapter, we looked at a few popular programming models to develop data-intensive applications. These programming models are powerful and used in many other applications. The programming APIs we see in data-intensive applications are built around data structures for these programming models. Chapter 6 will explore how we use messaging to execute distributed operations of applications at scale, and Chapter 7 will examine how we can execute these applications.

References

1. C. Kessler and J. Keller, "Models for parallel computing: Review and perspectives," *Mitteilungen-Gesellschaft für Informatik eV, Parallel-Algorithmen und Rechnerstrukturen,* vol. 24, pp. 13–29, 2007.

2. M. Snir, W. Gropp, S. Otto, S. Huss-Lederman, J. Dongarra, and D. Walker, *MPI--the Complete Reference: the MPI core. MIT press,* 1998.

3. D. G. Murray, F. McSherry, R. Isaacs, M. Isard, P. Barham, and M. Abadi, "Naiad: a timely dataflow system," in *Proceedings of the Twenty-Fourth ACM Symposium on Operating Systems Principles,* 2013, pp. 439–455.

4. P. Wickramasinghe *et al.,* "High-performance iterative dataflow abstractions in Twister2: TSet," *Concurrency and Computation: Practice and Experience,* p. e5998, 2020.

5. Y. Huang *et al.,* "Gpipe: Efficient training of giant neural networks using pipeline parallelism," *Advances in neural information processing systems,* vol. 32, pp. 103–112, 2019.

6. D. Narayanan *et al.,* "PipeDream: generalized pipeline parallelism for DNN training," in *Proceedings of the 27th ACM Symposium on Operating Systems Principles,* 2019, pp. 1–15.

7. T. Akidau *et al.,* "MillWheel: fault-tolerant stream processing at internet scale," *Proceedings of the VLDB Endowment,* vol. 6, no. 11, pp. 1033–1044, 2013.

8. S. Kamburugamuve, "Survey of distributed stream processing for large stream sources," 2013. [Online]. Available: `http://grids.ucs.indiana.edu/ptliupages/publications/survey_stream_processing.pdf`

9. M. Armbrust *et al.*, "Spark sql: Relational data processing in spark," in *Proceedings of the 2015 ACM SIGMOD international conference on management of data*, 2015, pp. 1383–1394.

10. E. Begoli, J. Camacho-Rodríguez, J. Hyde, M. J. Mior, and D. Lemire, "Apache calcite: A foundational framework for optimized query processing over heterogeneous data sources," in *Proceedings of the 2018 International Conference on Management of Data*, 2018, pp. 221–230.

Messaging

Large-scale data-intensive applications need coordination between the parallel processes to achieve meaningful objectives. Since applications are deployed in many nodes within a cluster, messaging is the only way to achieve coordination while they execute.

It is fair to say that when large numbers of machines are used for an application, performance depends on how efficiently it can transfer messages among the distributed processes. Developing messaging libraries is a challenging task and requires years of software engineering to produce efficient, workable, and robust systems. For example, the Message Passing Interface (MPI) standard–based frameworks celebrated 25 years of development and are still undergoing retooling thanks to emerging hardware and applications.

There are many intricate details involved in programming with networking hardware, making it impossible for an application developer to fashion a program directly using hardware features. Multiple layers of software have been developed to facilitate messaging. Some of these layers are built into the operating system, with others at the firmware level and many at the software library level.

Nowadays, computer networks are operating continuously everywhere, transferring petabytes of data that touch every aspect of our lives. There are many types of networks that are designed to work in various settings, including cellular networks, home cable networks, undersea cables that carry data between continents, and networks inside data centers. Since data-intensive applications execute in clusters inside data centers, we will look at networking services and messaging within a data center.

Network Services

Computer networks are at the heart of distributed computing, facilitating data transfer on a global scale. This is a complex subject with rich hardware and software stacks. It is outside the scope of this book to go into details on networking. Instead, we will focus on those services offered by the networking layer to the application layer.

Popular networks used today offer applications the option of byte streaming services, messaging services, or remote memory management services. On top of this, other quality-of-service features such as reliable messaging and flow control are available. Applications can choose from these services and combine them with the required quality of service attributes to create efficient messaging services that are optimum for their needs.

Ethernet and InfiniBand are the two dominant networking technologies used in data centers. There are many other networking technologies available, though none is quite as popular due to price, availability of libraries, APIs, and the knowledge required to program them.

TCP/IP

Transport Control Protocol/Internet Protocol (TCP/IP) provides a stream-based reliable byte channel for communication between two parties. TCP/IP only considers bytes and how to transfer them reliably from one host to another and has a built-in flow control mechanism to slow down producers in case of network congestion.

TCP is programmed using a socket API. It has a notion of a connection and employs a protocol at the beginning to establish a virtual bidirectional channel between two parties looking to communicate. Once the connection is formed, bytes can be written to or read from the channel. Since there is no notion of a message in the TCP protocol, the application layer needs to define messaging protocols.

There are two popular APIs used for programming TCP applications using the socket API. They are blocking socket API and nonblocking socket API. With the blocking API, calls to write or read bytes will block until they complete. As a result we need to create threads for handling connections. If there are many simultaneously active connections, this method will not scale. With a nonblocking API, the read or write calls will return immediately without blocking. It can work in an event-driven fashion and can use different thread configurations to handle multiple connections. As such, most applications that deal with a significant number of connections use the nonblocking API.

Direct programming on the socket API is a laborious task owing to the specialized knowledge required. Popular programming languages and platforms used today have TCP libraries that are well recognized and used throughout applications. Data analytics applications depend on these libraries to transport their data messages.

RDMA

Remote direct memory access (RDMA) is a technique used by messaging systems to directly read from or write to a remote machine's memory. Direct memory access (DMA) is the technology used by devices to access the main memory without the involvement of the CPU.

There are many technologies and APIs that enable RDMA, providing low latencies in the nanosecond range and throughput well beyond 100Gbps. These characteristics have contributed to them being widely used in the high-performance and big data computing domains to scale applications up to thousands of nodes. Due to the high communication demands of distributed deep learning, they are employed in large deep learning clusters as well. RDMA technologies are available in the following forms:

- **RDMA over Converged Ethernet (RoCE)**—RoCE is a network protocol that allows remote memory access over an Ethernet network. It defines the protocol used over Ethernet.

- **iWARP**—This is a protocol defined on Internet Protocol networks such as TCP to provide RDMA capabilities.

- **InfiniBand**—Networking hardware that supports RDMA directly. InfiniBand networks are used in high-performance computing environments. They are found in data centers and big data clusters to accelerate processing.

InfiniBand networks can bypass the CPU and operating system (OS) kernel for packet processing, freeing valuable resources for computations. RDMA technologies use polling to figure out network events rather than interrupts to avoid the OS kernel. Apart from RDMA, InfiniBand networks support other messages such as send/receive, multicast, and remote atomic operations. All these features are used to build highly efficient messaging solutions within data centers.

Messaging for Data Analytics

Peer-to-peer messaging is the most basic form of transferring data between processes. Unless hardware features of networking fabrics are used, messages are always transferred between two processes. Even the most complex messaging patterns are created using peer-to-peer messaging primitives.

Anatomy of a Message

Now, let us examine some of the important steps we need to take to send a message from one computer to another. Assume we have an object we need to send to the other party. The object can be an array, a table, or something more complex such as a Java object. Figure 6-1 shows the steps taken by an application to send data to another computer.

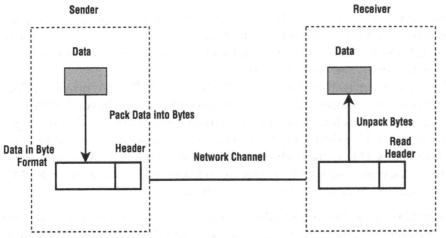

Figure 6-1: A message with a header. The header is sent through the network before the data.

Data Packing

First, we need to convert the data into binary format. We call this step *data packing* or *serialization,* and it depends on how we keep the data in the memory. In case our data is a C-style array, it is already in a contiguous byte buffer in the memory. If it is a table structure in a format like Apache Arrow, the data may be in multiple buffers each allocated for holding a data column of the table. In the case of Apache Arrow, there can be auxiliary arrays associated with the data arrays to hold information like null values and offsets. But the data is still in a set of contiguous buffers. In both a C-style array and an Arrow table, we can directly send the byte buffers without converting the original data structure.

If our data is in a more generic type such as a Java object, it is not in a contiguous buffer, and we may need to use an object serialization technology to convert it to a byte buffer. At the receiver, we need to unpack the data in the byte format and create the expected objects. To do this, we need information such as data types and the size of the message.

Protocol

A protocol is a contract between a sender and receiver so that they can successfully send messages and understand them. There are many messaging protocols available to suit our needs. Some are designed to work across hardware, operating systems, and programming languages. These protocols are based on open standards, with HTTP being familiar to most developers. Since such protocols are open, they sometimes present overheads for certain applications. For example, HTTP is a request-response protocol, but not every use case needs a response. The advantage of open protocols is that they allow various systems to be integrated in a transparent way.

Data-intensive frameworks tend to use internal protocols that are optimized for their use cases. The details of these protocols are not exposed to the user. Standard protocols are too expensive for the fine-grained operations occurring between the parallel processes of these frameworks.

There are two broad messaging protocols used for transferring data inside clusters. In the literature on messaging, they are called Eager Protocol and Rendezvous Protocol.

- **Eager Protocol**—The sender assumes there is enough memory at the receiving side for storing the messages it sends. When this assumption is made, we can send messages without synchronizing with the receiver. The Eager Protocol is more efficient at transferring small messages.

- **Rendezvous Protocol**—The sender first indicates to the receiver their intention to send a message. If the receiver has enough memory/processing to receive the message, it delivers an OK message back to the sender. Upon receiving this signal, the sender transmits the message. This protocol is mostly used for transferring larger messages.

The header contains the information needed by the receiver to process the message. Some common information in the header is listed here:

- **Source identifier**—Many sources may be sharing the same channel.

- **Destination identifier**—If there are many processing units at the receiver, we need an identifier to target them.

- **Length**—Length of the message. If the header supports variable-length information, we need to include its length.

- **Data type**—This helps the receiver to unpack the data.

As we can see, a header of a message can take up a substantial amount of space. If we specify the previous information as integers, the header will take up 16 bytes. If our messages are very small, we are using a considerable amount of bandwidth for the headers. After the receiver constructs the message, it can hand it over to the upper layers of the framework for further processing.

Message Types

A distributed data analytics application running in parallel needs messaging at various stages of its life cycle. These usages can be broadly categorized into control messages, external data source communications, and data transfer messages.

Control Messages

Data analytics frameworks use control messages for managing the applications in a distributed setting. The control messages are active in the initialization, monitoring, and teardown of the applications. Most are peer-to-peer messages, while some advanced systems have more complex forms to optimize for large-scale deployments. We touched upon control messages in an earlier chapter where we discussed resource management.

An example of a control message is a heartbeat used for detecting failures at parallel workers. In some distributed systems, parallel workers send a periodic message to indicate their active status to a central controller, and when these messages are missing, the central controller can determine whether a worker has failed.

External Data Sources

Data processing systems need to communicate with distributed storage and queuing systems to read and write data. This happens through the network as data are hosted in distributed data storages. Distributed storage such as file systems, object storages, SQL databases, and NoSQL databases provide their own client libraries so users can access data over the network. Apart from requiring the URL of these services, most APIs completely hide the networking aspect from the user.

We discussed accessing data storage in Chapter 2, so we will not go into more detail here. An example is accessing an HDFS file. In this case, the user is given a file system client to read or write a file in HDFS where the user does not even know whether that data is transferred through the network. In the HDFS case, the API provided is a file API. Databases offer either SQL interfaces or fluent APIs to access them. Message queues are a little different from other storage systems since they provide APIs that expose the messaging to the user. Reading and writing data to message queues is straightforward.

Data Transfer Messages

Once an application starts and data is read, the parallel workers need to communicate from time to time to synchronize their state. Let us take the popular big data example of counting words. To make things simple, we will be counting the total number of words instead of counting for individual words. Now, assume that we have a set of large text files stored in a distributed file system and only a few machines are available to perform this calculation.

Our first step would be to start a set of processes to do the computation. We can get the help of a resource manager as described in Chapter 3 and thereby manage a set of processes. Once we start these processes, they can read the text files in parallel. Each process will read a separate set of text files and count the number of words in them.

We will have to sum the word counts in different processes to get the overall total. We can use the network to send the counts to a single process, as shown in Figure 6-2. This can be achieved with a TCP library. First, we designate a process that is going to receive the counts. Then we establish a TCP connection to the designated receive process and send the counts as messages. Once the designated process receives messages from all other processes, it can calculate the total sums.

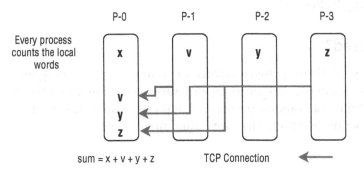

Figure 6-2: Processes 1, 2, and 3 send TCP messages to Process 0 with their local counts.

The previous example uses point-to-point messages, but collectively they are doing a summation of values distributed in a set of processes. A distributed framework can provide point-to-point messages as well as higher-level communication abstractions we call *distributed operators*.

- **Point-to-point messages**—This is the most basic form of messaging possible in distributed applications. The example we described earlier was implemented using point-to-point messages. These are found in programs that need fine-grained control over how parallel processes communicate.

- **Distributed operations**—Frameworks implement common communication patterns as distributed operations. In modern data-intensive frameworks, distributed operations play a vital role in performance and usability. They are sometimes called *collective operations* [1].

Most data-intensive frameworks do not provide point-to-point message abstractions between the parallel processes. Instead, they expose only distributed operations. Because of this, in the next few sections, we will focus our attention on distributed operations.

Distributed Operations

A distributed operation works on data residing in multiple computers. An example is the shuffle operation in map-reduce where we rearrange data distributed in a set of nodes. Distributed operations are present in any framework designed for analyzing data using multiple computers.

The goal of a distributed operation is to hide the details of the network layers and provide an API for common patterns of data synchronization. Underneath the API, it may be using various network technologies, communication protocols, and data packing technologies.

How Are They Used?

As discussed in Chapter 5, there are two methods of executing a parallel program: as a task graph or as a set of parallel processes programmed by the user. We can examine how distributed operations are applied in these settings. Irrespective of the setting, the operations achieve the same fundamental objectives.

Task Graph

Distributed operations can be embedded into a task graph–based program as a link between two tasks. Figure 6-3 details a computation expressed as a graph with a source task connected to a task receiving the reduced values through a Reduce link.

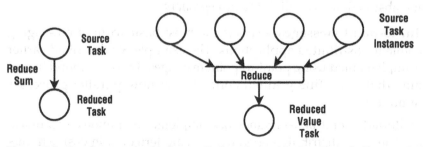

Figure 6-3: Dataflow graph with Source, Reduce Op, and Reduce Tasks (left); execution graph (right)

At runtime, this graph is transformed into one that executes on a distributed set of resources. Sources and reduced tasks are user-defined functions. The Reduce link between these nodes represents the distributed operation between them. The framework schedules the source and targets of the distributed operation in the resources according to the scheduling information. Figure 6-3 illustrates the transformed graph with four source task instances connected to a Reduce task instance by the Reduce distributed operation.

As we discussed in Chapter 5, the task graph–based execution is used in programs with a distributed data abstraction such as Apache Spark. The following Apache Spark example uses the Resilient Distributed Data (RDD) API to demonstrate a Reduce operation.

In this example, we have an array and partition it to 2 (parallelism). Then we do a Reduce operation on the data in the array. Note that Spark by default does the summation over all elements of the array and produces a single integer value as the sum. Spark can choose to run this program in two nodes of the cluster or in the same process depending on how we configure it. This API allows Spark to hide the distributed nature of the operation from the users.

```java
import java.util.Arrays;

import org.apache.spark.api.java.JavaRDD;
import org.apache.spark.api.java.JavaSparkContext;

public class SparkReduce {
  public static void main(String[] args) throws Exception {
    JavaSparkContext sc = new JavaSparkContext();

    // create a list and parallelize it to 2
    JavaRDD<Integer> list = sc.parallelize(
        Arrays.asList(4, 1, 3, 4, 5, 7, 7, 8, 9, 10), 2);

    // get the sum
    Integer sum = list.reduce((accum, n) -> (accum + n));

    System.out.println("Sum: " + sum);
  }
}
```

Parallel Processes

As previously described, the MPI implementations provide distributed operations so that we can write our program as a set of parallel processes. Table 6-1 shows a popular implementation of the MPI standard [2]. The standard provides APIs for point-to-point communication as well as array-based distributed operations called *collectives*.

Table 6-1: Popular MPI Implementations

MPI IMPLEMENTATION	DESCRIPTION
MPICH[1]	One of the earliest MPI implementations. Actively developed and used in many supercomputers.
OpenMPI[2]	Actively developed and widely used MPI implementation. The project started by merging three MPI implementations: FT-MPI from the University of Tennessee, LA-MPI from Los Alamos National Laboratory, and LAM/MPI from Indiana University.
MVAPICH[3]	Also called MVAPICH2, developed by Ohio State University.

With the default MPI model, the user programs a process instead of a dataflow graph. The distributed operations are programmed explicitly by the user between these processes in the data analytics application. Computations are carried out as if they are local computations identifying the parallelism of the program. This model is synonymous with the popular bulk synchronous parallel (BSP) programming model. In Figure 6-4, we see there are computation phases and distributed operations for synchronizing state among processes.

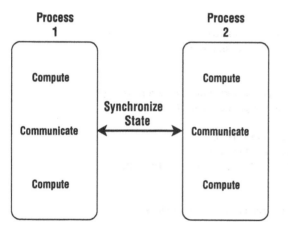

Figure 6-4: MPI process model for computing and communication

In the following source code, we have an MPI_reduce operation. Every parallel process generates a random integer array, and a single reduced array is produced at Process 0. The target is specified in the operation (in this case the 0th process), and the data type is set to Integer. Since the operation uses the MPI_COMM_WORLD, it will use all the parallel processes as sources. This API is a little more involved than the Spark version in terms of the parameters provided to the operation. Also, the semantics are different compared to Spark as the MPI program does an element-wise reduction of the arrays in multiple processes.

[1]https://www.mpich.org/
[2]https://www.open-mpi.org/
[3]https://mvapich.cse.ohio-state.edu/

```c
#include <stdio.h>
#include <stdlib.h>
#include <mpi.h>
#include <assert.h>
#include <time.h>

int main(int argc, char** argv) {
 MPI_Init(NULL, NULL);

 int world_rank;
 MPI_Comm_rank(MPI_COMM_WORLD, &world_rank);

 int int_array[4];
 int i;
 printf("Process %d array: ", world_rank);
 for (i = 0; i < 4; i++) {
   int_array[i] = rand() % 100;
   printf("%d ", int_array[i]);
 }
 printf("\n");

 int reduced[4] = {0};
 // Reduce each value in array to process 0
 MPI_Reduce(&int_array, &reduced, 4, MPI_INT, MPI_SUM, 0, MPI_COMM_WORLD);

 // Print the result
 if (world_rank == 0) {
   printf("Reduced array: ");
   for (i = 0; i < 4; i++) {
     printf("%d ", reduced[i]);
   }
   printf("\n");
 }

 MPI_Finalize();
}
```

With MPI's parallel process management and the ability to communicate between them, we can build various models of distributed computing. We can even develop task graph–based executions using the functions provided by MPI [3]. Since MPI provides only the basic and most essential functions for parallel computing, its implementations are efficient. Even on large clusters, microsecond latencies are observed for distributed operations.

On the other hand, the simplistic nature of these functions creates a barrier for new users. Most MPI implementations lack enterprise features such as gathering statistics and web UIs, which in turn make them unattractive for mainstream users. With deep learning frameworks, MPI is increasingly used for training larger models and continues to gain momentum in data analytics.

Anatomy of a Distributed Operation

Now, let us look at the semantics of distributed operations and the requirements of the APIs.

Data Abstractions

The semantics of a distributor operation depend on the data abstractions and application domain they represent. As discussed in Chapter 4, arrays and tables are the two most common structures used in data-intensive applications.

- **Arrays**—We use arrays to represent mathematical structures such as vectors, matrices, and tensors. Distributed operations on arrays define the common communication patterns used in parallel calculations over these mathematical structures.

- **Tables**—The operations associated with tables originate from relational algebra. Distributed operations on tables include these relational algebra operations and common data transfer patterns such as shuffle.

Distributed Operation API

As distributed operations are built on messaging, they need the information we discussed for messaging and more to produce higher-level functionality.

Data Types

Arrays and tables are composite data structures. The actual data within these data types can be of distinct types such as Integers, Doubles, or Strings. Some distributed operations need access to this information. For example, to sort a table based on a string column, the operation needs to know that the column contains strings. Arrays are associated with a single data type. A table can have distinct data types in its columns, and we call this data type information a *schema*.

Sources and Targets

Assume a distributed operation is transpiring among N processes. Between these processes, there can be many entities producing and receiving data in the same operation. We call the entities producing the data to be *source* and those consuming the data are *targets*. Sources and targets can overlap, and in some cases they can even be the same. In general, sources and targets are logical entities and can be mapped to more concrete resources such as processes or threads.

Edge/Stream/Tag

Now, what would happen if we deployed two instances of the same operation at the same time? The receivers can receive messages without knowing exactly what operation to which they belong. An instance of an operation needs an identifier so that the messages between different instances running contemporaneously can be distinguished from one another. Some systems call this identifier a tag, while others refer to it as an *edge* or *stream*. Certain systems generate the identifier automatically without the user even being aware of its presence.

User Functions

Some distributed operations accept user-defined functions. These can specify operations on data or specify how to arrange the data in a distributed setting. For example, they can accept custom reduction functions and partitioning functions.

Streaming and Batch Operations

So far, we have looked at a distributed operation as taking input and producing output working across parallel processes. There is a difference in how the operations are used in batch and streaming systems. Streaming distributed operations accept input data continuously and produce outputs continuously. The batch operations use a finite amount of input data and at the end, produce an output by processing the data.

Streaming Operations

Streaming systems are always modeled as task graphs, and they run as long-running tasks and communication links. So, the streaming operations are running continuously, connecting the tasks by taking input from source tasks, and producing output to the receiving tasks.

Batch Operations

Two variants of batch operations are possible depending on whether the operations are designed to process in-memory data or large data.

- **In-memory data**—For in-memory data, an operation can take the complete data at once and produce the output. This simplifies the operation API. For example, array-based operations in MPI are designed around this idea.

- **Large data**—To handle large data that does not fit into the memory, the operation needs to take in data piece by piece and produce output the same way. The operation design is much more involved, as it needs to take partial input, process this using external storage, and take more input until it reaches the end. At the end, it still needs to produce output one chunk at a time.

Distributed Operations on Arrays

As we discussed in Chapter 4, arrays are one of the foundational structures for computing. They are used in machine learning, deep learning, and computer simulations extensively. When we have multiple arrays distributed over a cluster, we can apply array-based distributed operations. Table 6-2 shows some widely used examples on arrays.

Table 6-2: Common Distributed Operations on Arrays

OPERATION	DESCRIPTION
Reduce, AllReduce	Elementwise reduction of array elements.
Gather, AllGather	Gathers multiple arrays together to form a larger array.
Broadcast	Sends a copy of an array to each target process.
Scatter	Partitions an array and sends those partitions to separate targets.
AllToAll	All the processes (sources) send data to all the other processes (targets).

Distributed operations consider arrays as a sequence of elements (vectors) and apply operations accordingly. Note, that we can consider a single value as an array with one element. The following sections assume arrays are present in several processes. The semantics for the operations are based on the MPI standard.

Broadcast

Broadcast is widely used by programs to send a copy of data to multiple processes from a single process. Broadcast is easy to understand and can be found in all major systems designed to process data in parallel. Figure 6-5 has five parallel processes with IDs assigned from 0 to 4. The 0th process has an array it must broadcast to the rest; at the end of the operation, all the processes will have a copy of this array.

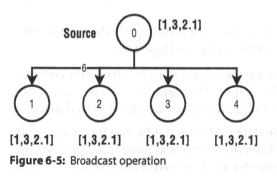

Figure 6-5: Broadcast operation

Broadcast does not consider the structure of the array, meaning it can be anything, such as a byte array created from a serialized object.

Reduce and AllReduce

Reduce is a popular operation for computations on arrays. A reduction is associated with a function, and the following are some popular examples:

- Sum
- Multiply
- Max
- Min
- Logical or
- Logical and

Commutativity is a key factor when considering Reduce functions. All those listed here are commutative functions. An example of a noncommutative function is division. A binary operator * is commutative if it satisfies the following condition:

$$A * B = B * A$$

If a reduction function is commutative, the order of how it is applied to data does not matter. But if it is noncommutative, the order of the reduction is important.

Now, let us look at the semantics of reductions on arrays. Each distributed process has the same size array. The values in every position of the array are reduced individually with the corresponding values from other arrays. The result is an array of the same size and data type. Here are four arrays:

A = [10, 12]

B = [20, 2]

C = [40, 6]

D = [10, 10]

The Reduce result for a sum function of these arrays is another array, R = [80, 30]. In Figure 6-6, the arrays are placed in tasks with IDs from 0 to 4. The Reduce result is given to Task 1.

AllReduce is semantically equivalent to Reduce followed by Broadcast, meaning reduced values are transferred to all the targets of the operation. This raises the question: why have a separate operation called AllReduce if Reduce and Broadcast already exist in the first place? First, this is a heavily used operation

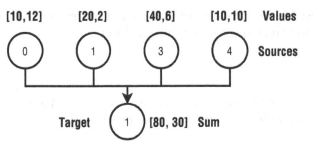

Figure 6-6: Reduce operation

in parallel programs. As such, it deserves its own place since it would be unrea-
sonable to expect users to use two operations for one of the most popular capabilities parallel programs require. Second, we can implement AllReduce in ways
that are more efficient than Reduce followed by Broadcast implementations.
Figure 6-7 shows the same example with AllReduce instead of Reduce. Now,
the reduced value is distributed to all the tasks.

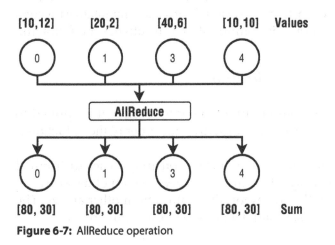

Figure 6-7: AllReduce operation

Gather and AllGather

As the name suggests, the Gather operation takes values from multiple locations
and groups them together to form a large set. When creating the set, implementations can preserve the source that produced the data or not, depending on
preference. In classic parallel computing, the values are ordered according to
the process identification number. Figure 6-8 shows a gather operation.

Similar to AllReduce, the AllGather operation is equivalent to combining
Gather followed by Broadcast. It is implemented as a separate operation owing
to its importance and the implementation optimizations possible. Figure 6-9
shows an AllGather example.

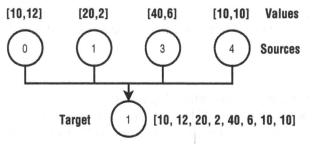

Figure 6-8: Gather operation

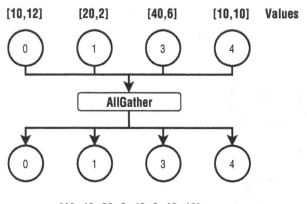

[10, 12, 20, 2, 40, 6, 10, 10]

Everyone has the same copy

Figure 6-9: AllGather operation

Scatter

Scatter is the opposite of the Gather operation, as it distributes the values in a single process to many processes according to a criterion specified by the user. Figure 6-10 shows the scatter operation from Process 0 to four other processes.

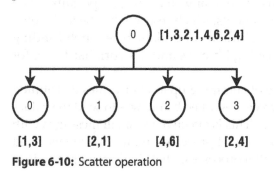

Figure 6-10: Scatter operation

In the preceding Scatter operation, the first two consecutive values are sent to the first target, while the second set of consecutive values go to the second target.

AllToAll

AllToAll can be described as every process performing a scatter operation to all the other processes at the same time. Figure 6-11 has four arrays in four processes, each with four elements. The 0th element of these arrays goes to 0th process, and the 1st element of these arrays goes to 1st process. Once we rearrange the arrays like this, four new arrays are created in the four processes.

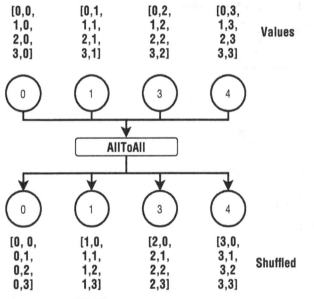

Figure 6-11: AllToAll operation

Optimized Operations

Messaging for parallel applications offers many challenges, especially when working in large, distributed environments. Much research has been devoted to improving these operations, with billions of dollars of research funding going toward enhancing the messaging libraries and network hardware for large-scale computations.

Let us take the previous example of summing up a set of values distributed over several processes. The approach we described before was to send the values from all processes to a single process. This is effective for small messages with a correspondingly small number of parallel processes. Now, imagine we need to send 1MB of data from 1,000 parallel processes. That single process needs to receive gigabytes of data, which can take about 1 second with a 10Gbps Ethernet connection with a theoretical throughput. After receiving 1GB of this data, the process must go through and add them as well.

When 1,000 processes try to send 1MB messages to a single process, the network becomes congested and drastically slows down, such that it can take several seconds for all the messages to be delivered. This can lead to network congestion and large sequential computations for a single process. In the 1980s, computer scientists realized they could use different routing algorithms for sending messages to avoid these problems. Such algorithms are now called collective algorithms and are widely used in optimizing [4] these distributed operations.

Broadcast

The simplest approach to implement Broadcast is to create N connections to the target processes and send the value through. In this model, if it takes t time to put the Broadcast value into the network link, it will take $t \times N$ times to completely send the value to all N processes. Figure 6-12 illustrates this approach. It is termed a *flat tree* as it forms a tree with the source at the root and all the other workers at the leaves. This method works better if N is small and takes much longer when either N or the message size increases.

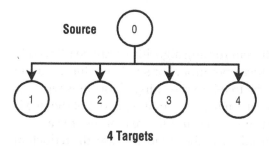

Figure 6-12: Broadcast with a flat tree

There are methods that can perform much better for many processes. One such option is to arrange the processes in a binary tree, as shown in Figure 6-13, and send the values through the tree. The source sends the value to two targets; these in turn simultaneously send the value to four targets, which transfer the value to eight targets, and so on until it reaches all targets. The parallelism of the operation increases exponentially, and as it expands, it uses more of the total available bandwidth of the network. Theoretically, it takes about $\log N$ steps to broadcast the values to all the nodes. When N is large, this can reduce the time required significantly.

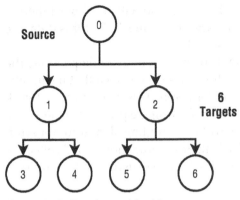

Figure 6-13: Broadcast with a binary tree

The tree approach works well only for smaller values that do not utilize the network fully. In the case of large messages, there is still a bottleneck in this approach since every node other than the leaves tries to send the value to two processes at the same time. The operation can be further optimized for larger data by using methods such as chaining and double trees. It is important to note that some computer networks have built-in capabilities to broadcast values, and implementations sometimes exploit these features.

Reduce

Depending on the message sizes, different routing algorithms can be utilized to optimize the performance of the Reduce operation. For smaller values, routing based on tree structures is optimal. The tree-based routing algorithms work by arranging the participating processes in an inverted tree. The root of the tree is the target that receives the final reduced value, and the rest of the tree are the sources producing the data to be reduced. As in the broadcast case, the reduction can be done in log N steps for N parallel processes.

AllReduce

The simplest form of AllReduce implementation is a Reduce operation followed by a Broadcast. This works well for small messages. When the message size is large, however, the network is not fully utilized. To optimize the network bandwidth utilization, a ring-based routing algorithm or recursive doubling algorithm can be used.

Ring Algorithm

In this version, data from each process is sent around a virtual ring created by the ith process connecting to the $(i+1) \bmod N$ where N is the number of processes. In the first step, each process sends its data to its connected process. In the next step, each process sends the data it received in the previous step to its connected process. This is done for $N-1$ steps. The algorithm fully utilizes the available network bandwidth by activating all the network links equally at every step. It is best suited for large data reductions. Figure 6-14 shows a reduced set of values in four processes in three steps.

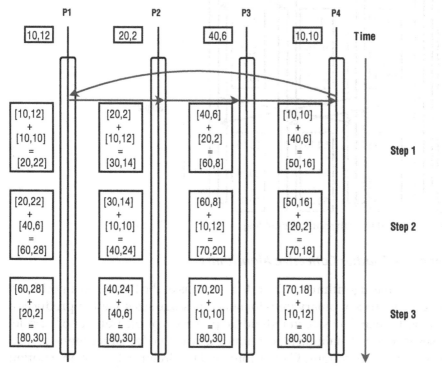

Figure 6-14: AllReduce with Ring

Recursive Doubling

Figure 6-15 shows the recursive doubling algorithm. Each process will start by sending data to a process at distance 1. For example, process 0 will send data to process 1. At each step i, this distance will double until $2i$ steps are completed. This algorithm takes $\log N$ steps to communicate the data between the processes. Figure 6-15 demonstrates how this algorithm works for four processes. The algorithm has better latency characteristics than the previous one but does not utilize the network as efficiently.

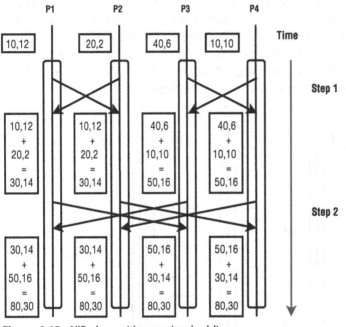

Figure 6-15: AllReduce with recursive doubling

Gather and AllGather Collective Algorithms

Gather collective algorithms are inverted versions of the Broadcast algorithms. We can use flat trees or binary trees for small message sizes. Gather produces a large dataset when data size in individual processes or the number of parallel processes increases. Chaining algorithms are available for larger messages.

For AllGather operations, Gather followed by Broadcast is a viable option for small messages with a small number of processes. AllGather can transfer larger messages as it needs to distribute the gathered value to all the other processes. For these cases, one can use the ring algorithm or the recursive doubling algorithm described in the AllReduce.

Scatter and AllToAll Collective Algorithms

Scatter utilizes collective algorithms found in Broadcast for sending the values present in a single process to multiple processes. AllToAll can involve many communications as a result of sending data from each process to all the other processes. It can be optimized using a chaining algorithm. This algorithm works by arranging the processes in a dynamic chain configuration. At the kth step, the process i sends data to the $(i+k) \bmod N$ where N is the number of processes. We will discuss this algorithm later along with shuffle.

Distributed Operations on Tables

As mentioned, data management systems are built around table abstractions. Whether Pandas DataFrame or Spark RDD, the processing semantics associated with them are similar because they have the same goal of representing data as a table. The operations in these systems are based on relational algebra [5] and SQL. Shuffle is the most widely used operation for implementing many of the relational algebra operations in a distributed setting. Table 6-3 lists some of the widely used operations we discussed in the previous chapter.

Table 6-3: Distributed Operations for Tables

OPERATION	DESCRIPTION
Shuffle	Partition the tables and redistribute them.
Joins	Distributed joins using join, left outer join, right outer join, and full outer join.
GroupBy	Group the rows according to a key.
Aggregate	Aggregate functions such as SUM, MIN, MAX, AVG.
Sort	Sorting of tables based on columns.
Union	Union of two tables.
Difference	Set difference of two tables.
Broadcast	Broadcast a table to workers.

Like with array based distributed operations, we have tables in a distributed setting. These can be partitions of a larger table depending on how our program models computations. For this discussion, we assume horizontal partitioning by rows. In the next few sections, we will look at how these operations are implemented.

Shuffle

The shuffle operation is designed to rearrange table data among a distributed set of workers. Shuffle is like AllToAll operation for arrays and works on tables instead. Since shuffle has AllToAll semantics, each node is potentially distributing data to all the other participating nodes.

Figure 6-16 demonstrates the major steps of shuffle. We have a table with two columns and four partitions distributed in a cluster. We are going to apply a shuffle operation to this data using the key as column K. After the shuffle, records with Key 1 will create Partition 0, records with Key 2 will create Partition 1, and so on.

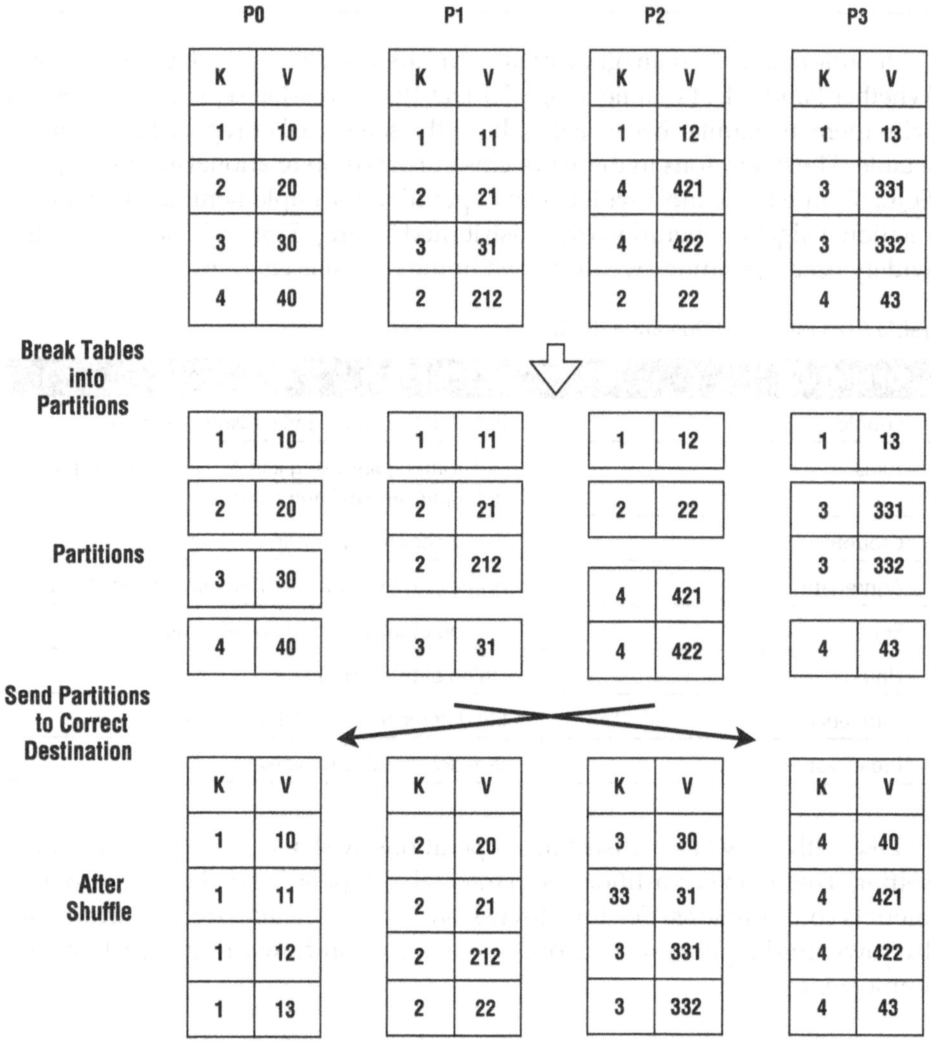

Break Tables into Partitions

P0 K	P0 V	P1 K	P1 V	P2 K	P2 V	P3 K	P3 V
1	10	1	11	1	12	1	13
2	20	2	21	4	421	3	331
3	30	3	31	4	422	3	332
4	40	2	212	2	22	4	43

Partitions

K	V	K	V	K	V	K	V
1	10	1	11	1	12	1	13
2	20	2	21	2	22	3	331
3	30	2	212	4	421	3	332
4	40	3	31	4	422	4	43

Send Partitions to Correct Destination

After Shuffle

K	V	K	V	K	V	K	V
1	10	2	20	3	30	4	40
1	11	2	21	33	31	4	421
1	12	2	212	3	331	4	422
1	13	2	22	3	332	4	43

Figure 6-16: Shuffle operation

The shuffle operation is given the original tables. The first step it must take is to create local partitions according to the key, as shown in Figure 6-16. These partitions are then sent to the correct destinations. A receiver will get many partitions from different processes and combine them to create the final table.

Systems can use different algorithms to create the partitions and send them to the correct destinations.

Partitioning Data

For larger datasets, partitioning can take a considerable amount of time. The common partitioning schemes used in data-intensive frameworks are hash partitioning and radix partitioning.

Hash Partitioning

Assume we are going to create n partitions from a dataset, and these are numbered from 0 to n. We can apply a hashing function to the attribute value we are using to partition the data. The new partition p of a record with attribute value v can be calculated by the following:

$$p = hash(v) \bmod n$$

This operation can be time-consuming when large numbers of records need to be processed. If we have multiple attributes, we can use those values in the hash function. A hash function such as murmur or modulo [6] can perform the hashing.

Radix Partitioning

Radix partitioning [7] is a widely used technique in databases. It starts by creating a histogram of 2^N buckets using a radix of size N. For example, if the radix is 10, it will create 2^{10} buckets. Then it goes through the data and counts the number of items for each bucket. This is done using N bits of each attribute value. Here is a code snippet for calculating histogram for a 32-bit integer value:

```
histogram[input >> (32 - N)]++
```

Now, using this histogram, we can calculate boundaries for P partitions where $P \leq 2^N$. We then go through the data again and assign them to the correct partitions.

In a distributed setting, we need to calculate a global histogram from all the partitions. We can calculate a histogram for each partition and combine them using a Reduce operation to create the global histogram.

Load Balancing

When we shuffle the data, the resulting partitions assigned to a CPU core can be skewed. Imagine in our previous example we chose the partitioning scheme as Keys 1 and 2 going to the 0th partition, Key 3 going to the 2nd partition, and

Key 4 going to the 3rd partition. Now data in the 1st partition is empty, while the 0th partition has twice the data as 2nd and 3rd partitions. This was a hypothetical example, but this scenario is common in practice, so choosing the correct partitioning method is important.

Depending on the number of buckets and the data distribution, radix can create an imbalanced partitioning. It is possible to increase the number of buckets in the histogram to reduce the load imbalance, but we may need more memory to create the histogram. A simple hash partitioning produces imbalanced partitions in numerous practical use cases. Depending on the data, we may need to use a custom partitioning method to make sure the resulting partitions are balanced.

Handling Large Data

Handling data larger than memory means we cannot keep all the data at once in memory. Therefore, we need to design the shuffle operation to take a stream of inputs to handle data larger than memory. Also, its output should be streamed out piece by piece. Since we are taking a stream of inputs, we can keep only part of the data in the memory at any instant.

To keep the parts that are not in memory, shuffle operation needs to tap into disk storage. Disks are orders of magnitude slower than the main memory and cheaper per storage unit by comparison.

The code works by reading a part of the data into memory and inserting that into the shuffle operation, as shown in Figure 6-17. The shuffle operation creates

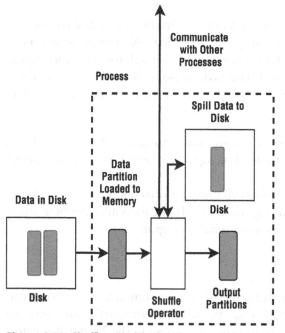

Figure 6-17: Shuffle with data that does not fit into memory

partitions and send them to the correct destinations. Once the receivers have these partitions, they can write them to disk so that they have enough memory to handle the next batch. Then we read the proceeding partitions from the disk and repeat the same until all the data are read from the disk.

At this point, the operation can start outputting data in a streaming fashion one partition at a time. Shuffle has an option to sort records based on a key associated with that record. When sorting is enabled, an external sorting algorithm can be used. For example, at the receiver we can save data to the disk after sorting. When reading, we merge the sorted partition data.

Next, we will look at a few algorithms for implementing shuffle operation.

Fetch-Based Algorithm (Asynchronous Algorithm)

The fetch-based algorithm is a popular approach adopted by current big data systems that adopts asynchronous execution. We will discuss it in Chapter 7. Figure 6-18 illustrates how the input data to the operation is split into buffers. When the buffer becomes full, the data is spilled to the disk. To achieve maximum performance from a disk, read and write needs to be done with larger chunks and on contiguous regions.

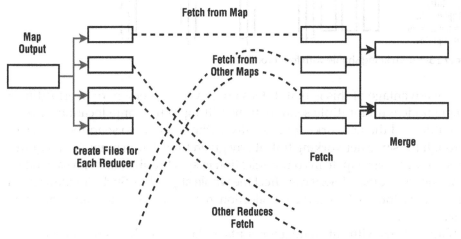

Figure 6-18: Fetch-based shuffle

The sources update a central server with the data location of partitions, and the targets get to know about the data to receive from this server. Bear in mind central synchronization does hold the risk of introducing potential performance bottlenecks when there are many parallel workers trying to synchronize all at once. After the target fetches data from multiple sources, they merge them utilizing the disk.

Distributed Synchronization Algorithm

The shuffle can be implemented as a distributed synchronization algorithm without a single point for coordination, as shown in Figure 6-19. This algorithm works by arranging the tasks in a chain configuration. The algorithm is self-synchronizing and can be used in high-performance clusters.

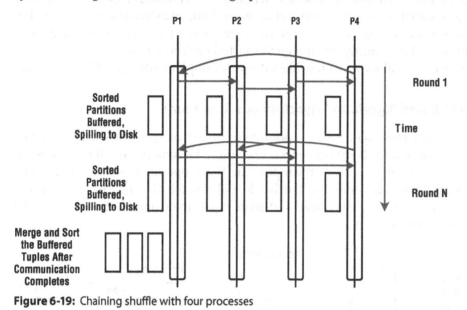

Figure 6-19: Chaining shuffle with four processes

The advantage of this is that it does not have the problem of overloading a single node with multiple senders transmitting to the same location. Also, it can utilize all the networking links fully without trying to send the messages through the same networking link at any given time. Unfortunately, it requires every node to participate in communication in synchronization with each other. If one node becomes slow, it can affect the whole algorithm. Such slowdowns can be due to factors such as garbage collection, network congestion, and operating system noise.

Shuffle deals with substantial amounts of data over phases of computation, communication, and disk I/O. By overlapping these phases, resources can be utilized to the fullest and improve the throughput. Most implementations found in big data systems support such overlapping to various degrees.

GroupBy

GroupBy followed by an aggregation operation is a popular method in big data systems. The original map-reduce paradigm was a GroupBy operation where a set of data in the form of a table (key, value) is shuffled and then grouped according to the key. It applies a Reduce (aggregate) operation to the values of the same key.

Figure 6-20 demonstrates the GroupBy operation with a summation aggregation. First, we shuffle the tables so that the same key goes to the same process. Then we do a local aggregation on the values of that key.

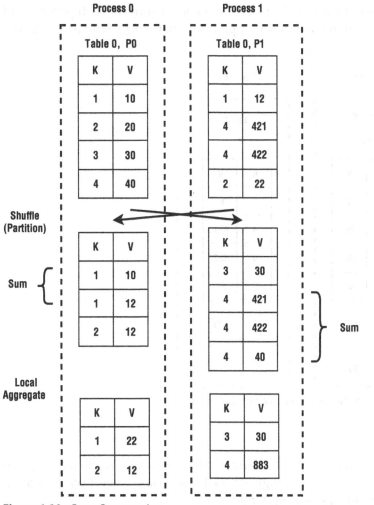

Figure 6-20: GroupBy operation

Aggregate

We looked at Reduce operations for arrays earlier. Aggregate operations in tables are like Reduce operations in arrays but with slightly different semantics. Aggregate operations are applied to a column of a table.

Let us take the example of a summation aggregate function. When applied to a column, the summation function adds up values of that column. When applied to a table distributed over a cluster, the aggregate function computes a global sum of the column values. In contrast, an array-based reduction adds up values in the same array indexes.

Figure 6-21 shows a SUM aggregate function on column V of the table distributed over two processes. We calculate the local sum for each process and then do a global sum using a reduce operation that works with arrays (array with one element).

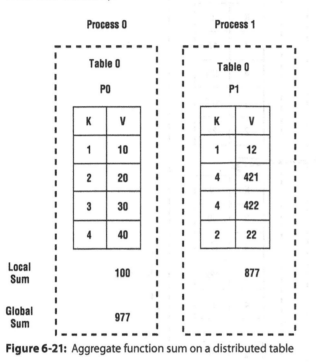

Figure 6-21: Aggregate function sum on a distributed table

Join

Joins are time-consuming when large datasets are involved. A join requires two input datasets and outputs a single dataset. There are several types of joins available in data management systems:

- Inner join
- Left outer join
- Right outer join
- Full outer join

With the help of an example, let us look at the semantics of these operations. Here are two datasets we are going to use for the joins shown in a table format. Each dataset has a common attribute called Customer ID.

Data Set A (Customer details)

CUSTOMER ID	NAME	EMAIL	PHONE
1	John Doe	john@fdia.com	891-234-9245
2	Smith Rosenberry	smit@rose.com	934-234-2321
3	Jack Igor	jack@123.com	421-234-1234
4	Ana Kelse	ana@out.com	233-123-4423

Data Set B (Orders)

ORDER ID	CUSTOMER ID	ORDER DATE
103	1	2020-02-10
223	3	2020-02-21
321	4	2020-02-11

Inner Join (Join)

An inner join creates a dataset with records that have matching values in both input datasets. Inner joins with equal conditions are one of the most often used in practice. Joins with equal conditions are called *equijoins*. Inner joins are referred to simply as *joins*. To find the relevant information of those customers who have an order, let us look at the output dataset for joining A and B with an equijoin using Customer ID as the key. The following table shows the results of this inner join:

CUSTOMER ID	NAME	EMAIL	PHONE	ORDER ID	ORDER DATE
1	John Doe	john@fdia.com	891-234-9245	103	2020-02-10
3	Jack Igor	jack@123.com	421-234-1234	223	2020-02-21
4	Ana Kelsey	ana@out.com	233-123-4423	321	2020-02-11

Left (Outer) Join

Left join outputs the left dataset completely while taking the records from the right dataset where the join condition is met. For records from a left dataset without matching records from the right dataset, the right table fields are filled with NULL values.

Still using the current example, we are going to select all the customers and any order they might have. Note that the customer with Customer ID 2 does not have any orders, so their corresponding columns are set to NULL.

CUSTOMER ID	NAME	EMAIL	PHONE	ORDER ID	ORDER DATE
1	John Doe	john@fdia.com	891-234-9245	103	2020-02-10
2	Smith Rosenberry	smit@rose.com	934-234-2321	NULL	NULL
3	Jack Igor	jack@123.com	421-234-1234	223	2020-02-21
4	Ana Kelsey	ana@out.com	233-123-4423	321	2020-02-11

Right (Outer) Join

Right join is the mirror of the left join, with all the records from the right dataset in the output. If the left join example's datasets are exchanged (the right dataset becomes the left, and the left dataset becomes the right) and applied to the right join with the same condition, it would produce the same results.

Full (Outer) Join

A full join produces a dataset by combining the results of both left and right outer joins and returns all rows irrespective of a match from the datasets on both sides of the join.

Dataset A

A	B
1	x
2	y
5	z

Dataset B

A	C
1	p
2	q
4	r

Here is a simple example of joining Dataset A and B on attribute A (equality) using a full join. There are two rows that match, and they share attributes for all. For nonmatching rows, the row from one table is given with missing values from the other table.

A	B	C
1	x	p
2	y	q
5	z	NULL
4	NULL	r

Join Algorithms

In most databases, the join algorithm occurs in a single machine, whereas with big data systems the joins take place in a distributed setting at a much larger scale. It is important to understand the mechanics of a join in a single machine to apply it on a larger scale. Hash join and sorted merge join algorithms are the most popular. Many frameworks implement both as they can be efficient for several types of joins with varying parameters. Depending on the situation, the correct join can be selected by the framework or the user.

Hash Join

Hash joins work by creating an in-memory hash map from one dataset. The algorithm has two phases:

- **Hashing phase**—Creates a hash map using one of the datasets. The key of the hash map is the join attribute, and the value is the actual record. The hash map should support a super-efficient lookup of values by way of the key. Usually this can be an $O(1)$ lookup. The smaller relation is used for building the hash map.

- **Joining phase**—After the hash map is created, the other table can be scanned and matched against the hash table. If a value is found in the hash table, these are then joined. Since the hash and equality are used for looking up the key, this method can only support joins with equal conditions.

We usually choose the smaller relationship to create the hash map.

Sorted Merge Join

The naive approach to joining two datasets is to take one record from a dataset and compare it against the entire next relationship to find if there are records matching the join condition. The pseudocode for this is shown in the following with datasets A and B:

```
For a in A
    For b in B
        If a and b matches join condition
            Add to output a,b
```

This approach needs a *no of records A × no of records B* comparison, which can become huge as the size of the datasets increases. Imagine joining a million tuples against another million tuples. The previous algorithm requires 1,000 billion comparisons to complete. To avoid that many comparisons, the datasets can be sorted using the joining keys. The sorting can be done in $N \log N$ time, and after this one scan through both datasets, it can join them together. If the number of records in relation A is N and the number of records in relation B is M, the complexity will be $N \log N + M \log M + M + N$.

The algorithm is shown next and can be described in just a few steps. Initially, both datasets are sorted with the join key. Note that this algorithm works only for equijoins. The algorithm defines a function called advance that scans a given dataset starting with a given index. This function outputs the records with a key equivalent to the starting index of the scan. Since the datasets are sorted, it only needs to look at the consecutive elements. The moment it sees anything different, it can return the current set.

```
function sortMergeJoin(dataset L, dataset R, key k)
    dataset output = {}
    // sort L and R with key k
    list lSorted = sort(L, k)
    list rSorted = sort(R, k)
    key lKey, rKey
    set lSubset, rSubset
    advance(lSubset, lSorted, lKey, k)
    advance(rSubset, rSorted, rKey, k)
    while not empty(lSubset) and not empty(rightSubset)
        if lKey == rKey
            add cartesian product of lSubset and rSubset to output
            advance(lSubset, lSorted, lKey, k)
            advance(rSubset, rSorted, rKey, k)
        else if left_key < right_key
            advance(lSubset, lSorted, lKey, k)
        else
            advance(rSubset, rSorted, rKey, k)
    return output
```

```
function advance(subset out, sortedData inout, key out, k in)
    key = sortedData[0].key(k)
    subset = {}
    while not empty(sortedData) and sortedData[0].key(k) == key
        subset.insert(sorted[0])
        sortedData.remove(0)
```

After the `advance` function finds records for each dataset, if the keys are equal, the Cartesian product is taken of the two outputs of the advance, and then the `advance` function is run on both datasets. If the keys of a dataset are less than the other dataset, the algorithm runs the `advance` routine on the dataset with the lesser key starting from the previous end index. This assumes an ascending order sorting of the relationships. The algorithm does this until it reaches the end of one dataset. Figure 6-22 shows two relationships with two fields per record. The first field is taken as the joining key.

A	1,1	3,5	3,6	5,1	5,0	8,0	8,9

B	3,1	3,2	3,3	4,0	5,1	8,1	9,9

Figure 6-22: Sorted merge join

The output of the equijoin will be as follows:

```
[3,5,1], [3,5,2], [3,5,3], [3,6,1], [3,6,2], [3,6,3], [5,1,1], [5,0,1], [8,0,1],
[8,9,1].
```

Notice how it takes the Cartesian product of the matching records of the two datasets. This algorithm works much more efficiently compared to two sets done naively for larger datasets. Sorting an enormous number of records can take a significant amount of time. When data larger than memory is involved, an external sorting algorithm is of great help.

Distributed Joins

The idea behind the distributed join is simple. It first redistributes data with the same keys from both datasets into the same processes. After this, the data in each process is joined separately using one of the join algorithms mentioned earlier [8]. Figure 6-23 shows an example of such where Process 0 and Process 1 has two tables 0 and 1. Process 0 has the 0th partition of these tables, and Process 1 has the 1st partition. First the data is shuffled so that Keys 1 and 2 go to Process 0 and Keys 3 and 4 are sent to Process 1. After the shuffle, the tables are joined locally.

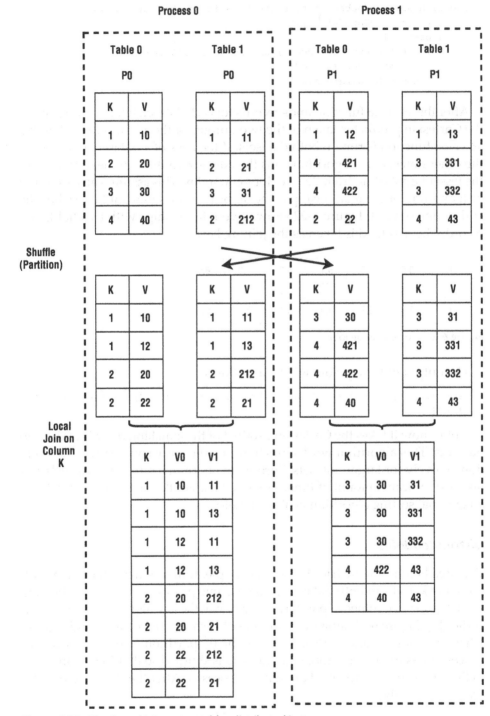

Figure 6-23: Distributed join on two tables distributed in two processes

Performance of Joins

We described the basic structure of a join here, and in practice they are implemented to efficiently use the cache and reduce the TLB misses. First, the tables are partitioned into small datasets. This is done so that individual partitions fit into the cache to make sorting or hashing efficient.

A join can produce a dataset that is many times bigger than the input datasets. In classic implementations, the hash join is slightly better than the sort-merge join. Sort-merge join is a more popular implementation as it can handle all the join scenarios. The performance of these two algorithms depends on the implementation and programming environment.

The performance evaluations of the algorithms found in research literature are done mostly in ideal conditions. In practice, factors such as data representation in the memory and size of the data and whether disks are used can determine which implementation is faster. With such a complex set of circumstances, it is better to consult the performance numbers of specific frameworks and their recommendations to figure out the correct algorithm for certain situations.

There are many other optimizations available as well. For example, if one relationship is comparatively small, instead of reshuffling both tables, we can send the small table to all the processes and do the join at each process. This avoids the shuffling of the larger table that can take a considerable time.

More Operations

Table 6.4 shows a few other operations and how they are implemented in a distributed setting. All the operations in the table use shuffle, and some use a few other communication operations as well.

Table 6.4: Table-Based Operations and Their Implementations

OPERATION	DESCRIPTION	IMPLEMENTATION
Union	Set union with duplicate removal.	Shuffle based on hash and local union.
Sort	Sorting values so there is a global ordering. For example, 0th process gets the lowest sorted values, 1st process gets the next sorted values, and so on.	Do sampling to determine the global partition boundaries. Requires a Gather operation and a broadcast for determining the partitioning using sampling. Then do shuffle and local sorting.
Difference	Set difference.	Shuffle based on hash and take local difference.

Advanced Topics

There are many factors to consider when a system is configured to run large-scale data analytics applications. Primarily, the networking layer at the OS level needs to be configured to handle a high number of connections efficiently. The frameworks have many configuration knobs that need tuning in order to achieve maximum performance for our applications.

Data Packing

We need to put the user data into the network layer as a set of bytes. *Data packing* and *data serialization* are two terms used when referring to the techniques involved.

Memory Considerations

Memory management is key to efficient messaging, as most of the overhead occurs when in-memory user-defined data types are transferred to the network buffers. This is especially problematic for higher-level languages such as Java and Python, where objects are created in heap memory. When numerous small objects are made in heap memory, transferring them to the network buffers can be costly due to many random memory accesses that occur.

Java-based frameworks use object serialization technologies such as Kryo or Avro to serialize user-defined objects into byte format. For these applications, serialization incurs a significant overhead when large numbers of small messages are transferred.

On the other hand, high-performance frameworks restrict the users to define data types that fit into the networking buffers without additional processing. For example, compact formats like Apache Arrow use buffers that can be directly applied in network transfers. This is the most efficient form of designing applications as there is no need to pack the user-defined object into a buffer.

Message Coalescing

Small messages in the network lead to the underutilization of network bandwidth. To fully take advantage of the network, messages must be as big as possible. Message size is dictated by the applications, and frameworks can coalesce or group these small messages to increase network bandwidth use.

Sending groups of messages increases bandwidth utilization, but individual messages can observe higher latencies. This effect is more important for streaming applications where latency is critical. Also, message coalescing requires the use of CPU and additional memory.

Compression

Message compression can be applied to reduce the number of bytes transferred through the network. There are many compression schemes available with varying degrees of compression capabilities. Usually when a compression ratio of an algorithm is high, it demands more computing power to operate. A user can choose the algorithm based on the availability of spare CPU power. Since compression is a compute-intensive operation, it is not suitable for every situation.

Compression should be used when a data transfer is bounded by the network bandwidth and there are spare CPU cycles. Another situation where compression can be used is when network transfers incur monetary costs compared to using the CPU.

When records are small, it is harder for the communication algorithms to utilize the full bandwidth of the network. Larger size records can saturate the network, so we may consider compression algorithms in such cases. We should note that small messages can be combined to form larger messages.

Stragglers

Large-scale messaging performance can degrade owing to slow computers and congested network links. The shuffle operation implemented with a chaining algorithm can be a good example to explain this phenomenon. If one link or a node becomes slow in each round, all the other nodes are affected by this because they need messages from or coming through the slow node to complete. Often such random slowness can have a ripple effect on the performance, which tends to amplify as the operation progresses.

In large-scale parallel computing, even operating system noise can cause such ripple effects where microsecond-level latencies are observed. Memory-managed languages such as Java and Python can observe these effects due to garbage collection. In such environments, we can use off-heap memory to minimize garbage collection during communication operations to reduce these effects.

Nonblocking vs. Blocking Operations

There are two main variations of communication operations, namely, blocking and nonblocking operations. Nonblocking operations are more general in the sense that they can be used to implement blocking operations, so most messaging systems first implement the nonblocking primitives and then use them to build the blocking primitives.

Blocking Operations

When invoked, blocking operations wait until a network operation fully completes. The biggest issue with blocking operations comes from the fact that network operations work with distributed resources and can take considerable time to complete.

When the network operation is the only task the program has to do, there is no harm in waiting. But this is a rare circumstance in a complex program. Usually a program needs to communicate with multiple entities simultaneously, and they have other tasks that can complete while network operations are pending. The shuffle operation is one such application, where the targets receive multiple values from various sources. While they obtain values from the source, the program can sort and store the already received data into the disk.

If we are working with blocking operations, we need to use separate threads for doing other tasks while some threads wait for network operations. Spawning threads unnecessarily can seriously affect the performance of a program, especially when there are many of them. Most data-intensive applications use a conservative approach for creating threads and try to keep the thread count close to the number of CPUs assigned to a process. To achieve this objective, they have no choice but to use nonblocking APIs for communication.

Nonblocking Operations

A nonblocking operation does not have the requirement of creating separate threads for handling each concurrent connection. A carefully written nonblocking networking program can use up to N number of threads for handling N connections. In a nonblocking API, calls such as read or write do not wait for completion. Because of this, we need to check periodically to see whether there is data ready in the network channels. This checking is called a *progression loop* and can be found in nonblocking network APIs.

Once an operation has begun, unless the progression loop is invoked, the network will not advance. Such progression loops allow programmers to control the threads used for networking operations. This applies from low-level to high-level APIs offered for handling messages. The following is an example of how this principle can be applied to a distributed operation AllReduce:

```
// this call returns immediately without finishing,
// it returns a reference to the pending nonblocking operation
R = IAllReduce(dataset)
// loop until the operation is complete, we use the reference to check
While (not isComplete(R)) {
    // do other work
}
```

The `isComplete` call is necessary as it performs the network handling and the completion of the operation. Without this, the operation cannot progress as there is no other thread to check on the network. Various frameworks provide different names for the `isComplete` method such as `test`, `probe`, `select`, etc. But they all achieve the same goal of checking whether the operation is complete and proceeding with the underlying network operations.

Summary

Messaging libraries glue various components of data analytics systems together and enable them to function. This chapter discussed how parallel messaging operations are used to coordinate the distributed workers of a large-scale application. The distributed performance of an application is a direct function of the messaging it uses.

There are many hardware choices for messaging with different delivery guarantees, semantics, and quality-of-service attributes. Most of the application developers are hidden from these details by many layers of software stacks ranging from operating systems to firmware to libraries and frameworks. Even though such details are hidden, it is important to be aware of their existence to write and manage applications at large scale using these rich technologies and systems.

References

1. J. Pješivac-Grbović, T. Angskun, G. Bosilca, G. E. Fagg, E. Gabriel, and J. J. Dongarra, "Performance analysis of MPI collective operations," *Cluster Computing*, vol. 10, no. 2, pp. 127–143, 2007.

2. M. Snir, W. Gropp, S. Otto, S. Huss-Lederman, J. Dongarra, and D. Walker, *MPI–the Complete Reference: the MPI core*. MIT press, 1998.

3. S. Kamburugamuve, K. Govindarajan, P. Wickramasinghe, V. Abeykoon, and G. Fox, "Twister2: Design of a big data toolkit," *Concurrency and Computation: Practice and Experience*, vol. 32, no. 3, p. e5189, 2020.

4. U. Wickramasinghe and A. Lumsdaine, "A survey of methods for collective communication optimization and tuning," *arXiv preprint arXiv:1611.06334*, 2016.

5. C. Widanage *et al.*, "High performance data engineering everywhere," in *2020 IEEE International Conference on Smart Data Services (SMDS)*, 2020: IEEE, pp. 122–132.

6. K. Kara and G. Alonso, "Fast and robust hashing for database operators," in *2016 26th International Conference on Field Programmable Logic and Applications (FPL)*, 2016: IEEE, pp. 1–4.

7. F. M. Schuhknecht, P. Khanchandani, and J. Dittrich, "On the surprising difficulty of simple things: the case of radix partitioning," *Proceedings of the VLDB Endowment*, vol. 8, no. 9, pp. 934–937, 2015.

8. C. Barthels, I. Müller, T. Schneider, G. Alonso, and T. Hoefler, "Distributed join algorithms on thousands of cores," *Proceedings of the VLDB Endowment*, vol. 10, no. 5, pp. 517–528, 2017.

Parallel Tasks

A task represents an abstract unit of work in a program. It can be fine-grained, such as reading a file from the disk or sending a message to a receiver. Conversely, it could also be coarse-grained, for instance, predicting the next word in a sentence or simulating the weather over the course of a few days. It is important to understand a program as a collection of tasks, and just like deciding how granular a task should be, there are other factors we must consider when orchestrating tasks to produce data-intensive applications.

CPUs

The CPU is synonymous with data analytics. Even if we use accelerators like GPUs, we need the CPU to invoke those programs running in the GPUs. Getting the best out of a CPU for data analytics applications depends on many factors, including memory access (data structures), cache utilization, thread programming, and accessing shared resources.

Cache

Cache is one of the most important structures when it comes to performance in large data analytics. Data transfer between main memory and CPU is governed by throughput and latency. Throughput is the amount of data that can be transferred from the memory to CPU per second. Latency is how much time it takes for a CPU to issue a command to get data from memory and receive that data.

Memory bandwidth has increased over the years, but latency has remained mostly the same for a while now. A modern CPU can invoke many operations in the time it takes to fetch data from the main memory. If we always fetch data from main memory, it will waste many CPU cycles waiting for the data to arrive. To avoid this, CPUs use two strategies:

- Keep a fast memory called *cache* near the CPU core. Access to this memory is much quicker compared to main memory.
- Prefetch the data before executing instructions.

Even with the cache and prefetching, a CPU eventually runs out of data in the cache and needs to wait for more. This is called a CPU *stall*. In the previous chapters, we looked at the importance of cache in terms of data structures. We cannot control the cache directly from our programs, but we can write our programs in such a way that a CPU is able to utilize this important structure.

Data is transferred between memory and cache in fixed-size blocks called a *cache line*. Even if the program requests a single byte of memory, the data will be transferred as a block that includes that byte.

False Sharing

False sharing [1] occurs because of multiple threads sharing the same cache line, causing the OS to invalidate it every time a write happens to one of the variables. These writes may occur at different offsets of the cache line, but the entire line is still affected.

Figure 7-1 shows an example. Two variables, X and Y, are loaded from memory to the same cache line of L3. These are then loaded to the cache lines of L2 and L1 caches for CPU 0 and CPU 1, respectively. In this example, let us assume Thread 1 in CPU 1 modifies Y, and Thread 0 in CPU 1 modifies X, in that order.

When Y is modified in L1 of CPU 1, all other cache lines must be invalidated to maintain cache coherency. This will cause the update for X to wait and will invalidate everything, causing it to reload. This subtle effect adds a significant overhead, which could lead to diminishing returns as the number of threads increases.

False sharing is best avoided by analyzing the code and identifying such cases. Usually this happens with array access, where threads may access nearby elements. One way to eliminate that is to let threads work at indices farther apart than the length of a cache line. Padding can also be used with data structures to align them to a cache line so that no two access attempts touch the same one.

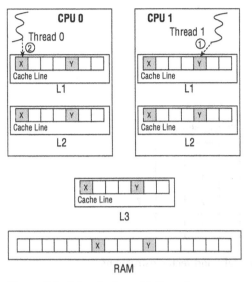

Figure 7-1: False sharing with threads

Vectorization

Vectorization is an automatic code parallelization technique available in modern CPUs. It performs the single instruction multiple data (SIMD)–style parallelization of loops in your code.

Figure 7-2 shows a simple case of adding elements of two integer arrays. In the absence of vector instructions, this addition would be carried out in a loop where each corresponding pair of integers would be loaded to two registers and added. If we assume it takes one clock cycle to perform addition, for this example to complete, it will take four clock cycles.

By contrast, vector instructions load multiple elements to multiple registers. The addition is done in parallel on these data elements in a single clock cycle. Therefore, the same example would take only a single clock cycle to compute. The number of elements the vector processing unit can load and operate on a single cycle is called the *vector length*. This corresponds to the possible speedup you could achieve by vectorizing your code as well.

Figure 7-3 shows the evolution of vector operations in Intel processors. The first was Multimedia Extensions (MMX) in the late 1990s. This was followed by Streaming SIMD (SSE) instruction versions 1 to 4.2 in the following years. The biggest trend toward automatic vectorization, however, occurred with the Advanced Vector Extensions (AVX) 512 introduction in 2016. This enabled 512-bit vector lengths supporting double precision operations, giving a theoretical maximum speedup of 8 for double precision computations.

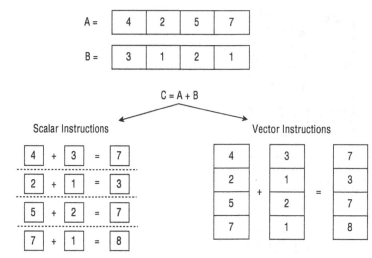

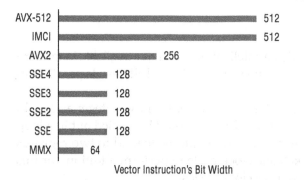

Figure 7-2: An example of array addition using scalar and vector instructions

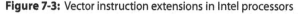

Figure 7-3: Vector instruction extensions in Intel processors

As shown earlier in Figure 7-2, vectorization parallelizes loops. The common approach is to let the compiler vectorize loops as it sees fit. Alternatively, one can also call the intrinsic vector functions such as `_mm512_load_pd()`, `_mm512_add_pd()`, and `_mm512_store_pd()`. However, this approach leads to less portable and maintainable code, so it is preferable to use automatic vectorization with directives such as `#pragma omp simd`. These directives can be used to instruct vectorizing an outer loop, as opposed to the innermost loop that is done by default.

The following shows a simple C++ loop that will be vectorized:

```cpp
#include <iostream>

int main()
{
```

```
const int n=1024;
int A[n] __attribute__((aligned(64)));
int B[n] __attribute__((aligned(64)));

for (int i = 0; i < n; ++i)
{
    A[i] = B[i] + 1;
}

std::cout << A[1023] << std::endl;

return EXIT_SUCCESS;
}
```

For example, using g++, we can see what is vectorized using the following compiler flags. It clearly shows that the `for` loop in line 9 was vectorized. This can be further investigated by producing the assembly output for the curious reader.

```
g++ -O3 -ftree-vectorizer-verbose=7 -fopt-info-vec-all -march=native vec.cpp

vec.cpp:9:23: optimized: loop vectorized using 32 byte vectors
vec.cpp:3:5: note: vectorized 1 loops in function.
vec.cpp:14:24: missed: statement clobbers memory: _10 = std::basic_
ostream<char>::operator<< (&cout, _3);
/usr/include/c++/9/ostream:113:13: missed: statement clobbers memory:
std::endl<char, std::char_traits<char> > (_10);
/usr/include/c++/9/iostream:74:25: missed: statement clobbers memory:
std::ios_base::Init::Init (&__ioinit);
/usr/include/c++/9/iostream:74:25: missed: statement clobbers memory:
__cxa_atexit (__dt_comp , &__ioinit, &__dso_handle);
```

Automatic vectorization has limitations as well. The number of iterations must be known, so `while` loops that terminate on a runtime predicate are not vectorized. Also, if subsequent operations are dependent on previous ones, such loops cannot be vectorized due to data dependency. For example, the following code snippet will not be vectorized:

```
const int n=1024;
int A[n] __attribute__((aligned(64)));
int B[n] __attribute__((aligned(64)));

for (int i = 1; i < n; i++)
{
    a[i] += a[i-1];
}
```

However, if the dependency was on a subsequent element, then it is safe to vectorize, as shown in the following code:

```
const int n=1024;
int A[n] __attribute__((aligned(64)));
int B[n] __attribute__((aligned(64)));

for (int i = 1; i < n; i++)
{
    a[i] += a[i+1]; // Updating a[i] does not depend on a previous update,
so vectorizable.
}
```

Threads and Processes

Modern CPUs are equipped with many cores. As discussed in previous chapters, we can use multiple processes, each with single or multiple threads, to process the data. Even in the case of a single process model, more than one thread is often used for other tasks such as statistics collection and communicating with management nodes.

Concurrency and Parallelism

In a machine with n number of cores, we can create m threads to execute tasks simultaneously. If $m > n$, the operating system can run only n out of m tasks at any instant. The other tasks are kept in the background without executing. This is done by the operating system scheduler. In this scenario, we can say our system is concurrently making progress on m tasks; if $m \leq n$, then both parallelism and concurrency will be equal. In other words, we can divide our work into the number of parallel tasks greater than the cores available, but our true parallelism cannot exceed the number of cores.

Context Switches and Scheduling

Context switching allows the operating system to save the state of a thread (or process), halt its execution, and switch to another thread. The halted thread can be resumed using the saved state later. This allows the operating system to run more threads (processes) than the CPU cores at hand.

There are several ways a context switch can occur:

- An execution ends (process or thread).
- The OS scheduler preempts; the process uses up its time slice or a higher-priority process becomes eligible.
- A process waits for resources such as I/O or a mutex.

A context switch is an expensive operation. When one occurs, it can invalidate the cache, flush the TLB (in the case of a process), and involve the operating system scheduler. To achieve the best performance, we need to avoid excessive context switching in data processing applications.

Our programs should reduce the context switches for I/O operations and mutexes whenever possible. We can tune the OS scheduler to reduce preempts. Also, oversubscribing the system with more threads than the cores available can force the OS to context switch.

Mutual Exclusion

Concurrent access to shared state by multiple threads can lead to correctness issues in programs that are difficult to pinpoint. When accessing and modifying shared variables (state), we need the following:

- **Exclusive access**—Only one thread can be modifying the shared state at a time.

- **Progress**—A thread requesting access to a shared region should eventually get it. No deadlocks.

There are many types of primitives used for facilitating orderly access to shared data by many threads. Table 7-1 lists some of the most popular primitives.

Table 7-1: Synchronization Primitives

PRIMITIVE	DESCRIPTION
Mutex (locks)	Mutex allows mutual exclusion of threads by only allowing a single thread to access a critical section that it guards.
Monitors (Conditional variables)	Monitors allow threads to have mutual exclusion and cooperation. They provide functions to make threads wait for certain conditions to be true.
Semaphores	Semaphores use a counting mechanism to allow threads to enter the critical section. This is a generalization of a mutex to allow more than one thread access to shared resources.
Recursive locks	A recursive lock is a special mutex where the thread holding the lock can acquire it recursively.
Atomics	The atomic variable type performs synchronized reads and writes without explicit locking from the programmer.

These synchronization primitives can be implemented using interrupts or busy waiting. An interrupt-based synchronization causes a context switch and puts the thread to sleep if it cannot acquire the lock. In a spin lock–based lock, the waiting thread is kept on a busy loop checking the lock continuously until it can acquire it.

Since it is waiting on a loop, a context switch does not need to occur. If we are in a system where we create more threads than the available CPU cores, the competing threads would have to be put into sleep by the operating system scheduler as it sees to the waiting threads with work to do (executing the loop). This can lead to performance degradation. As a result, busy waiting synchronization primitives are best for multicore systems with clearly load-balanced work for each thread.

User-Level Threads

In the past, there was a lot of emphasis on user-level threads for executing fine-grained task graphs. The normal threads we use have a one-to-one mapping with the kernel threads. This allows the kernel to schedule them and control their execution. However, they have high overhead due to OS scheduling.

User-level threads work at the user space, and the kernel is not aware of them, reducing the OS scheduling overheads. Since OS does not schedule them, the user needs to be careful not to allow one thread to execute forever. Furthermore, I/O is difficult in relation to user-level threads as it can block the complete program. Thread implementations in operating systems have come a long way in terms of performance, and because of this user level, threads are employed only in rare designs nowadays.

Process Affinity

Modern operating system schedulers try minimizing the movement of processes and threads among CPU cores as much as possible. For our desktops, which run mixed workloads with interactive applications and background applications with numerous threads, such shuffling is inevitable.

The dedicated servers that run data processing, on the other hand, are free from any other distractions, and the only tasks they run belong to the data processing applications. Additionally, the applications are not oversubscribed to the resources, meaning they do not usually create more executable threads than CPU cores available.

In these scenarios, we can bind the processes/threads to CPU cores to prevent the OS scheduler from moving them around to different cores. Linux provides a command called `taskset` to achieve this functionality. In most cases, we have seen increases in performance when we bind the processes to the CPU cores.

NUMA-Aware Programming

High-performance programming boils down to minimizing costs, namely, data movement and computing cycles. In this regard, NUMA programming is about being aware that the cost of data access is not uniform. As mentioned earlier, when multiple physical CPUs exist, it is called a *multisocket* configuration. Here, the word *socket* is used interchangeably with *CPU*. The main memory is zoned or partitioned among these sockets, which makes access to memory that is local to a socket faster than that of a remote socket.

Data placement is the first thing to be aware of when programming under NUMA. It defines the memory allocation policy, and by default operating systems set it to Local. The result of this is that any new memory allocation within a process would happen in the same NUMA node.

Interleave is another policy in which memory allocations are done in a round-robin fashion across NUMA domains. This might seem counterintuitive, as it spreads data in the memory, but it is useful if data is accessed at random offsets by different threads. While not the best in terms of memory access time, it helps to load-balance the access requests.

Strict and Preferred are two other NUMA memory placement policies. Strict tries to allocate memory on a given NUMA node and fails if memory cannot be allocated there. Preferred is similar, but it is free to allocate on a different memory node without failing.

A subtle point to note with NUMA policies is that specifying a certain policy such as Local does not necessarily guarantee all memory access will be local to the NUMA node. The reason is that memory policies hint to the operating system what to do when a new allocation happens. But especially in a multithreaded program, it is possible that a page is allocated by one thread, which is later accessed by another. The first thread to touch or write to a page will determine its location. This is known as *first touch* in NUMA nomenclature.

The second point to consider with NUMA is process affinity. Under normal operation conditions, the operating system is free to move processes and threads around CPUs. While this helps with load balance, performance-critical applications could suffer as memory access might no longer be local with the new process placement.

Accelerators

Accelerators come in many shapes and forms nowadays, and they go together with CPUs in modern computers. It is even common in other devices such as gaming consoles and cell phones as well. An accelerator is a custom hardware designed to perform a specific type of computation faster and more efficiently than a traditional CPU.

GPUs are the most common class of accelerators. Once intended only to accelerate graphics computations to drive computer displays, GPUs now support more general tensor operations, making them the heavy lifters behind the deep learning revolution as well. GPUs are designed to gain high throughput. They achieve this by having orders of more GPU cores compared to a CPU. These are identical to CPU cores, and recently, there are two flavors to them. NVIDIA's latest architectures, Volta and Turing, have CUDA cores, which are the usual GPU cores present in all NVIDIA architectures, and the Tensor cores, which are specialized to perform fast matrix multiply and add operations.

Like NVIDIA GPUs, a tensor processing unit (TPU) [2] is another accelerator type but created by Google. These were specifically made to make matrix multiplications faster. Multiplying two matrices can be made faster by having a systolic array, which is what TPU versions 2 and 3 employ internally.

Microsoft too employs FPGA-based custom accelerators to speed up cloud-scale DNN inference and training. In project Brainwave [3], a single CPU drives multiple ASICs, which in turn are networked hierarchically to form the training/inference cluster.

Amazon EC2 offers F1 instances, which are custom accelerators based on FPGAs as well. All these accelerators require specialized SDKs to program them. NVIDIA GPUs, for example, are programmed using the Cuda SDK. As these accelerators are built for specific computations, they typically need to handle things such as data type conversions, data padding, data tiling, and memory allocations specific to the accelerator when running user programs.

Task Execution

Monolithic software systems are almost nonexistent today, and layered architectures prevail in practice. Reusability of components, ease of programming, and maintainability are a few reasons for such layered design.

The bottom-most layer in Figure 7-4 represents hardware. While there could be many hardware components, we highlight four important ones: CPUs, accelerators (such as GPUs, FGPAs, and ASICs), memory subsystem, and network. On top of this layer sits the operating system, or a hypervisor in the case of virtualization. Software development kits and programming libraries follow next.

When writing data analytics solutions or other general software, programmers do not have to implement anything within these bottom three layers. Often programs are written against frameworks or libraries. It is therefore important to understand the abstractions provided by these layers to write code that performs well.

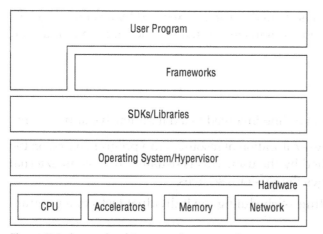

Figure 7-4: Layered architecture of programming

A distributed application for data processing consists of a set of distributed operations, local operations, state, input, output, and a resource specification, as shown in Figure 7-5. The local operations can be provided by the system or are programmed by the user. Distributed operations come courtesy of the system. Most frameworks do not allow users to define new distributed operations unless they change the system source code. An example of a distributed operation is a shuffle operation used to distribute a set of tables among a set of tasks.

How these operations are connected and work is defined by the programming model. The task graph model arranges the operations into a graph and allows the inputs and outputs of the operations to drive the computation.

To execute this program, the system creates an execution plan that assigns the instances of operations to specific resources (Figure 7-5). Since we are working with the task graph model, the operations translate into task instances that consume and produce data. The system can decide how the threads are allocated to execute these task instances.

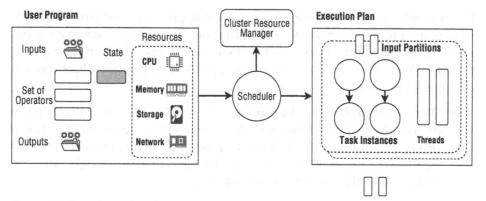

Figure 7-5: Transformation of a program into an executable plan

Once this execution plan is created, it can be executed by a set of processes allocated to the job. Different systems use different scheduling methods and execution models.

Scheduling

There are three levels of scheduling involved in a data-intensive application:

- **Resource scheduling**—Allocation of resources to a program based on the requirements specified by the user. This is usually done by an external program that manages the cluster resources.

- **Task graph scheduling**—Scheduling the individual tasks of a program to the processes.

- **Thread scheduling**—Scheduling of threads within a process to run various tasks of a program, including I/O operations and user functions.

We discussed the resource allocation in a previous chapter. Depending on the nature of the program, task scheduling and thread scheduling can be done with static or dynamic algorithms.

Static Scheduling

Static scheduling algorithms assign the work at the beginning, and the assignment remains the same once the processes or threads start running. Static scheduling is mostly found in regular applications with known workloads.

The work needs to be assigned to tasks in a way that everyone gets close to an equal amount of computing. If the application permits, static scheduling gives the best performance as there is not scheduling overhead at runtime.

Dynamic Scheduling

Dynamic scheduling [4] algorithms are used in applications with unpredictable computation requirements that arise at runtime. For example, when an application starts executing, it can generate more work depending on the input at runtime. Work sharing and work stealing [5] are two popular algorithms in dynamic scheduling.

- **Work stealing (pull)**—As shown in Figure 7-6, the scheduler initially divides the tasks into the available processors in some order. When a processor finishes all the tasks in its queue, it becomes a thief and tries to steal a task from another processor. As long as there is enough work, the processors will continue to process tasks.

■ **Work sharing (push)**—As in the work stealing system, the work is assigned initially to processors. At runtime, if a processor has excess work, it will try to send them to other processors with less work.

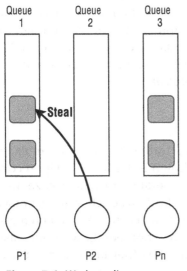

Figure 7-6: Work stealing

There are subtle differences in the two approaches, but mostly they perform similarly in practice. For example, in work stealing, an idle processor tries to steal work and there is no context switching. In work sharing, a busy processor tries to send work that can cause a context switch.

To schedule individual tasks of a graph across multiple processes dynamically, we need to monitor the work and transfer tasks to the processes at runtime. As this takes place in a distributed setting, it can be a significant overhead if the tasks we schedule are in the second or millisecond range to run. If the tasks involve larger computations that take hours to run, dynamic scheduling overheads can be negligible compared to the overall computation times.

Thread scheduling is local to a process, and we can use dynamic scheduling algorithms with less overhead compared to dynamic task scheduling across processes. So, in many cases, static algorithms are utilized in scheduling tasks and dynamic algorithms in scheduling threads within a process.

Loosely Synchronous and Asynchronous Execution

A parallel program has logical synchronization points to keep data in multiple processes coherent with one another. At a logical synchronization point, all the parallel tasks join to share information. Distributed operations are implicit synchronization points in a parallel application. A parallel framework may have explicit synchronization operations as well as implicit synchronization operations such as barriers.

How data synchronization operations are implemented, as well as how tasks are scheduled and executed, defines the nature of a parallel system. We can define a parallel system requiring all the parallel tasks in the program to execute at the same time, or we can run those tasks by decoupling them. We call the former a *loosely synchronous parallel system*, and the latter is termed an *asynchronous parallel system* or *fully distributed system*.

Loosely Synchronous Parallel System

We can illustrate a loosely synchronous parallel system with an example. Imagine we have four parallel tasks as shown in Figure 7-7. Upon completion of the tasks, they invoke a distributed operation to synchronize the data. Since the synchronous model assumes all four tasks to be active, it can implement the distributed operation assuming this fact. Thus, each task can send messages to other tasks directly. Between the synchronization points, a parallel task can execute its code without coordination with the other tasks, hence the name loosely synchronous.

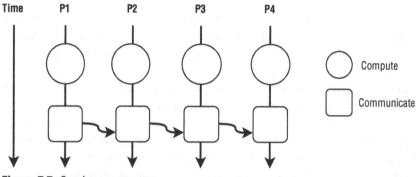

Figure 7-7: Synchronous system

The model assumes all parallel processes to be allocated up front, and so we need to wait until such requirements are satisfied in a cluster. Assume we have a cluster with five nodes and there is a job that is already running taking up four nodes. Now, if we want to run the next job that requires two nodes, we have to wait until the first job finishes.

Asynchronous Parallel System (Fully Distributed)

The asynchronous model does not assume all the tasks are present, so it cannot send messages directly from one task to another. Instead, messages should be buffered temporarily at a process that is running at the instant the message originated until the other tasks are ready to pick them up. We can think of them as having a message broker in the middle to temporarily hold the messages. This is shown in Figure 7-8, where the second process is not running when Processes 1, 3, and 4 are active. So process 1 buffers its messages until Process 2 becomes available. Once Process 2 starts executing, it is notified of the data it needs to receive from Process 1. This model allows the tasks to be scheduled independently of each other according to the resources available and has been perfected for high throughput computing.

In our previous example of five nodes, we can start the second job with only one computer, and once the already running job finishes, we can use the rest of the resources for the new job. As such, we are utilizing all the nodes and thereby increasing the throughput.

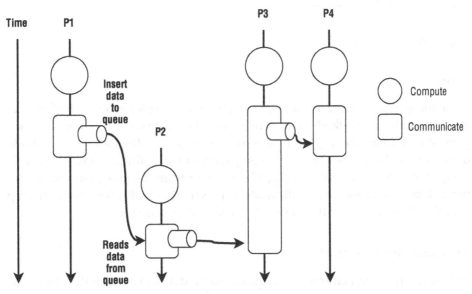

Figure 7-8: Asynchronous system

Further tasks can be scheduled at runtime in distinct locations, allowing the application to consider external factors such as data locality. This type of execution can be seen in frameworks such as Hadoop and Spark. Since the data locality is no longer as important as before, this argument may no longer hold the validity it did 10 years ago.

Actor Model

The actor model [6, 7] is a mathematical computation model for concurrent computation. It is built around the concept of an actor, which is the fundamental unit of computation. The model is asynchronous and uses the event-driven model. Figure 7-9 shows the overall model of an actor system where there are sets of actors and message passing (events) between them.

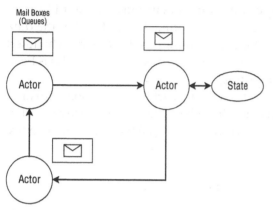

Figure 7-9: Actor model

Actor

An actor is a user-programmed entity with a set of rules around it. The code inside an actor is invoked when it receives a message (event). Once this happens, it can do local computations, send messages to other actors, and create more actors. Actors can be in a single process or distributed across multiple computers. The actor model is slightly different from the task graph model; in the task model, tasks are not allowed to spawn other tasks. An actor can keep a local state and modify this state upon receiving messages.

Asynchronous Messages

Actors are in an asynchronous computation model, and as such they have the concept of message queues. In some cases, they are called *mailboxes*. When an actor sends a message to another actor, that message is stored in a queue until the target task is scheduled to run. This queue can store multiple messages. If the target task is available at the moment the message is sent, it can be given immediately to that task as in the synchronous model.

Actor Frameworks

There are many actor frameworks in use today, all developed in different programming languages with slight variations. An actor framework contains a programming model for creating actors, a messaging layer, and a scheduler. Actor frameworks can work in a single machine using only threads or across machines via threads and processes.

As a computation model, actor model is more generic than the task graph model and can even be used to create one. Apache Flink uses an actor framework underneath to create tasks and execute them.

Execution Models

Whether it is a task graph, actor system, or MPI program, we can use a single thread or multiple threads within each process. This is the distributed memory versus hybrid model we discussed in Chapter 1. At runtime, we will have a set of processes and one or more threads inside those processes executing our application. This is shown in Figure 7-10, where there are multiple threads in executor processes and a separate thread scheduler.

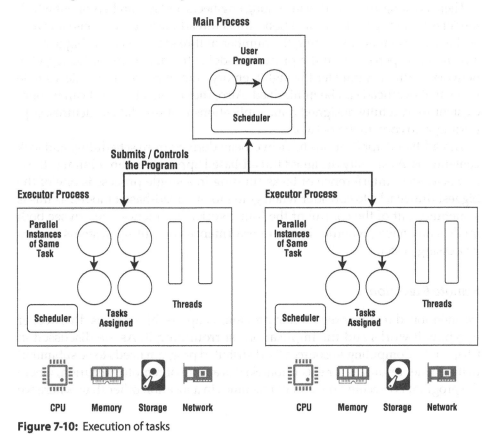

Figure 7-10: Execution of tasks

Process Model

In this model, a process executes a single task instance of the parallel application. Processes are created according to the parallelism of the application. This model gives a clean separation between tasks and allows them to execute without interfering with each other. We can use separate threads for I/O operations and computations.

We should note that in this model, only a single thread executes the parallel code. It may use other threads for tasks such as control messages and statistic gathering.

Thread Model

This is the hybrid calculation model. Multiple parallel tasks of the application are run within the same process, which allows tasks within the same process to share data quickly and reduces the network bandwidth usage. This model has the downside of multiple tasks running in the same process that can interfere with each other. In this model, we can use the same threads assigned for task execution to communicate or choose separate threads.

There is a long-running debate among engineers and researchers about which model is best for parallel applications. Most thread-based executions can work as the process model by setting the number of threads to one. The biggest disadvantage as perceived in the process model is the data sharing through the network. With data transfer through memory among processes inside a single node, that overhead can be minimized. Also, the serialization cost can be nonexistent for carefully designed data applications that use data structures, supporting zero copy to the network.

Thread-based applications have overhead derived from scheduling and lock contentions. A carefully designed thread-based application can minimize these issues as well. Interference of tasks running in a single process is one of the biggest drawbacks to consider when going for a thread-based model, as this is sometimes out of the control of the frameworks. In practice, we can see both models are viable, whether in high-performance computing systems or data processing systems.

Remote Execution

We mentioned remote execution in previous chapters. Now, let us dive deeper into how it works and the implications surrounding it. As we discussed in Chapter 3, "Computing Resources," a distributed program needs to be submitted to the cluster resources for execution. So it is a form of remote execution, where the program is executed on a set of machines in a location other than where we submit it. In general, there is a submitting program to get the resources from a cluster and execute the program. We often use this submitting program to monitor the status of the parallel program.

The remote execution extends this single program submission to multiple programs that can exchange data as discussed in Chapter 5. Figure 7-11 shows the steps taken by remote execution programs to submit computations to the cluster.

1. The driver program creates a computation and submits it to a manager.

2. The manager schedules the program to the compute nodes in the cluster.

3. The compute nodes start the computation.

4. After the computation, if there are results that need to be sent back to the driver, they are sent.

5. If the results need to be cached for the next computation, they are cached in the processes.

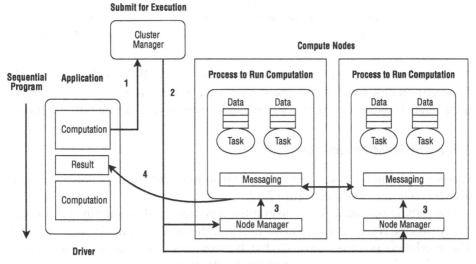

Figure 7-11: Remote execution from a driver program

When thousands of compute nodes are present, submitting a large number of computations can be an overhead. With this model, we should try to make the computations as big as possible to offset the overhead of the central submission. For example, if we submit 1,000 computations each taking only 1 millisecond to run and the submissions take 2 milliseconds, our overhead is 2 seconds to the total calculation time of 1 second.

Tasks for Data Analytics

Both batch and streaming systems use the task graph to model a computation. Table 7-2 shows how the task graph model is used in practice. Streaming systems always use a single task graph to execute. The batch systems can use the remote execution method, single graph, or dynamic multiple graph models.

Table 7-2: Use of Task Graph Model for Data Analytics

PROGRAMS	TASK GRAPH	FRAMEWORKS	EXECUTION
Streaming	Static single graph	Storm	Loosely Synchronous
		Flink	
Batch	Remote execution of multiple graphs	Spark	Asynchronous
		Dask	
	Static single graph	Hadoop	Asynchronous
		Flink	
	Multiple graphs on the same process	PyTorch	Loosely Synchronous

The last column of Table 7-2 illustrates whether a fully asynchronous mode of execution or a synchronous execution are used. Streaming systems always use a asynchronous execution, while batch systems can handle both methods.

SPMD and MPMD Execution

A task graph can be scheduled to run on resources both in the SPMD style and MPMD style, as shown in Figure 7-12.

In an SPMD execution, the same graph is scheduled in the distributed processes. Every process runs the source tasks first and the next compute tasks, and so on. This model of execution is seen in batch programs. For example, PyTorch uses this style of execution for data parallel model training.

In MPMD-style execution, parts of the graph are scheduled on different processes. In Figure 7-12, instances of task A are scheduled to worker 0, and instances of B are scheduled to worker 1. This is a more general form of scheduling compared to an SPMD case and is used in streaming programs. Some batch programs use this execution style for specific problems such as pipeline parallel as we described in Chapter 5.

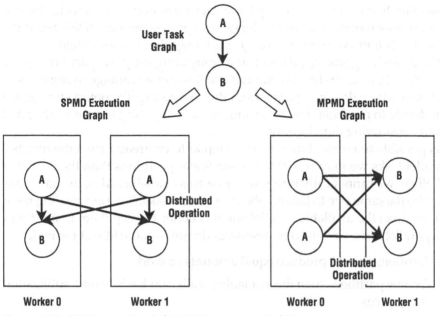

Figure 7-12: SPMD execution (left); MPMD execution (right)

Batch Tasks

A batch application terminates after processing input and producing output. It can be modeled as a set of tasks and links in a graph. They need to individually terminate upon completion. A batch execution partitions the data among parallel tasks, schedules the tasks to run on these partitions, and executes the tasks along with the communication to synchronize data between tasks.

Data Partitions

Data processing applications need to partition the data so that tasks can work on them in parallel. How we divide a dataset into multiple partitions depends on the application and the nature of the data. For instance, if it is a table-like dataset, we can divide it into rows or columns. If the data is a matrix in binary form, we may choose to divide it into eight blocks (subset of rows and columns in one block), rows, or columns.

This data is stored in either a distributed file system, object storage, or a database. The storage itself imposes a distribution of the data. For example,

Parquet files that we use for storing table data are stored in row blocks. We can map these row blocks directly to a block storage system like HDFS. But if the Parquet file is housed in object storage, such mapping is nonexistent.

If the underlying storage, dataset, and computing supports partitioning the data so that it preserves locality, we can use it to our advantage in some cases. In a cluster where data is separate from the computing like object storage, we might decide to partition data according to the computing resources allocated without considering data locality.

It is possible to create data partitions equal to or greater than the number of parallel tasks we may run. If we create fewer partitions than the available parallelism, we cannot fully utilize the resources available. Also, the partitions need to be the same size to balance the load across tasks. If we are creating more partitions than the available parallelism, it is better to keep them in multiples of the parallel tasks so that some resources do not become idle at the end.

- Partitions should produce equal amounts of work.

- Too few partitions than the available parallelism leads to underutilization of resources.

- More partitions than the available parallelism can lead to a small amount of work per task. This increases the overhead of task creation compared to the work performed.

- If the partitions are not divisible by the parallelism and we have more partitions than available parallelism, some computers will be idle at the end.

The following code shows the base interface of the Apache Spark RDD API to create the initial partitions when reading the data. Spark uses the Hadoop's APIs for reading the data. Here, each split corresponds to a data partition. For every data partition, it creates a record reader to read the contents.

```
public interface InputFormat<K, V> {

  /**
   * Logically split the set of input files for the job.
   *
   * @param job job configuration.
   * @param numSplits the desired number of splits, a hint.
   * @return an array of {@link InputSplit}s for the job.
   */
  InputSplit[] getSplits(JobConf job, int numSplits) throws IOException;

  /**
   * Get the {@link RecordReader} for the given {@link InputSplit}.
   *
```

```
 * @param split the {@link InputSplit}
 * @param job the job that this split belongs to
 * @return a {@link RecordReader}
 */
RecordReader<K, V> getRecordReader(InputSplit split,
                                   JobConf job,
                                   Reporter reporter) throws IOException;

}
```

Data partitioning, scheduling, and execution are closely related in data processing systems.

Operations

Now, let us look at some of the programming constructs used by frameworks nowadays. A programming construct and an actual task executed by the framework have a complex relationship, as multiple user-defined functions can be combined to form a task, or a user-defined operation can be broken down into multiple tasks.

Table 7-3: Sample Local Operations

OPERATION	DESCRIPTION
Map	Inputs a record and outputs a record
FlatMap	Inputs a record, and output can be multiple records
Filter	Filters records by applying a function
Sort	Sorts the records

Table 7-4: Sample Distributed Operations on Tables

OPERATION	DESCRIPTION
Join	Joins two tables based on a set of keys
Union	Concatenates two tables, removing duplicates
Partition	Redistributes table data into the computer
GroupBy	Groups rows based on values of a key set
Drop duplicates	Drops the duplicate records
Distributed sort	Sorts tables so that they have a predefined distributed order

Here is an example set of operations in an Apache Spark program. Figure 7-13 shows the corresponding task graph created by Spark. This program reads a set of data files and counts the number of characters in it. This is a superficial example where it first repartitions the data to 4 and then applies map and reduce operations. In the case of Spark, reduce is a terminating operation that sends the results to the driver program.

```
SparkConf conf = new SparkConf().setAppName("RDD Example");
JavaSparkContext sc = new JavaSparkContext(conf);

JavaRDD<String> distFile = sc.textFile("/path/to/files").repartition(4);
int lengthSum = distFile.map(new Function<String, Integer>() {
  @Override
  public Integer call(String s) throws Exception {
    return s.length();
  }
}).reduce(new Function2<Integer, Integer, Integer>() {
  @Override
    public Integer call(Integer int1, Integer int2) throws Exception {
      return int1 + int2;
    }
});
```

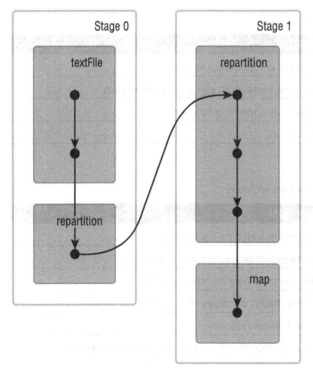

Figure 7-13: Spark task graph

Like ETL operations, deep learning operations that get executed on accelerators do create tasks as well. To better understand this, Figure 7-14 presents a distributed configuration of an accelerator cluster like GPUs. It shows multiple CPUs that each connect multiple accelerators using PCIe. The CPUs communicate over a TCP or InfiniBand network. The accelerators can also communicate, bypassing the CPU over some back-end network such as GPU Direct RDMA.

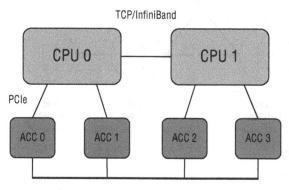

Figure 7-14: The architecture of an accelerator cluster

Typically, deep learning operations such as MatMul, Conv2d, Relu, etc., get broken down into a collection of matrix multiplications and vector operations. These are then executed in the accelerators associated by data transfers from CPUs to the accelerator.

Task Graph Scheduling

Think of a task graph consisting of parallel regions and distributed operations, as shown in Figure 7-15. A parallel region begins at the source or receive tasks of a distributed operation and ends in the sink tasks or source tasks of a distributed operation. In this discussion, we assume a synchronizing distributed operation. For a parallel region to begin, the previous parallel region needs to finish (unless it is not the first one).

Normally, tasks of a parallel region that work with the same partitions are scheduled to the same processes. The communication between those tasks can be done through memory.

If we are using a dynamic scheduling that can allocate tasks at different machines as discussed in the previous section, the scheduler can schedule the tasks in stages. When running a static schedule, we might even schedule the complete graph and let the events drive the application.

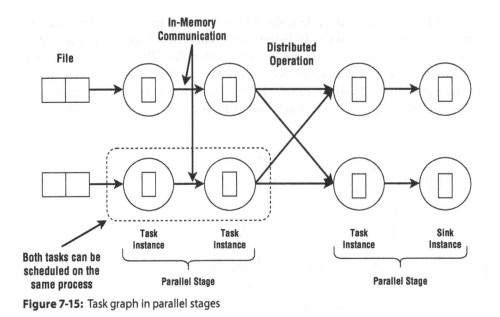

Figure 7-15: Task graph in parallel stages

All the parallel instances of a task can theoretically use this full number of CPUs and full memory minus memory for any state from previous computations while they are running.

Threads, CPU Cores, and Partitions

True parallelism of an application is the number of threads (cores) that are available to run an application. This can be illustrated by the following example.

Assume we have two computers, each with 24 CPU cores to process data. Additionally, we have a large dataset we are going to split into 100 partitions, and we intend to process these partitions using 100 tasks (threads). Even if we have created 100 tasks, only 48 tasks can run at a time in our 2 nodes. So, our true parallelism is 48 even if we created 100 tasks and 100 partitions. As there are now more tasks than processes available, the system can use a dynamic scheduling algorithm to assign them to processors.

We create 48 threads that are assigned the 100 partitions. They can be run as a dynamic scheduling system with work stealing to process the 100 partitions. As such, we have the following options to run an application.

If we look at our application so far, creating 100 partitions, and hence 100 tasks, seems arbitrary. Instead, we have only 48 processors and create 48 partitions. This will allocate a fixed task for each CPU core, and we can avoid the overhead from dynamic scheduling of tasks. To summarize, our options are as follows:

- Create threads equal to the number of cores available.
    - If partitions are equal to threads, we can statically assign them to threads.

- If there are more partitions than threads available, we can use a static or dynamic (i.e., work stealing) scheduling of partitions to threads.

- Create threads equal to the number of partitions. The operating system is responsible for scheduling the threads.

The second option is rarely used in systems, as granting an operating system control over scheduling and subscribing the threads can be inefficient. Also, with the second option, we cannot control the execution, and depending on the OS scheduling, all the partitions can be loaded into memory, which may not be the desired behavior.

Data Locality

Data locality–aware scheduling assigns tasks to computers that are closer to the data partitions. To understand how data locality influenced modern data processing systems, let us look at a four-machine cluster with one CPU core in each. We have a program to process some data, and we are allocating only two CPU cores for this application. The data is in four partitions distributed in all four machines.

In this model, we will create a task for each partition. The execution is shown in Figure 7-16. Initially two task instances are created in Machines 1 and 2 to process the partitions in each. Once they are finished, another two tasks are created in Machines 3 and 4 to process partitions there. Afterward, the data is shuffled to two task instances. This dynamic approach requires allocating resources dynamically while a computation is running. In this example, even if we read the data locally, the distributed (i.e., shuffle) operation requires us to read data from all four nodes through the network.

The other approach as shown in Figure 7-17 is to just use two nodes and read the partitions from nodes 1 and 2 followed by 3 and 4. This approach is simple in that it does not require resources and tasks to be allocated dynamically. The data is read through the network from nodes 3 and 4, but the shuffle happens only between two nodes.

When scheduling tasks according to data locality, we can proceed in the following order, giving priority to in-memory data:

1. Data local to the process

2. Data local to the machine

3. Data local to the rack

So, if we cannot get a task running within the same node as the data, we should aim to get a node from the same rack.

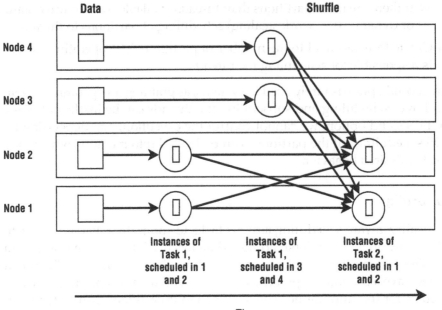

Figure 7-16: Scheduling with data locality

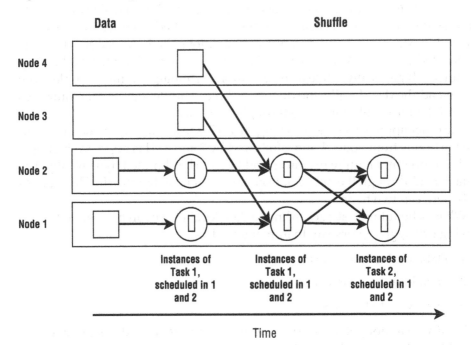

Figure 7-17: Scheduling without data locality

Dynamic allocation of tasks is much more complex in practice than stated here. In a shared cluster, we may need to get the processors from a resource manager to achieve dynamic allocations for a single application. Such allocations can suffer from significant overhead in practice and may not guarantee an allocation, as there can be other applications already running. Additionally, if we are reading from an object store, a data locality argument is hard to apply.

Execution

The tasks within a parallel region can be executed in an event-driven way within the memory of a single process. Once the execution reaches the distributed operation, it must wait until that operation completes by receiving data from all the participating task instances. At this point, we can begin executing the next parallel region.

In general, one or more task instances can be assigned to a process to execute. If process model is used, usually one instance of a task is executed at a time, as parallelism within a process is one. If multiple threads are used, multiple instances of the same task can be assigned to utilize the available parallelism within a process. Depending on how the work is assigned, we can use dynamic thread scheduling to execute the tasks inside a process.

Streaming Execution

When dealing with data that does not fit into memory, a system needs to process it in a streaming fashion by handling data part by part. Figure 7-18 shows a streaming execution of large data files. To achieve the streaming execution, a partition is divided into records. A record can be a single line of a text file or multiple lines combined. We need to keep in mind that computations on larger datasets are normally more efficient than those on single records. The tasks process these records and output records.

The parallel regions of the task graph are executed in a streaming fashion until it comes to a distributed operation. Usually a distributed operation such as a shuffle or a join needs to look at the complete dataset. Because of this, we must save the records in the disk again at the distributed operation. Disk usage is mandatory at the end of the distributed operation as it needs to stream the data to the proceeding tasks. Some frameworks choose to spill the records to the disk at the source ends of the distributed operation as well.

Once the distributed operation is completed, the following tasks can stream the data from the disk.

State

State is an essential component of any computation. A distributed application can keep state in the local process, in a remote location like a driver program, or in a separate distributed data store such as a file system or a database. State can be simple, such as keeping an integer count, or complex like maintaining a large two-dimensional array or a table.

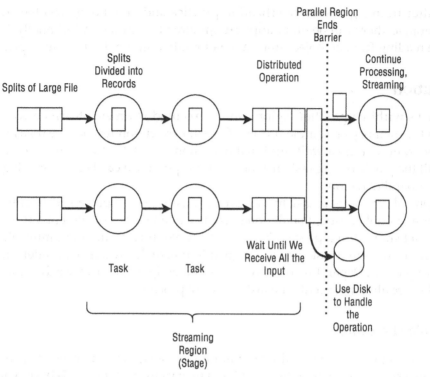

Figure 7-18: Streaming execution of tasks

State is closely related to fault tolerance because we need to restore state when recovering from failures. We will discuss state and its relationship to fault tolerance in Chapter 9.

Immutable Data

Data processing systems often do not allow data to be updated. Instead, when operations are applied on a dataset, it creates a new dataset. This simplifies the design of applications and reduces user errors. Sometimes this can lead to unnecessary memory utilization and extra CPU power. The immutable data is enforced by the APIs by giving the operations access to a read-only copy of the data.

State in Driver

In a centrally controlled execution, some states can be held in the driver. One example is parameters read from the command line to control the execution of the job. Sometimes we must send state in the driver to the compute functions in the graph. In these instances, we can use a broadcast operation.

Here is an example from Spark where we keep a variable in Driver program and broadcast it to the filter functions:

```java
public class SparkBroadcast {
  public static void main(String[] args) {
    SparkConf conf = new SparkConf().setAppName("RDD Example");
    JavaSparkContext sc = new JavaSparkContext(conf);

    // this value is in the driver
    Integer value = 5;
    Broadcast<Integer> valueBcast = sc.broadcast(value);
    List<String> words = Arrays.asList("Test", "Example");
    long wordsCount = sc.parallelize(words).filter(new Function<String,
Boolean>() {
        @Override
        public Boolean call(String s) throws Exception {
          //access the broadcast value
          int threshold = valueBcast.getValue();
          return s.length() > threshold;
        }
    }).count();
    System.out.println("WORDS COUNT: " + wordsCount);
  }
}
```

Distributed State

Distributed state is created at the compute nodes when running the program. Distributed data is made either by reading data or as a result of a computation. Depending on the programming model, distributed state can be used differently. For instance, in a centrally controlled execution of Spark, distributed state is created using a cache operation. This operation saves a large dataset in the memory of compute nodes or in disks to be used by a later computation.

In a bulk synchronous parallel program like MPI or data parallel deep learning application, each process can keep its own state.

Streaming Tasks

Streaming tasks are different from batch tasks in that they process data continuously. It is necessary to assign streaming tasks to compute resources so that they are available to process data continuously.

Streams and Data Partitioning

The most common data source for streaming applications is message brokers. Message brokers have queues and topics (events) that streaming frameworks subscribe to in order to receive events (messages). A streaming application can work on messages coming from any number of queues. To process the data in parallel, there should be a partitioning of data coming to a queue. In some message brokers, we need to create multiple queues for partitioning data, and certain message brokers can further divide a queue into partitions.

Partitions

When processing data in parallel, some applications need to consider the order of the messages. If it is necessary to process data in the order it is received, we cannot easily partition that data to process in parallel. For example, it might be a data stream coming from a video camera where we need to maintain the frames in the order they are produced. Even if we cannot process data from a single camera in parallel, it is possible to process data from many cameras connected to the streaming application in parallel.

Modern message brokers such as Kafka have stream partitioning built-in for topics. If a topic has N partitions, the maximum parallelism of a stream processing application that needs to preserve the message ordering for each partition will be N. In our previous example of cameras, data from a single camera will always go to the same partition. If the application can process data in any order, we can easily partition the data from N topic partitions to M parallel instances of the streaming application sources.

Messages are partitioned using an attribute or a combination of such. For example, we can imagine each camera in the previous example possesses a unique identifier that we use to send the messages from the same camera to the same partition. Table 7-5 summarizes the different partitioning strategies for streaming applications.

Table 7-5: Partitioning Strategies

PARTITIONING	DESCRIPTION	CONSTRAINTS
Random	Randomly assigns events to partitions according to a uniform distribution.	Cannot process ordered streams.
Round-robin	Assigns events to partitions in a round-robin way.	Cannot process ordered streams.
Key-based	Assigns events with same key to the same partition.	Streams can be skewed.

Operations

It is possible to have the same operations we see in the batch operations in the streaming applications. They work on either a batch of data or single records. If the operations handle a batch of data, we call them windowed operations. You might think of a single record of a data as a batch with size 1, but most streaming systems have different mechanisms for processing windows and single messages. The operations shown in Tables 7-6, 7-7, and 7-8 apply to a single stream or multiple streams.

Table 7-6: Local Operations on Streams

OPERATION	DESCRIPTION
Map	Inputs a record and outputs a record
FlatMap	Inputs a record and output can be multiple records
Filter	Filters records by applying a function
Reduce	Rolling reductions on a continuous stream
Aggregations	Rolling aggregations on a continuous stream
Union	Combines elements from two streams to create one

Table 7-7: Windowed Operations

OPERATION	DESCRIPTION
Window	Creates a window from a stream of data
Map	Applies a function considering all the data in the window
Reduce	Reduces the values in the window, i.e., batch reduce
Aggregations	Applies aggregate function to the values in the window, i.e., batch aggregation
Join	Joins data from two streams

Table 7-8: Distributed Operations

OPERATION	DESCRIPTION
Partition	Partitions the data
Broadcast	Broadcasts values to all the processing units
Gather	Gathers elements from multiple partitions

Here is a simple Flink streaming application and its corresponding task graph. This example is taken from the Flink documentation; it counts words in time windows of five seconds. It has a source, a map, and a window along with a sum. As shown in Figure 7-19, Flink has concatenated a few operations into one task.

```java
public class FlinkStreaming {
  public static void main(String[] args) throws Exception {
    StreamExecutionEnvironment env =
                    StreamExecutionEnvironment.getExecutionEnvironment();
    DataStream<Tuple2<String, Integer>> dataStream = env
        .socketTextStream("localhost", 9999)
        .flatMap(new Splitter())
        .keyBy(value -> value.f0)
        .window(TumblingProcessingTimeWindows.of(Time.seconds(5)))
        .sum(1);
    dataStream.print();
    env.execute("Window WordCount");
  }

  public static class Splitter implements
    FlatMapFunction<String, Tuple2<String, Integer>> {
      @Override
    public void flatMap(String sentence,
                    Collector<Tuple2<String, Integer>> out) throws Exception {
      for (String word : sentence.split(" ")) {
        out.collect(new Tuple2<String, Integer>(word, 1));
      }
    }
  }
}
```

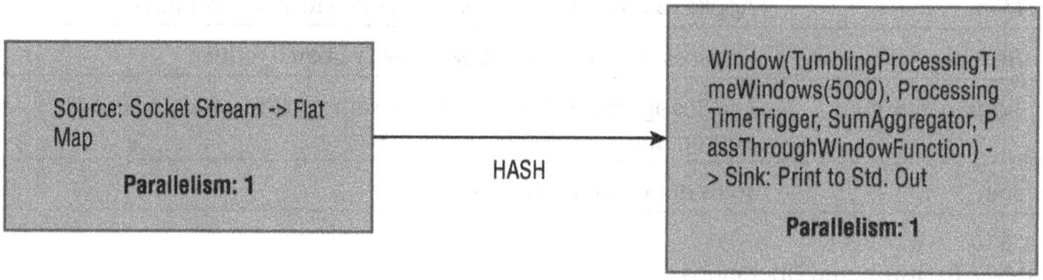

Source: Socket Stream -> Flat Map	HASH	Window(TumblingProcessingTimeWindows(5000), Processing TimeTrigger, SumAggregator, PassThroughWindowFunction) -> Sink: Print to Std. Out
Parallelism: 1		**Parallelism: 1**

Figure 7-19: Flink streaming graph

Scheduling

Streaming task graph scheduling is different from batch scheduling because all the streaming tasks need to run at the same time to process a stream of data.

To illustrate the requirements of stream task scheduling, let us assume we have four computations to execute on a stream of messages, with each computation taking t CPU time. If we have four CPUs available, the data rate is one message per t CPU time, and we run all four tasks on a single CPU as shown in Figure 7-20, it takes $t \times 4$ time to process one message, and the computation cannot keep up with the stream using one CPU.

Instead, we must load balance between the four CPUs, in which case the order of the processing is lost unless explicitly programmed with locks to keep the state across four CPUs. But it is worth noting that the data remains in a single thread while the processing takes place, thus preserving data locality. If we perform the schedule as shown in Figure 7-20, it will be able to process the incoming stream. The data locality is lost, but the task locality is preserved.

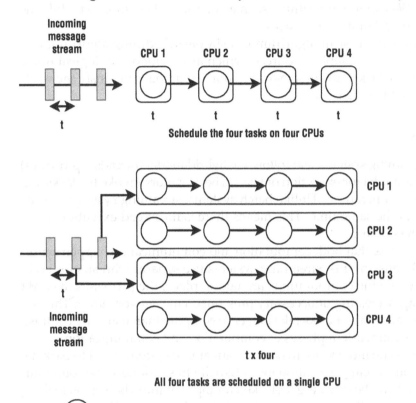

Figure 7-20: Stream graph scheduling

The role of a streaming scheduling algorithm is to allocate tasks to the available compute resources, thus satisfying their CPU and memory requirements. Further, they try to minimize the data movement among computers to reduce the latency and increase the throughput of applications. Apart from the instances we described earlier, streaming scheduling algorithms are different from batch scheduling algorithms because they work with tasks that have different memory and CPU requirements.

Uniform Resources

The simplest method to allocate tasks to processes is to assume every task needs the same number of resources. With this assumption, we can use algorithms such as round-robin scheduling, which allocates tasks to resources in a uniform way. When allocating the tasks, we need to minimize the communications among them.

Resource-Aware Scheduling

Separate parts of a streaming application may require different resources, such as memory. We can use algorithms such as first fit or best fit to schedule the tasks to the logical units of resources.

For example, the first-fit algorithm is a simple scheduling algorithm that keeps track of the available resources, which are divided into logical units, and allocates the task to the first logical resource unit that can satisfy the task's memory and CPU requirements.

Execution

There are streaming systems that follow the hybrid model (threads + processes) or the process model for execution of tasks. The executors invoke the tasks and communication operations. Unlike batch systems, streaming systems execute all the tasks at the same time. This means there is no staged execution as we saw on batch systems.

In addition, note that both computation and communication happen simultaneously. Because of this, streaming systems use separate threads for both. Otherwise, while the computations are taking place, the processes may not accept messages, creating unnecessary pressure on the network layer. This can be especially important if tasks take longer to compute than usual. By contrast, batch systems can work in phases of computation and communication.

When there is no more work to be done, streaming systems need to park the threads without running execution logic. Usually this is done at the communication layer, where the threads get blocked for input. If threads keep on looking for input even when there is no work, the CPU can be stuck at 100 percent, thus wasting energy.

Dynamic Scaling

Streaming applications can see fluctuations in traffic. When traffic increases, frameworks can scale the application to additional nodes. The user can specify a maximum resource allocation for the job and a default resource allocation. At runtime, the application will be scaled to the maximum resources if the load increases and there are resources available.

Dynamic scaling depends on resource availability. Relying on dynamic scaling can result in an application not being able to handle requests because resources are not available to handle the excess load. In resource-limited environments, it is best to run with the maximum capacity because of this. In public clouds, where there is a large number of resources available, we can always get more compute nodes when required, eliminating the previous problem.

Back Pressure (Flow Control)

Streaming tasks might produce data faster than the downstream tasks can handle, as shown in Figure 7-21. When this occurs, the system can no longer process the data, and it may be forced to drop messages to continue. This can be due to the following:

- A downstream task is slow to process messages. Some reasons for this are machines running the task might become slow, the task may be running low on memory, or the network becomes slow.

- An upstream task receives data faster than expected. The data sources may get an unexpected amount of data due to reasons beyond the control of the system, such as a spike in the usage of the application.

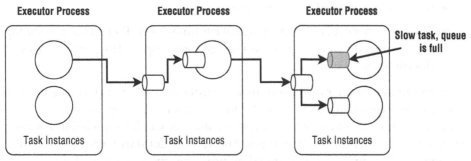

Figure 7-21: Back pressure on a set of streaming tasks

To avoid this scenario, the systems need to detect such slowdowns and notify the sources to limit the output [8]. Should this take place, the data sources can lean on the message brokers to store the excess data until the situation becomes manageable for the tasks affected by it. We call this controlling of the data flow "back pressure" or "flow control." Flow control is an extensively studied area in computer networks, and the concepts used in streaming systems originate from flow control in computer networks and other communication channels.

Every messaging system has protocols built in at the software or hardware level. Since streaming systems use the network for transferring messages between tasks, they can piggyback on the flow control at the network layer. But streaming systems cannot solely rely on the network layer flow control for slowing down the sources due to these implementation reasons:

- The tasks that are slow can be many hops down the task graph. It might take time for all the network links to become congested and propagate the issue to the sources.

- There may be several tasks within the same process, and these could be connected using a shared network channel and buffers. If we allow the network to congest because one task is slow, the other tasks may suffer as a result.

In any flow control system, the sender cannot figure out the status of the receiver until a message is sent and a reply comes back. If we send each message after we get the feedback from the receiver, the maximum message rate we can achieve is limited. To utilize the network fully we must send messages without knowing the status of the receiver. The flow control systems define how the sender can infer the status of the receiver without knowing the complete picture of the receiver in this blind mode.

Rate-Based Flow Control

In a static rate–based flow control, the source sets a fixed maximum rate for sending the messages. It can be something like number of bytes sent per second. This approach has the following issues:

- It is difficult to predict the consumer capacity.
- The consumer capacity can change at runtime depending on the processing requirements of different messages and operating environment fluctuations.

Owing to this, static rate–based flow control can lead to underutilization of resources in a dynamic environment and sometimes message drop.

In a dynamic rate–based control system, the rate can be adjusted at runtime based on feedback from the consumer. The system can start with an initial rate, and this can be adjusted at runtime depending on the consumer state.

Credit-Based Flow Control

In a credit-based flow control system, the sender keeps track of a parameter that helps it to infer the state of the receiver. For example, it can be a buffer count at the receiver. When a sender sends a message, it reduces the buffer count (credit) by one. When the buffer count reaches zero, it cannot send messages anymore until it gets some credit (acknowledgments back from the receiver). The credits from the receiver can come anytime during transmission, allowing the sender to update its credit. Sliding window is a popular credit-based flow control mechanism used in the TCP protocol.

Figure 7-22 demonstrates how Apache Storm handles back pressure. Storm monitors the input queues of the tasks, and if the queues are full, it sets a flag in the central data storage ZooKeeper. The worker processes listen to these flags at the ZooKeeper and notify the spouts to slow down in case the tasks become congested.

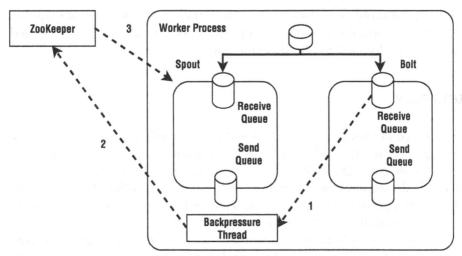

Figure 7-22: Apache Storm back-pressure handling

State

As streaming computations work with continuous data streams, oftentimes the user functions (tasks) need to keep state of the continuing computations. In a distributed streaming engine, state is closely related to fault tolerance as we need it to restore an application in case of a failure. In a streaming application, we can keep the state in the local process or a distributed state store, such as a file system or a database.

- **Local store**—In normal applications, we keep the state in the same memory as the program. Following this approach, a streaming application's state can be saved in the process memory of every task. Keeping state locally in the process is efficient but requires frequent checkpoints to a durable store to recover from failures.

- **Distributed store**—A streaming framework might choose to keep state in a distributed store for durability. In case of a failure, the tasks can be started pointing to the state in the durable storage. Usually, a hybrid approach is used where the state is kept in local storage and backed onto distributed storage from time to time.

Frameworks provide abstractions so that they hide where the state is stored. Users can use the same API to store and retrieve state, and configuration parameters are used to specify the actual state storage. This simplifies the programming of the tasks without consideration for where the state is stored. Compared to batch applications, the streaming application does not deal with distributed state data that does not fit into main memory.

Summary

Execution combines communication and tasks together to create large-scale programs. We are all familiar with CPU programming to write our applications. To utilize the CPU fully, we must consider the efficient use of memory, cache, NUMA, threads, network, and I/O, among many other things. Because of this, writing efficient programs that scale to thousands of nodes to process substantial amounts of data is a challenge.

Data-intensive application frameworks take most of this burden away from the user, with highly optimized local and distributed operations. Even with these frameworks, it is beneficial to know the underlying principals governing the execution of our large-scale programs so that we can develop and manage them more efficiently. Lately, more and more computations are being moved from CPUs to accelerators like GPUs and FPGAs.

References

1. J. Torrellas, H. Lam, and J. L. Hennessy, "False sharing and spatial locality in multiprocessor caches," *IEEE Transactions on Computers*, vol. 43, no. 6, pp. 651–663, 1994.

2. N. P. Jouppi *et al.*, "In-datacenter performance analysis of a tensor processing unit," in *Proceedings of the 44th annual international symposium on computer architecture*, 2017, pp. 1–12.

3. E. Chung *et al.*, "Serving dnns in real time at datacenter scale with project brainwave," *iEEE Micro*, vol. 38, no. 2, pp. 8–20, 2018.

4. G. Manimaran and C. S. R. Murthy, "An efficient dynamic scheduling algorithm for multiprocessor real-time systems," *IEEE Transactions on Parallel and Distributed Systems*, vol. 9, no. 3, pp. 312–319, 1998.

5. J. Dinan, D. B. Larkins, P. Sadayappan, S. Krishnamoorthy, and J. Nieplocha, "Scalable work stealing," in *Proceedings of the Conference on High Performance Computing Networking, Storage and Analysis*, 2009: IEEE, pp. 1–11.

6. D. Charousset, R. Hiesgen, and T. C. Schmidt, "Caf-the c++ actor framework for scalable and resource-efficient applications," in *Proceedings of the 4th International Workshop on Programming based on Actors Agents & Decentralized Control*, 2014, pp. 15–28.

7. S. Tasharofi, P. Dinges, and R. E. Johnson, "Why do scala developers mix the actor model with other concurrency models?," in *European Conference on Object-Oriented Programming*, 2013: Springer, pp. 302–326.

8. A. Floratou, A. Agrawal, B. Graham, S. Rao, and K. Ramasamy, "Dhalion: self-regulating stream processing in heron," *Proceedings of the VLDB Endowment*, vol. 10, no. 12, pp. 1825–1836, 2017.

Case Studies

Over the years, numerous frameworks have been developed to process data, written in different programming languages and aimed at a variety of applications. These frameworks are written to work with extract, transform, load (ETL), exploratory data analytics, machine learning, and deep learning systems. Some systems support multiple types of applications while some support only a single type. Those designed for one purpose are sometimes used in several domains. We will look at a representative set of frameworks including Apache Hadoop, Apache Spark, Apache Storm, Kafka Streams, PyTorch, cuDF, and Cylon.

Apache Hadoop

Apache Hadoop was the first open source large-scale data processing system built.[1] It was inspired by the Google Map-Reduce paper [1]. The Hadoop Project includes the Hadoop Distributed File System (HDFS), Hadoop Map-Reduce, and Hadoop Yarn projects. Hadoop Map-Reduce provides the computational capability, while Hadoop Yarn is a cluster resource manager. Here we will focus on the Hadoop Map-Reduce computation capabilities.

---

[1]https://hadoop.apache.org/

Hadoop Map-Reduce provides a simple API with only two functions called map and reduce. These functions are connected by a shuffle distributed operation. Hadoop has a key-value-based data abstraction that is equivalent to a two-column table in modern data processing systems. In such terms, the distributed operation of Hadoop can be thought of as a GroupBy operation.

Hadoop employed the HDFS and disk extensively for large-scale computations. In addition, since a single job could have only two operations connected by a distributed GroupBy operation, it was limited in both functionality and performance required for more complex applications. As Hadoop was the only option available in the early stages of large-scale processing, engineers found different workarounds to hide its intrinsic limitations. But eventually these limitations caught up to it, and Hadoop is now being replaced by more modern systems like Spark.

Programming Model

Hadoop programming involves a set of input/output functions and map and reduce functions. Map and reduce are connected by the shuffle operation. Therefore, we can think of Hadoop as a framework with a fixed graph, as shown in Figure 8-1. It is an SPMD program with a data parallel programming model.

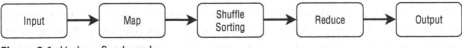

Figure 8-1: Hadoop fixed graph

The input and output functions are exposed along with data partitioning steps. Input allows Hadoop to read large datasets split into partitions and process them in parallel. Although input is not discussed in the map-reduce paradigm, it plays an integral part in the execution and programming model of Hadoop.

Output saves the partitions of the Hadoop program data into multiple files. By default, Hadoop provides input functions to read from common sources such as text files, CSV files, and Parquet files. The default input functions are programmed to efficiently work with block storage such as HDFS considering the data locality of the blocks.

Input data of a map function comes directly from the input function. If the input function reads a text file and outputs it line by line, the map function gets the line as the input. As such, the interface is presented to the function in a streaming fashion. If the input function reads the whole file as a single entity, the map function will have the whole file content at the same time.

The output of the map function is a key-value pair. A shuffle operation distributes these key-value pairs to the reduce function such that the same key goes to the same reduce function. On top of that, the keys are sorted. Values for the same key are grouped into a list and presented to the reduce function.

In database terms, this is a GroupBy function, where the reduce function is left to the user to program. There is also an optional combiner that can be applied to the output of the map function in case we intend on doing a reduction at the reduce stage.

This model is simple but generic enough to solve a substantial number of use cases. Initially, there were even machine learning libraries created on the Hadoop interface. But as we know, GroupBy reduce is not the only function required to create a data processing application. There are many other operations, such as joins and unions, that need special consideration and implementation to be efficient.

To illustrate the differences, let us look at a variant of the famous word count program, as shown here. Instead of counting words, we will try to count all the words with more than five characters. Since map-reduce is a GroupBy operation on keys, what we need is a single group with a summation. So, from the map function, we will output a predefined grouping key. In this example, we are outputting 1 as the key.

```java
public static class TokenizerMapper
    extends Mapper<Object, Text, IntWritable, IntWritable> {
  private final static IntWritable one = new IntWritable(1);

  public void map(Object key, Text value, Context context
  ) throws IOException, InterruptedException {
    StringTokenizer itr = new StringTokenizer(value.toString());
    while (itr.hasMoreTokens()) {
      String w = itr.nextToken();
      if (w.length() > 5) {
        // write 1 to the group 1
        context.write(one, one);
      }
    }
  }
}


public static class IntSumReducer
    extends Reducer<IntWritable, IntWritable, IntWritable, IntWritable> {
  private final IntWritable result = new IntWritable();
  public void reduce(IntWritable key, Iterable<IntWritable> values,
                     Context context
  ) throws IOException, InterruptedException {
    int sum = 0;
    for (IntWritable val : values) {
      sum += val.get();
    }
    result.set(sum);
    context.write(key, result);
  }
}
```

```
public static void main(String[] args) throws Exception {
  Configuration conf = new Configuration();
  Job job = Job.getInstance(conf, "word count");
  job.setJarByClass(WordCount.class);
  job.setMapperClass(TokenizerMapper.class);
  job.setCombinerClass(IntSumReducer.class);
  job.setReducerClass(IntSumReducer.class);
  job.setOutputKeyClass(Text.class);
  job.setOutputValueClass(IntWritable.class);
  FileInputFormat.addInputPath(job, new Path(args[0]));
  FileOutputFormat.setOutputPath(job, new Path(args[1]));
  System.exit(job.waitForCompletion(true) ? 0 : 1);
}
```

Now, we can clearly see outputting 1 as the key is something unnecessary in this program. We should be able to just output the counts and get the sum without involving a key.

Architecture

A Hadoop cluster has a main program that manages the job and set of workers called *task trackers*, which in turn execute the map, reduce, and shuffle operations.

Figure 8-2 illustrates how the map and reduce functions are invoked in a Hadoop cluster. The job is submitted to the application primary, which orchestrates the execution of the tasks in the TaskTrackers.

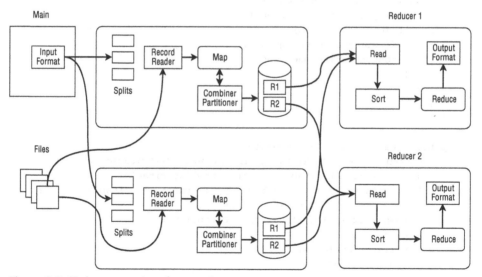

Figure 8-2: Hadoop execution of map-reduce

First, the data is partitioned into splits. These are read by the task trackers by means of the record reader and fed into the map tasks assigned to them. The output of the map tasks goes through an optional combiner that can reduce the size of the data. Output is saved into disk and reduce tasks are scheduled to run, after which the output is shuffled according to the output key.

Reduce tasks can be scheduled on the same task trackers that ran the map tasks or different ones. They read the output of the map tasks and then combine and sort them before invoking the reduce tasks. The output goes to the persistent storage such as HDFS.

Big data systems such as Spark and Flink possess a similar architecture in the shuffle operation. There have been improvements made, such as keeping the data in-memory or doing parts of the shuffle computation while the map tasks are executing.

Cluster Resource Management

Hadoop works with Yarn resource manager to allocate tasks for its jobs. Yarn is part of the Hadoop project. Originally, Hadoop did not possess a resource manager and worked only on clusters that were dedicated to it. Yarn was developed to solve this problem, restricting the resource management from the original Hadoop project to the Yarn project. Hadoop map-reduce has a close relationship to Yarn as it is the only resource manager it supports.

Apache Spark

Apache Spark is a distributed in-memory data processing engine[2] [2]. The data model in Spark is based on Resilient Distributed Datasets (RDDs) [3]. RDD is an abstraction to represent a large dataset distributed over the cluster nodes.

The logical execution model is expressed through a chain of transformations on RDDs by the user. The graph created by these transformations is termed the *lineage graph*. It also plays an important role in supporting fault tolerance. Spark was created to support batch applications and later was extended to include streaming applications.

Programming Model

A Spark application is written inside an executable code that has a main function called a *driver*. The driver program usually runs in a separate computer, and the parallel jobs created in the driver program are shipped to the cluster to be executed. It is necessary to create a context object that manages the connection to the cluster and the dependencies between jobs. So, Spark provides a workflow model with a distributed data API. The workflow model is limited to execute data transformation operations supported by Spark.

---

[2]https://spark.apache.org/

With this model, complex control flow operations that need to run serially (such as iterations and "if" conditions) run in driver, while parallel data flow operations are executed in worker nodes.

Apache Spark application is specified as a set of transformations on RDDs, DataFrames, DataSets, or as an SQL script. The user can cache or persist intermediate data for jobs so that the next job can use those data. This is especially important for iterative computation where the same datasets are being used repeatedly.

The transformations on distributed data structures are termed *lazy* because they build a task graph only until an action is performed. The "actions" act as end indicators of the task graph. When an action is applied, the task graph is submitted and executed in the cluster.

> **NOTE**   A Spark application is a program with a single Spark context. Within this context, Spark can submit many jobs consecutively or simultaneously to the cluster. A job creates a task graph to be executed.

RDD API

RDD is a generic data structure representing a distributed dataset with key value data or just values. A value or a key can be an object to represent complex data. Spark uses the Hadoop input and output functions to read and write RDDs. RDDs can be read in from a file system such as HDFS, and transformations are applied to them.

The following code is the same program we did in Hadoop to count words with more than five characters. Notice that instead of a shuffle operation (GroupBy), we can use Spark reduce operation. Also, we can have any number of operations combined in our program. In this program, reduce is an "action" that sends the graph to execute. The result of the reduce operation is sent to the driver. You can see that the last print statement is running in the driver program.

```
public class RDDExample {
    public static void main(String[] args) {
        SparkConf conf = new SparkConf().setAppName("RDD Example");
        JavaSparkContext sc = new JavaSparkContext(conf);

        JavaRDD<String> distFile = sc.textFile("data.txt");
        int lengthSum = distFile.map(new Function<String, Integer>() {
            @Override
            public Integer call(String s) throws Exception {
                return s.length() > 5 ? 1 : 0;
            }
        }).reduce(new Function2<Integer, Integer, Integer>() {
            @Override
```

```
        public Integer call(Integer t1, Integer t2) throws Exception {
            return t1 + t2;
        }
    });
    System.out.println("Count Length > 5: " + lengthSum);
}
}
```

SQL, DataFrames, and DataSets

In Spark, RDD can be considered to represent one-column or two-column (key, value) tables. The DataFrame and DataSet APIs take this to the next level by generalizing to any number of columns.

DataSet is a strongly typed SQL API for data processing. The SQL queries are written using programming language constructs. DataFrames can be thought of as DataSet<Row>, where Row represents a row in a table. DataSets are type-safe, and queries can be checked at compile time, while with DataFrames only some type of safety is provided.

We can write the previous example using the DataSet<Row> API, as shown next. Here, we need to treat the file as a table with a single column. Each row in this table has one string value. As Spark is now using a full table abstraction, it is a more natural fit for SQL queries.

```
public class DataSetExample implements Serializable {
    public static void main(String[] args) {
        SparkSession spark = SparkSession
            .builder()
            .appName("Java Spark SQL basic example")
            .config("spark.some.config.option", "some-value")
            .getOrCreate();

        Dataset<Row> df = spark.read().text("data.txt");
        int lengthSum = df.map(new MapFunction<Row, Integer>() {
            @Override
            public Integer call(Row row) throws Exception {
                return row.getString(0).length() > 5 ? 1 : 0;
            }
        }, Encoders.INT()).reduce(new ReduceFunction<Integer>() {
            @Override
            public Integer call(Integer t1, Integer t2) throws Exception {
                return t1 + t2;
            }
        });
        System.out.println("Count Length > 5: " + lengthSum);
    }
}
```

Architecture

Figure 8-3 displays the Apache Spark architecture. The driver is connected to a set of worker processes through the Spark master process. The worker processes can run in a cluster of machines, each assigned a set of resources at its disposal to allocate toward applications.

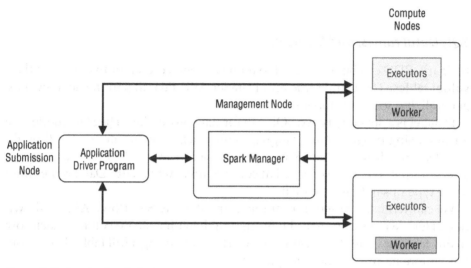

Figure 8-3: Apache Spark cluster

When a user submits a job, the driver converts the code, containing transformations and actions performed on the Spark data structures, into a directed acyclic task graph. When converting to this task graph, Spark can apply optimizations to improve the execution, which are based on relational algebra.

Spark decomposes a parallel job according to data partitions. Each partition is executed in a task; therefore, tasks and partitions have a one-to-one mapping in Spark. The user program running in the driver asks Spark to execute set operations combined in a graph in the cluster. Spark schedules these tasks on the workers, who then spawn separate JVMs to run the tasks for the user-submitted graph. These processes are called *executors*. The physical execution plan for executing this graph contains a set of stages.

Resource Managers

Spark can work with several resource managers to acquire and manage cluster resources for its applications.

- **Standalone** —Simple resource allocator for clusters dedicated to Spark applications
- **Yarn, Mesos, Kubernetes**—External resource managers to the Spark Project

Spark job scheduling is done via these resource managers. By default, Spark allocates the requested resources for an application up front and uses them throughout the execution. A Spark application can specify the memory and number of CPU cores required for it and can dynamically share CPUs with other applications in Mesos, although those deployments are not common as Mesos is no longer being actively developed.

Within an application, Spark can submit multiple task graphs (jobs) to the cluster to execute simultaneously. In this case, Spark relies on a fair scheduler or first in first out (FIFO) scheduler to allocate resources.

Task Schedulers

Task schedulers oversee individual jobs within an application. When a user performs an action on a set of transformations, a job is submitted to the cluster. Spark has two schedulers called DAGScheduler and TaskScheduler to execute the tasks of a single job:

- **DAGScheduler**—Works in the Spark Driver and decomposes a graph into stages according to distributed operations. It optimizes the graph to create a minimal graph, after which the TaskScheduler executes it.

- **TaskScheduler**—TaskScheduler gets a set of tasks submitted to it from the DAGScheduler for each stage and sends them to the cluster, retries if there are failures, and handles stragglers. The task scheduler does not know about the dependencies between tasks.

Executors

Now, let us aim to understand how Spark maps a computation to the available resources. This involves two concepts called *executors* and *executor cores*. An executor is a process spawned to perform the tasks of the Spark job. If there are n executors for a job, Spark will spawn n processes. Executor cores define how many threads are assigned to an executor. A Spark job is configured with a fixed number of executors, each of which is assigned a set of cores. The total available parallelism of a Spark job is defined as follows:

$$parallelism = no\ of\ executors \times executor\ cores$$

To understand the parallelism of a Spark job, say we are reading a set of text files and applying a map function followed by a distributed sorting operation. The data emerging from the sorting operation is saved into a file system using another function.

Now, let us assume we have four compute nodes to execute jobs, each containing four cores. Our file is large, so we are going to divide it into 100 partitions across the nodes, meaning there are 25 partitions to process, and we have four executor cores (threads) available. Spark will run the map function as a task for each of these partitions. There will be 25 task instances created in one executor, but at any given time there can be only four tasks running as we have only four cores. The number of partitions in a Spark job should be equal to or higher than the available parallelism to utilize the resources fully.

Communication Operations

The distributed operations in Spark can change the number of output partitions from the input partitions. The local operations applied to a partition do not change the number of partitions. An example of a local operation is a map function, and a distributed operation is a partition operation.

OPERATIONS	DESCRIPTION
Shuffle	Redistributes the tuples randomly or based on a key
Broadcast	Broadcasts a value from driver to executors
Reduce	Reduces values and transfers them to the driver

Spark employs the Netty communication library to implement its communication operations [4]. The most widely used communication operation is shuffle, as it is found in all the major operations, including joins, GroupBy operations, and a variety of others.

Apache Spark Streaming

Unlike other streaming engines, Apache Spark uses its batch engine for streaming applications. As we can see in Figure 8-4, instead of processing streams one message at a time, Spark creates mini-batches. These mini-batches are then treated by the Spark workers as though they were simply processing a small dataset, like in the case of batch processing.

Figure 8-5 shows the flow of the Spark streaming execution. When we start a Spark streaming job, Spark initiates a set of receiver tasks in the executors. These tasks listen to external sources and gather the data. Spark has a configuration that determines the interval at which the receiver gathers the data for creating a mini-batch. Once this interval is over, the accumulated data becomes a mini-batch and is reported to the Spark context running in the driver. Data are treated as an RDD from this point onward. The driver then initiates a batch computation on this RDD data using the Spark core engine.

This model has the obvious disadvantage of invoking a batch engine for a small amount of data. The constant costs associated with scheduling and executing a set of batch tasks for each mini-batch compared to the data processing

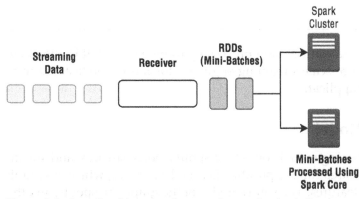

Figure 8-4: Overall architecture of a streaming application in Spark

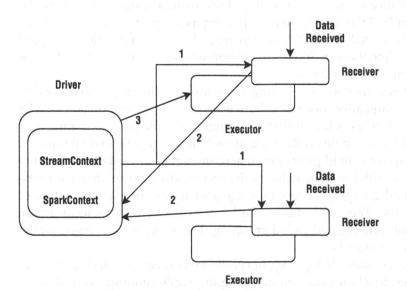

Figure 8-5: Spark streaming with mini-batches

times can be significant. With these persistent overheads, Spark streaming is bounded by the minimum latency it can achieve for processing a message.

When the batch sizes grow larger, the overhead associated in the batch computation compared to the actual computation becomes small. Since data are processed in larger batches, the computation can achieve higher efficiency, and the throughput increases. Thus, this model is ideal for streaming applications that are computationally expensive with larger window sizes.

Apache Storm

Apache Storm[3] is a real-time stream processing framework [5]. It is one of the first open source large-scale streaming engines. Storm uses the task graph to model a streaming application.

Programming Model

The Storm programming model consists of spouts, bolts, streams, and stream groupings. A Storm streaming application is called a *topology*, which is a graph consisting of these features. The source nodes of the graph are spouts, and the rest are bolts. Links between the tasks are stream groupings and implemented as communication links.

Stream events are injected into a topology from a spout. A spout can be listening to an HTTP port, or it may be pulling messages from a queue. When the topology is created, it specifies how many tasks to run in parallel for a spout or a bolt. We view these as logical execution units and tasks as the physical instances of the spouts and bolts.

In Storm, tasks are connected using a streaming grouping, which is a distributed communication operation between two sets of task instances. The simplest of such rules is the shuffle grouping. In shuffle grouping, messages between the tasks are delivered such that each task will get an equal number. Another grouping is field grouping, where messages are keyed on an attribute, and those with the same value as the chosen attribute are directed to the same task. In all groupings, every message goes to the corresponding task of the receiving bolt. There are other examples like direct grouping, local shuffle grouping, nongrouping, and global grouping. These can be used based on the application requirements.

Figure 8-6 is an example topology at runtime where Spout 1 and Spout 2 are both connected to a bolt using shuffle grouping while running two instances. As a result of the shuffle grouping, every instance of a spout sends messages to both instances of the bolt.

Storm is a task parallel program model with multiple program multiple data (MPMD)–style execution because it runs tasks with different programs on different processes.

Here, we have a code example with two spouts sending messages to a bolt that then joins the messages from the two streams. The join is implemented in another bolt by Storm. In other systems like Spark or Flink, the join occurs at the system level as a distributed operation. Note how the `TopologyBuilder` class is used to create the graph by adding the nodes and the communication links.

---

[3]`https://storm.apache.org/`

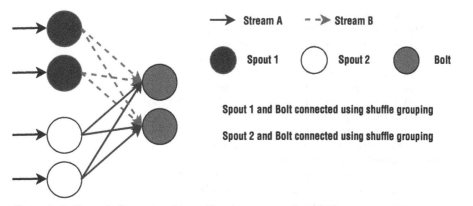

Figure 8-6: Example Storm topology with two spouts and one bolt

```
public static class AgeSpout extends GenSpout {
  private int i = 0;
  public AgeSpout(Fields outFields) {
    super(outFields);
  }
  @Override
  public void nextTuple() {
    i++;
    collector.emit(new Values(new Values(i, i + 20),
        UUID.randomUUID().toString()));
  }
}

public static class GenderSpout extends GenSpout {
  private int i = 0;
  public GenderSpout(Fields outFields) {
    super(outFields);
  }
  @Override
  public void nextTuple() {
    i++;
    String gender = i % 2 == 0 ? "male" : "female";
    collector.emit(new Values(new Values(i, gender),
        UUID.randomUUID().toString()));
  }
}

public static void main(String[] args) throws Exception {
  GenSpout genderSpout = new GenderSpout(new Fields("id", "gender"));
  GenSpout ageSpout = new AgeSpout(new Fields("id", "age"));

  // build the graph
  TopologyBuilder builder = new TopologyBuilder();
```

```
// add the nodes
builder.setSpout("genderSpout", genderSpout, 2);
builder.setSpout("ageSpout", ageSpout, 2);
// join is implemented as another bolt, after a shuffle
JoinBolt joiner = new JoinBolt("genderSpout", "id")
    .join("ageSpout", "id", "genderSpout")
    .select("genderSpout:id,ageSpout:id,gender,age")
    .withTumblingWindow(
        new BaseWindowedBolt.Duration(10, TimeUnit.SECONDS));
// add the grouping, i.e. communication
builder.setBolt("joiner", joiner)
    .fieldsGrouping("genderSpout", new Fields("id"))
    .fieldsGrouping("ageSpout", new Fields("id"));
builder.setBolt("printer", new PrintBolt() {
  }).shuffleGrouping("joiner");

Config conf = new Config();
try (LocalCluster cluster = new LocalCluster()) {
  cluster.submitTopology("join-example", conf,
      builder.createTopology());
  Thread.sleep(10000);
  }
}
```

Architecture

There are three sets of processes in a Storm cluster: Nimbus, Supervisor, and Worker. These are shown in Figure 8-7.

- **Nimbus**—Nimbus is the management node of a Storm cluster. It is responsible for distributing work on the applications to workers, assigning tasks to them, and monitoring the tasks for failures. In case of failure, Nimbus can reassign tasks to other workers. Nimbus keeps all its state in ZooKeeper and can be restarted from a save state.

- **Supervisor**—Supervisor runs on the cluster nodes to manage the actual worker processes that execute the tasks of the job. It is responsible for creating, starting, and stopping worker processes to perform the tasks assigned to that node. Supervisor stores all its state in ZooKeeper and can be restarted without affecting the cluster. If a worker process exits unexpectedly, the supervisor can respawn it.

- **ZooKeeper**—Storm uses the ZooKeeper cluster for exchanging control data between Nimbus and Supervisors [6]. The complete state of the cluster is saved in ZooKeeper, allowing individual components to fail and restart without affecting the overall performance of the cluster.

- **Worker process**—The Worker process executes the actual tasks (spouts, bolts) assigned to it using threads. A worker runs tasks on a single application. They handle communication for the tasks by creating network channels between the worker processes.

▪ **Executors and tasks**—Executors are threads running tasks (spouts and bolts). They listen to incoming messages and execute the tasks with the input.

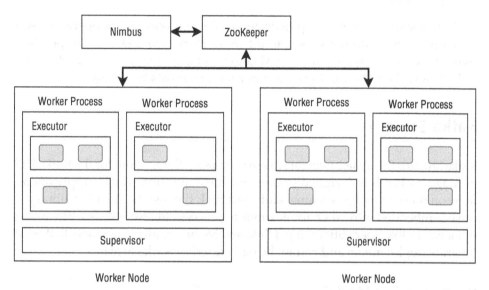

Figure 8-7: Apache Storm cluster

When a job is submitted, it goes to the Nimbus. Nimbus distributes this job to worker nodes and asks the supervisor to start the worker processes to execute it. Spouts and bolts are assigned to workers. Note that at runtime, many instances of spouts and bolts will be created depending on the parallelism specified by the user. A worker node has threads that execute the spouts and bolts based on an event-driven approach.

Cluster Resource Managers

Unlike with Spark, Storm does not have a built-in mechanism for working with cluster resource managers. Since streaming applications run for a long time without termination, they can be thought of simply as long-running processes. A user may allocate a set of containers in a cluster like Kubernetes and run the required Storm servers to start a Storm application.

Storm was developed early in the big data frameworks timeline and did not have the required architecture to support cluster resource managers. Later systems such as Flink [7] and Apache Heron [8] have built-in support for different resource managers.

Communication Operations

Storm has two main distributed operations:

- **Shuffle**—Redistributes the tuples randomly or based on a key
- **Broadcast**—Broadcasts values from task instances to all the target task instances

Storm's shuffle is not as sophisticated as the Hadoop/Spark operation as it deals only with continuously streaming in-memory data. The shuffle operation connects N source task instances to M target task instances. As such, each source task instance has M outgoing communication channels to M tasks.

Kafka Streams

Kafka Streams [9] is a lightweight stream processing library built for the Kafka [10] message broker. It is designed to consume messages from Kafka, apply operations on those message streams, and send back the results. As it is a library, it can be embedded into other applications to process data from Kafka. Streaming frameworks like Spark Streaming, Flink, and Storm are all frameworks that need separate deployments and cannot be embedded as Kafka Streams.

Programming Model

Kakfa Streams has a similar programming model to other stream processing engines and represents the computation as a streaming task graph called a *topology*. There are stream *sources*, *sinks*, and *stream processors* (nodes) connected by streams (links). The following is the source code from Kafka streams that counts words coming through a Kafka topic. The output is also sent to a Kafka topic. It is a modified version of the famous word count program where it only counts words with a length greater than 5.

```
final StreamsBuilder builder = new StreamsBuilder();
final KStream<String, String> source = builder.stream("input-topic");
final KTable<String, Long> counts = source
    .flatMapValues(new ValueMapper<String, Iterable<String>>() {
      @Override
      public Iterable<String> apply(String s) {
        List<String> words = new ArrayList<String>();
        String[] splits = s.split("\\W+");
```

```
      for (String sp : splits) {
        if (sp.length() > 5) {
          words.add(sp);
        }
      }
      return words;
    }
  })
  .groupBy((key, value) -> value)
  .count();
counts.toStream().to("output-topic", Produced.with(Serdes.String(),
Serdes.Long())));
final KafkaStreams streams = new KafkaStreams(builder.build(), props);
try {
  streams.start();
  Thread.sleep(100000);} catch (final Throwable e) {
  System.exit(1);
}
```

When we define a stream topology, it will be applied to the streams coming from the Kafka topic partitions separately. The stream partitions are processed in isolation from each other using different instances of the topology. As a result, stream processing is always local to the partition of a topic, and if we need to work across different partitions, we have to go through the Kafka broker as a separate application. In a stream processing engine like Storm or Flink, we can combine the streams deriving from different partitions at the processing layer.

Architecture

Kafka Streams has the concept of a task as the unit of *parallelism*. Kafka stream parallelism is connected to the Kafka topic partitions. An application's true parallelism cannot be greater than the number of partitions of a topic.

A task is connected to one or more Kafka topics. It can consume from a single partition of the Kafka topic. Tasks are assigned statically to one of the partitions, and this assignment cannot be changed. A task runs the processor topology for a partition using threads. An application might have many threads, each of which runs one or more tasks inside that application.

Figure 8-8 highlights the execution of a Kafka streaming application in three machines. The application derives from two topics, each with four partitions. Application Instance 1 runs two threads and two tasks. Application Instances 2 and 3 run only a single task and a single thread.

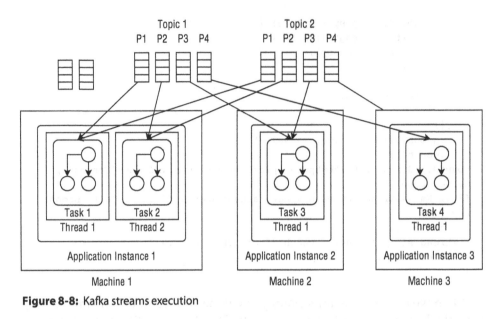

Figure 8-8: Kafka streams execution

PyTorch

PyTorch [11] is a tensor processing framework designed to develop and train deep learning models with ease. It is one of the leading deep learning frameworks from Facebook, alongside Tensorflow from Google. In its core is a tensor abstraction that can primarily be used in both CPUs and GPUs. Other accelerator devices such as TPUs are also supported in recent versions of PyTorch. Operations on these tensors define a PyTorch program.

Programming Model

The programming model in PyTorch implicitly defines a task graph of tensors. The graph is implicit because PyTorch evaluates operations eagerly without requiring the creation of a static graph like in Tensorflow. While this graph is applicable to any PyTorch program, it is easier to visualize when it involves a neural network model.

Figure 8-9 shows a simple model that performs tensor multiplication. We can use the code snippet shown on the right to produce this graph using PyTorch's built-in Onnx support. Onnx is an open format to exchange neural networks as graphs. This graph also highlights how data structure and the operations around it define a data analytics framework, as mentioned in Chapter 5. For example, the elements 0, 1, and 2 in this figure are the tensors in PyTorch, and MatMul is the tensor operation.

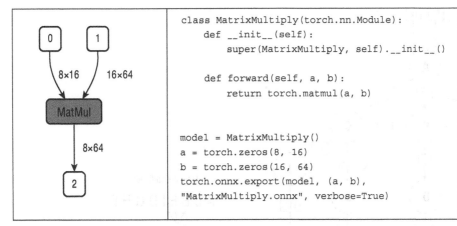

```
class MatrixMultiply(torch.nn.Module):
    def __init__(self):
        super(MatrixMultiply, self).__init__()

    def forward(self, a, b):
        return torch.matmul(a, b)


model = MatrixMultiply()
a = torch.zeros(8, 16)
b = torch.zeros(16, 64)
torch.onnx.export(model, (a, b),
"MatrixMultiply.onnx", verbose=True)
```

Figure 8-9: An example tensor graph for matrix multiplication

PyTorch is a general tensor processing framework, so it can be used to write programs other than neural networks as well. In such cases, the programming model becomes a sequence of tensor transformation and algebraic operations. However, one difference that we observe with PyTorch compared to other data processing frameworks is that it supports both forward and backward computations as required by neural network training.

Forward Computation

Evaluation of the tensor operations graph, from input tensor nodes through to the end, is known as the *forward computation*. In the previous model, computing the matrix multiplication would be the forward pass. In complex computation graphs, forward computation would follow the topological order of nodes.

Topological order of nodes organizes operations such that if some operation Y is dependent on the output of another operation X, then Y comes after X in the ordered list. To illustrate, consider the graph in Figure 8-10. The computation starts with operation A, where one of its output gets fed into B and F, while the other is an input to C. At this point, only C can be executed next as other operations have unsatisfied dependencies from prior operations. After C, all of B, E, and I can be executed at the same time.

Backward Computation

Backward computation refers to computing gradients of the output with respect to each input in every node in the computational graph.

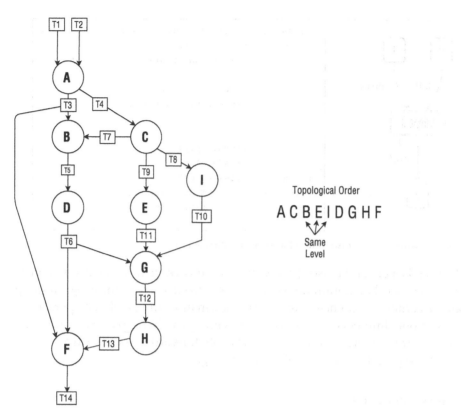

Figure 8-10: Topological order for computation graph

Figure 8-11 shows an example computation graph for a single perceptron training with two inputs. Here the two weights, W1 and W2, are learnable parameters. During the forward computation, the inputs X1 and X2 are multiplied with weights and summed together to feed the sigmoid function in the perceptron. The output (Y) of this computation is used to compute the loss (L) against ground truth.

Backward computation is what adjusts the weights to minimize the loss on the next pair of inputs. To do this, it needs to find out the partial derivatives of L with respect to W1 and W2. Once these are known, weights can be adjusted depending on the chosen weight update method. For example, a simple weight update scheme would be to set $W = W - \alpha \left(\frac{dL}{dW} \right)$, where α is called the *learning rate*. There are more advanced schemes than this, but the general idea remains the same.

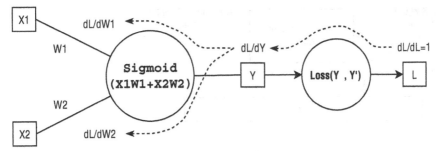

Figure 8-11: Perceptron learning

As loss is the output of several function compositions, we can utilize chain rule to compute the gradients starting at the output, called *backward computation*. For example, $\frac{dL}{dW1} = \left(\frac{dL}{dY}\right) * \left(\frac{dY}{dW1}\right)$ using the chain rule.

Autograd

As may be obvious by now, writing code to compute gradients needed during backward pass is quite tedious. Therefore, PyTorch implements an automatic gradient computation library called Autograd.

Despite its name, there is no magical way to know what the gradient for a given function is. So, for each function that Autograd supports, the backward gradient computation needs to be provided. It then propagates gradients up the call tree. Also, if the function is just a composition of already known functions, there is no need for the developer to explicitly define the gradient calculation.

Figure 8-12 shows how Autograd gets its knowledge about how to compute gradients for a particular node. During the forward pass, the developer has the option to save any required input to a context that is shared during the backward pass as well. As Autograd is a chain of operations; during the backward pass of this node, it will receive the derivate of the loss (or final output) with respect to its inputs. Then the developer only needs to implement what derivatives must be propagated back from this node to those nodes preceding it. This is where stashed values from the context will be used.

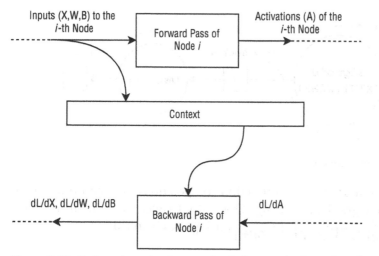

Figure 8-12: Backward pass implementation in Autograd using a shared context

Execution

During normal execution, PyTorch resorts to CPU-based implementations of tensor operations. However, the widespread practice is to offload these kernel executions to GPUs. For example, if one GPU is available, this can be represented as `cuda:0` to which any tensor or model can be ported using the `to()` function call. To port the previous model in Figure 8-9 to a GPU, we can add the `model.to(torch.device("cuda:0"))` line after creating the model. It is worth noting that, excluding distributed operations, PyTorch tensor operations will not work if the participating tensors are not all in the same device.

Distributed Execution

PyTorch also supports distributed tensor operations and, in turn, distributed training of models. The distributed execution model is single program multiple data (SPMD). There are three distributed abstractions currently supported. These are Distributed Data Parallel (DDP), Remote Procedure Call (RPC), and collective communications. The last of the three is a bit misleading as it also includes peer-to-peer send and receive primitives. Nevertheless, it is about primitive tensor communication like one would find in MPI. Also, these communication primitives come from PyTorch's underlying tensor library, C10.

DDP and RPC are two abstractions written on top of the communication primitives, where DDP utilizes collective calls such as AllReduce, whereas RPC is based on send and receive operations. Of these two abstractions, DDP is more restricted than RPC, where its purpose is to support only data parallel training over distributed resources.

As shown in Figure 8-13, the model is replicated across workers but fed different data samples, which is why it's called *data parallel*. The backward pass gradients from these replicas are all-reduced before updating the weights. In DDP, each of the forward to optimizer chains would run on a separate process. The horizontal communication arrows show the synchronization AllReduce construct. DDP resembles the Bulk Synchronous Parallel (BSP) execution model.

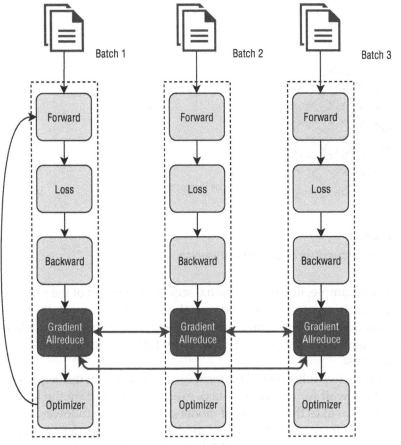

Figure 8-13: PyTorch Distributed Data Parallel

Data parallel is one of several types of parallelisms you can introduce to train a model, as shown in Figure 11.13. The other two types are model parallelism and pipeline parallelism. Note that neural networks have an inherent dependency between layers, which means that to achieve efficient pipeline parallelism, one needs to stream mini-batches. Otherwise, there would be larger bubbles in the pipeline, where work would sit idle waiting for data from either previous layers (for forward computations) or subsequent layers (for backward computations).

As shown in Figure 8-14, implementing other types of parallelisms requires less restricted support from PyTorch than DDP, and RPC is introduced as a solution. It is not attached to a particular parallelization of a model but rather provides a general framework to send data from one worker to another as well as reference remote data. It is typical to employ a leader and follower pattern when using RPC, though it is not strictly required.

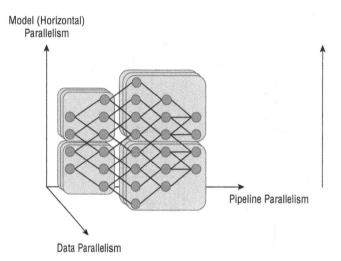

Figure 8-14: Different types of parallelism in deep learning

Figure 8-15, for example, illustrates a partial sequence diagram of the pipeline parallel implementation of the Resnet50 model using RPC support. It shows only the initialization and the forward pass, as internal implementation details are hidden (executed over distributed followers by PyTorch) for the backward and optimizer steps.

The leader and the two followers all perform `rpc.init_rpc()` in the beginning. The followers then wait for any remote task executions issued by the leader. Initially, the leader invokes the creation of model shards in each follower. These calls return remote references to the created models. Then the leader continues with the training loop, where for each mini-batch per batch, it first invokes the forward implementation on follower 0. This returns a remote reference to the forward output of shard 0.

It is then used subsequently to invoke the forward pass on follower 1 for shard 1 of the model. This returns a future object that can be queried later for the result when execution is completed. Note both these calls return immediately by spawning a task on the remote follower.

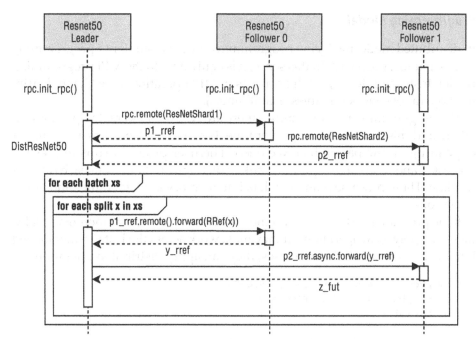

Figure 8-15: Pipeline parallelism of Resnet50 using RPC support in PyTorch

During the backward pass, which is not shown in the sequence diagram, the remote reference output of forward passes, along with remote references to all model parameters of shard 0 and shard 1, will be used by the distributed optimizer implementation to perform distributed gradient computation and weight update.

Cylon

Cylon[4] is a high-performance distributed memory data-parallel library developed for processing data in tabular form [12]. Its execution and programming models are different compared to other frameworks we discussed. Cylon implements a set of relational operations to process data. While "core" Cylon performs using system-level C/C++, it has Python and Java interfaces.

Its flexible C++ core and language interfaces allow Cylon to be used as a library for applications or run as a stand-alone framework. Internally it uses a compact Apache Arrow data format. In the distributed mode, it relies on MPI to execute its processes and handle the communication [13].

---

[4]https://cylondata.org/

Programming Model

In distributed mode, the Cylon programming model is similar to programming a set of parallel processes. In this sense, it is equivalent to the MPI programming model. Instead of dealing with arrays as in MPI operations, the Cylon distributed operations work on tables (DataFrames).

The programming model assumes there are N processes created per computation, and this does not change over time. N can range from 1 to any number depending on the parallelism we need. The user program runs in these N processes and relies on the process rank to distinguish them from each other at runtime. These processes can load data into memory as DataFrames and apply operations.

If the program needs to work on the DataFrame loaded into memory locally, they can apply local operations. If they must work across the DataFrames loaded into the memory of all the processes, they can apply distributed operations.

```
from pycylon import DataFrame, CylonEnv
from pycylon.net import MPIConfig
import random

df1 = DataFrame([[1, 2, 3], [2, 3, 4]])
df2 = DataFrame([[1, 1, 1], [2, 3, 4]])
df2.set_index([0])

# local join
df3 = df1.join(other=df2, on=[0])
print("Local Join")
print(df3)

# distributed join
env = CylonEnv(config=MPIConfig())
df1 = DataFrame([random.sample(range(10*env.rank, 15*(env.rank+1)), 5),
                 random.sample(range(10*env.rank, 15*(env.rank+1)), 5)])
df2 = DataFrame([random.sample(range(10*env.rank, 15*(env.rank+1)), 5),
                 random.sample(range(10*env.rank, 15*(env.rank+1)), 5)])
df2.set_index([0], inplace=True)
print("Distributed Join")
df3 = df1.join(other=df2, on=[0], env=env)
print(df3)
```

Architecture

Figure 8-16 shows the Cylon architecture. At the core of Cylon is a set of relational algebra operations and distributed communication operations. A C++ API is built on top of these for processing data. Above the C++ API, it has a Python API and a Java API. A user can choose either the PyArrow API or the Arrow Java API to manipulate in-memory data tables. The distributed execution is managed by the MPI process management.

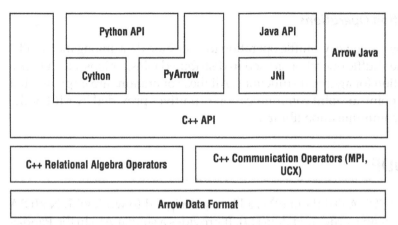

Figure 8-16: Cylon architecture

Execution

The distributed execution assumes a process model with a single thread calling distributed operations. The user can write the program as they wish since it does not depend on any programming model like a task graph. The user is responsible for creating the threads and I/O threads in case they need such executions, but most people can just utilize the main thread of the program to execute within a process.

Inside the processes, the user calls local operations and distributed operations. Since Cylon does not create any threads, these are executed on the calling threads of the program, as shown in Figure 8-17.

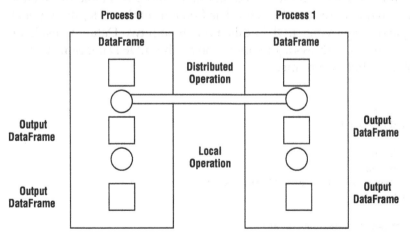

Figure 8-17: Cylon program execution on two processes

Communication Operations

Cylon uses the in-memory shuffle operation to distribute data among the parallel processes. The shuffle operation is used in distributed joins, unions, etc. It uses a reduce operation for aggregate functions. All these operations are implemented on top of the point-to-point communication primitives provided by MPI or the UCX library communication library.

Rapids cuDF

Rapids cuDF (CUDA DataFrame)[5] is a library designed to work with NVIDIA GPUs for processing structured data [14]. It provides a similar API to the Pandas DataFrame through its Python interface. The core of cuDF is written in C++ and Cuda [15]. It has language bindings in Python and Java.

At the core of cuDF is an in-memory (GPU memory) table and a set of data operations around it. The operations are inspired by Pandas DataFrame operations. We can use cuDF as a library on our C++, Python, or Java applications, similar to using Pandas DataFrame in a Python application. Internally, cuDF uses the Apache Arrow columnar format for representing data in-memory. This allows cuDF to work seamlessly with other systems such as PyTorch and TensorFlow.

Programming Model

When used as a library, the cuDF programming model is similar to a Pandas DataFrame. It provides an API to load data into memory in a table format and apply relational operations on this data. The first part of the code, shown next, is an example of employing cuDF in this mode to join two DataFrames. Later in the same program, it shows a join operation on the cuDF DataFrame backed by the Dask distributed runtime.

```
import os
import cupy as cp
import pandas as pd
import cudf
import dask_cudf
import numpy as np
from dask.distributed import Client, wait
import dask_cudf

client = Client('localhost:8786')

df_a = cudf.DataFrame()
```

---

[5]https://rapids.ai/

```
# first dataframe with 'key', 'vals_a' columns
df_a['key'] = [1, 2, 3, 4, 5]
df_a['vals_a'] = [float(i + 10) for i in range(5)]

# second dataframe with 'key', 'vals_b' columns
df_b = cudf.DataFrame()
df_b['key'] = [2, 3, 5, 6, 7]
df_b['vals_b'] = [float(i+100) for i in range(5)]

# join operation
merged = df_a.merge(df_b, on=['key'], how='inner')
print(merged)


# dask_cudf
left = dask_cudf.from_cudf(df_a, chunksize=5)
right = dask_cudf.from_cudf(df_b, chunksize=5)
# join operation on dask frame
joined = left.set_index("key").join(
    right.set_index("key"), how="inner", lsuffix="l", rsuffix="r"
)
merged = joined.compute().to_pandas()
print(merged)
```

Architecture

Figure 8-18 shows the cuDF architecture. cuDF provides a distributed execution on the Dask framework, which is built on a UCX [16] communication framework-based distributed backend. This API allows users to run cuDF on a cluster with multiple GPUs distributed over many machines. Since it has UCX, cuDF can use network hardware such as InfiniBand for communication.

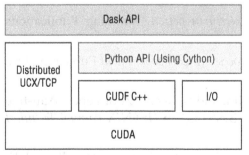

Figure 8-18: CUDF architecture

As a library, cuDF does not impose any execution model and relies on the user program to execute its operations. When paired with Dask, the execution is like what Apache Spark provides with a remote execution model. The user program is run in a driver program, which submits individual task graphs to be executed in the cluster.

Summary

We introduced a set of Java-based frameworks and Python/C++ frameworks for data analytics. The Java-based frameworks discussed here are designed to manage large datasets. C++ frameworks with Python APIs are increasingly found in data science workflows, which are highly interactive with a lot of human involvement.

References

1. J. Dean and S. Ghemawat, "MapReduce: simplified data processing on large clusters," *Commun. ACM*, vol. 51, no. 1, pp. 107–113, 2008.

2. Matei Zaharia, Mosharaf Chowdhury, Michael J. Franklin, Scott Shenker, and Ion Stoica, "Spark: Cluster Computing with Working Sets," presented at the 2nd USENIX Workshop on Hot Topics in Cloud Computing (HotCloud '10), Boston, June 22, 2010. [Online]. Available: `http://www.cs.berkeley.edu/~franklin/Papers/hotcloud.pdf`

3. M. Zaharia *et al.*, "Resilient distributed datasets: A fault-tolerant abstraction for in-memory cluster computing," in *9th {USENIX} Symposium on Networked Systems Design and Implementation ({NSDI} 12)*, 2012, pp. 15–28.

4. N. Maurer and M. Wolfthal, *Netty in action*. Manning Publications New York, 2016.

5. Q. Anderson, *Storm Real-time Processing Cookbook*. Packt Publishing Ltd, 2013.

6. P. Hunt, M. Konar, F. P. Junqueira, and B. Reed, "ZooKeeper: Wait-free Coordination for Internet-scale Systems," in *USENIX Annual Technical Conference*, 2010, vol. 8, p. 9.

7. P. Carbone, A. Katsifodimos, S. Ewen, V. Markl, S. Haridi, and K. Tzoumas, "Apache flink: Stream and batch processing in a single engine," *Bulletin of the IEEE Computer Society Technical Committee on Data Engineering*, vol. 36, no. 4, 2015.

8. S. Kulkarni *et al.*, "Twitter heron: Stream processing at scale," in *Proceedings of the 2015 ACM SIGMOD International Conference on Management of Data*, 2015, pp. 239–250.

9. W. P. Bejeck and N. Narkhede, *Kafka streams in action*. Manning Publications Co., 2018.

10. J. Kreps, N. Narkhede, and J. Rao, "Kafka: A distributed messaging system for log processing," in *Proceedings of the NetDB*, 2011.

11. A. Paszke *et al.*, "Pytorch: An imperative style, high-performance deep learning library," *arXiv preprint arXiv:1912.01703*, 2019.

12. C. Widanage *et al.*, "High performance data engineering everywhere," in *2020 IEEE International Conference on Smart Data Services (SMDS)*, 2020: IEEE, pp. 122–132.

13. E. Gabriel *et al.*, "Open MPI: Goals, concept, and design of a next generation MPI implementation," in *European Parallel Virtual Machine/ Message Passing Interface Users' Group Meeting*, 2004: Springer, pp. 97–104.

14. B. Hernández *et al.*, "Performance Evaluation of Python Based Data Analytics Frameworks in Summit: Early Experiences," in *Smoky Mountains Computational Sciences and Engineering Conference*, 2020: Springer, pp. 366–380.

15. J. Sanders and E. Kandrot, *CUDA by example: an introduction to general-purpose GPU programming*. Addison-Wesley Professional, 2010.

16. P. Shamis *et al.*, "UCX: an open source framework for HPC network APIs and beyond," in *2015 IEEE 23rd Annual Symposium on High-Performance Interconnects*, 2015: IEEE, pp. 40–43.

Fault Tolerance

Fault tolerance is a necessity in large-scale data processing systems. In this chapter, we will look at why we need to handle faults, the techniques available to support failure handling, and the trade-off between them. We will start with a general discussion on faults in distributed systems and narrow our discussion to batch and streaming data processing systems.

Dependable Systems and Failures

A computer consists of many parts: a motherboard, central processing unit (CPU), random access memory (RAM), hard drives, graphic processing units, power units, and network interface cards. Some of these components can be built into a single circuit board. For example, the Ethernet network interface cards are included in most motherboards. Each component has a probability of failure that increases with its use. In large distributed systems, computer networks connect thousands of computers with additional hardware thrown into the mix, including network switches, cooling systems, and power systems. Owing to the number of hardware components involved in large-scale distributed computations, the probability of part failure during a computation only increases.

Software failures are equally evident in large distributed applications. This includes operating system issues, insufficient resources such as memory, hard disk space, or network resources, and even bugs in the software. Applications encounter software failures more often than hardware failures in the initial stages of production deployments due to undiscovered bugs and missed configurations.

With the increased probability of failures, applications working in distributed environments need mechanisms that can safeguard them. Distributed applications tend to encounter errors in a few components. These are called *partial failures*. Some components of the distributed application may be affected by the failure, and some may work properly. On the other hand, a nondistributed application can completely crash when it encounters an error, which are referred to as total failures.

We say a data processing application has failed when it cannot continue the computation it was designed to carry out. The cause of the failure is called the *fault*. The goal of fault-tolerant distributed data processing systems is to automatically recover from failures without affecting the overall system performance.

Fault Tolerance Is Not Free

Making applications work amid failures comes at a cost of performance and resources. It is observed that the more protected the application is from faults, the slower it will be, as well as requiring more resources. Developers often make compromises in terms of performance versus failure recovery. If a failure occurs once or twice a year, should we be making thousands of runs of an application 20 percent slower while spending more money on the resources? The answer can be a definite yes in some situations, but there can be ways to mitigate such failures without compromising on performance and resources.

It is almost impossible to develop distributed applications that can work in every failure scenario. Practical systems implement mechanisms to lower the probability of loss to businesses by handling the most probable failure cases. Application developers and administrators need to be aware of these limitations and devise mechanisms to safeguard against issues that are not covered by the systems. For example, the Hadoop file system uses replication to keep data safe in case of hard disk failures. If a replication factor of three is used and all three of the hard disks containing the same data fail at the same time, the data will be lost. To avoid this, the replication factor can be increased to four, but that does not solve the problem of four hard disks failing all at once. When the replication factor is increased, the cluster will require more hard disks, possibly more machines, and will be slow in writing operations.

Data storage and management is the first piece when applying data analytics, while data processing is the second. For most practical applications, handling failures at the data storage is more critical than at the processing steps. For an analytics application, if a failure happens at a processing step, the application can be executed again from the beginning or from a known state if the data it worked on is kept untouched. If a set of data records are lost from a file system or a database, it may be hard to recover them unless there are backups.

There are many methods available to recover from failures depending upon the type of system. A distributed data processing application can have multiple processes running in various nodes of a cluster. Some of these processes are spawned for managing the applications, while others do the actual computations. If an application has one process for managing the cluster and 1,000 worker processes for computations, the probability of worker process failure is much higher. Owing to the functionality of management processes and computations being different, applications need to employ a variety of techniques to handle failures when they occur. Nowadays data processing frameworks are converging toward a template set of fault handling techniques in practice. We will focus on these widely used techniques for current systems.

Dependable Systems

Fault tolerance is closely related to the concept of dependable systems [1]. Dependability is associated with four properties:

- **Availability**—Readiness of the system to use at any given time.
- **Reliability**—How long the system can run without failing.
- **Safety**—Avoiding catastrophic or adverse events. For example, a system controlling an airplane should never fail.
- **Maintainability**—How easy it is to bring a system that fails back to working order.

Availability and reliability are closely related, but there is a subtle difference. If a system crashes for a small period every day, it is highly available but unreliable. If a system needs to be taken out of service for a month for maintenance but otherwise never crashes, it is reliable but not available.

There are metrics associated with hardware that show their probability of failure.

- Mean time to failure (MTTF) is the average time until a part fails.
- Mean time to repair (MTTR) is the average time to repair a failed part.
- Mean time between failures (MTBF) is the expected time between two failures of a repairable system. A component fails, it is replaced (MTTR), and then the component again fails (MTTF). $MTBF = MTTR + MTTF$.

Each hardware part has these values specified. When building systems if these numbers are low (i.e., more failures), we should take more precautions at the software level to mitigate failures. A good example is a Hadoop cluster made of mechanical hard disk drives versus one made of SSDs. If SSDs are used, it may be possible to apply a replication factor of 2, while with HDDs we should consider a factor of 3 or more. The usage patterns of hardware also determine how likely they will fail. If a CPU or a hard disk is used infrequently, its probability of failure is low compared to a CPU or hard disk that is used all the time.

Failures

Before delving into the details of fault recovery methods, it is important to understand what type of failures are commonly seen in data analytics systems. Depending on the nature of the fault, they are generally classified as transient, intermittent, or permanent. A transient fault occurs once and never shows up again. They are very hard to find and diagnose. An intermittent fault can occur from time to time. Most intermittent failures are due to concurrent resource access to shared resources. A permanent fault persists until the malfunctioning parts are replaced. These last are the easiest types of faults to detect. They typically imply something like a process crash or a node crash due to hardware failure.

In general, there are two main types of failures seen in distributed systems: crash faults and Byzantine faults. The data analytics systems only deal with crash faults, so we will only discuss Byzantine faults briefly for completeness of our discussion. Crash faults can occur due to software bugs or hardware failures. We will not consider catastrophic events such as data center failures (i.e., power outages) in this section as they are mostly relevant to databases that span multiple data centers.

Process Failures

Process failures are common in data analytics systems mostly due to bugs in applications or frameworks. In production applications, these bugs are seen in execution paths that occur rarely due to input data and environmental changes. Because of this, they are not detected in common tests and occur in real production scenarios infrequently.

A bug in a program can be due to a coding error or a configuration issue. For example, the code may be written to expect an integer in a data field, and there can be a string in that field on rare occasions causing the program to fail. A common configuration error in large data applications is related to insufficient memory allocations. Applications can demand different amounts of memory for different datasets. A good example is a distributed join operation where the number of output records from the join depends on the data distribution of the input datasets. A join operation can produce 10 times as much data as the input datasets or 1/10th as much data. If the large output case occurs rarely and we did not program or configure the application to handle it, the application can run out of memory easily at runtime. In most cases, it is impossible to recover from these faults without any effects on the data processing. To recover, we need to fix the application and restart it.

Network Failures

Network failures are not as common in modern data centers but can still occur nonetheless. They are especially hard to detect and recover from in distributed data processing applications. There are true network failures that stem from hardware issues, or there can be cases where it seems like only the network has failed. The latter takes place when processes or nodes become too slow to respond.

Two major hardware issues cause network failures. They are link failures and device failures. A link failure is defined as a lost connection between two networking interfaces. When one occurs, two nodes in the cluster may not be able to communicate while others can communicate properly. A device failure is the malfunctioning of a network device such as a switch or router. These can happen due to failure of hardware, power, or rarely software. When they do occur, the effects are visible to a larger number of nodes.

Node Failures

A node failure takes place when hardware issues make the node completely or partially unusable. If an important piece of hardware such as a memory module or a CPU fails, the node may completely collapse. In case of a single hard disk failure among many in a node, the node can continue to work, and we may be able to replace the hard drive without restarting it. In the case of hard disk failure, depending on how the application is configured, it may fail.

Software such as Kubernetes or Slurm that manage the cluster can detect node failures. In a distributed setting, it is harder to know whether a node or its network failed, as it would report the same error to other nodes trying to reach it.

Byzantine Faults

Crash faults are attributed to unintentional bugs in software or hardware failures. The distributed processes may not respond in a reasonable time or even at all. But in a crash fault, they will not act as a rogue agent inserting invalid data into the network. A Byzantine fault is when one or more nodes of a cluster start changing or forging data. Because these nodes are parts of the cluster, another node cannot figure out whether the data is correct or not.

Byzantine faults are harder to detect and solve. If a system is designed to protect against them, it can demand much more resources than a normal one. Data analytics applications are executed inside secure networks of organizations with many firewalls between them and the public. The probability of their being hijacked to act as rogue agents is extremely low. So, data analytics systems do not consider Byzantine faults as a possibility and do not implement measures to handle them.

Failure Models

As we have seen, there are many types of errors that can lead to failure in a distributed system. Even though different hardware and software can break down, these cases are visible to a distributed application differently. For example, both a process crash and a compute node crash might be designated by other processes solely as a process crash. A malfunctioning network and a simply slow process may produce network timeouts. Because of this, the failures can be classified to indicate what is observed by the distributed system. One such classification has the following failure models:

- **Crash failure**—A server that was working properly comes to a halt prematurely.

- **Omission failure**—There are two types of omission failures: receive omissions and send omissions. Sent messages may not be correctly received in receive omissions. Messages are not sent that should have been sent in send omissions.

- **Timing failures**—Outputs are provided but outside of a required period.

- **Response failures**—Outputs are incorrect.

- **Arbitrary failures**—Any failure can occur, sometimes even unnoticed.

In data processing systems, we do not see response failures. All other failure models can be viewed in data processing systems.

Failure Detection

To recover from failures, a distributed data application first needs to detect them. When a fault happens, there are faulty and nonfaulty processes in the system. The nonfaulty ones need to figure out what processes are at fault. In practice, a form of ping messaging is used to detect whether a process is alive. Ping messages use a time-based approach for detecting failures. In some cases, the processes send ping messages to a controlling entity in regular time intervals. If this controller does not receive a ping message within this period, it marks the process as failed. This is not an exceptionally reliable way of detecting a failure, as timeouts can occur even without failures. For example, the process may be so busy doing a computation it may not be able to send the ping request on time. To avoid such false positives, applications can wait for multiple ping message omissions, or they can send a message to ensure the process is alive.

Another way to detect failures is through regular communication. If an error occurs when a process tries to communicate with another, applications can mark the process that gave the error as failed. Again, network slowness and busy processes can derail this approach as well. Also, this approach assumes there are frequent communications between distributed data applications.

A combination of ping messages and normal messages are often used for detecting a failure. If either of these cases occurs, the application can try to figure out whether the process failed.

Another issue is to distinguish between a node and network failures. To a correctly working node, these can appear to be the same in a faulty node. In such cases, instead of one process deciding the fault, many processes can try to contact the fault server to get a better idea of the underlying error.

Independent monitoring by a third-party application such as a resource manager is a commonly used method to detect failures. For example, in case of a process failure the resource manager which started the process will detect the event immediately. The application can listen to events from the resource manager to detect the failure.

Recovering from Faults

Most applications choose the simplest form of fault recovery, which is to restart the application. We have all experienced this method for both software and hardware. Restarting an application from the beginning is acceptable once. But if the application takes hours or days to run, restarting it from the beginning can waste valuable resources. Also, restarting from the beginning is not an option for streaming applications that process continuous streams of data, as it can lead to a large number of messages being queued while the application restarts. This in turn leads to large latencies that are a burden to the applications.

Ideally, we would like our applications to recover from failures as if nothing happened or without any side effects. Some common side effects from failures are an increase in time to complete, increased latency, decrease in throughput, and data loss. In practice, data analytics frameworks impose limitations on what type of recovery is possible and its parameters. This limits our recovery options, so we need to find a balance between the ideal recovery and what is possible. The fewer side effects the application has from failures, the more resources, and hence the more money it costs to run.

Batch and streaming systems are the main branches of data processing systems. Expectations and requirements of fault recovery are different for streaming and batch applications. In batch applications, recovery from a failure always means without any loss of data. Otherwise, the accuracy of the batch application results may be incorrect. Streaming applications allow more lenient forms of recovery, because they can tolerate data loss to some extent. Different batch systems tend to use similar techniques for handling failures while streaming processing systems are also converging on a similar set of techniques to recover from failures.

Recovery Methods

There are two major approaches used to recover from failures in data processing systems: checkpointing and replication. Checkpointing saves the state of the application from time to time. If an incident occurs, this saved state can be used to restart the application without going back to the beginning. Replication uses additional resources to run a copy of the processes that contain a valid state of the process that they mirror. In case of failure, the replicated instance can take over for the failed instance. Since the replicated processes are already running, the time to recover can be minimized. Owing to the additional resources needed in replication, it is not a popular option among data processing frameworks.

In general, fault recovery is closely associated with the application state. When an error happens, we can assume one or more processes of the distributed application is going to fail. The state stored in the volatile storage (memory) of these processes is lost. If we have the complete state of the failed processes right before the failure occurs, we may be able to start them at a point before the error. This is easier said than done in practice due to the size of the state that needs to be saved and the fact that there are messages inflight between processes that can be considered as part of the state. When we start an application, it has a program counter that points to which instruction it is executing and variables in the memory that hold values. The state of a program at a given moment in time is defined by these two things. If the program does not change the outside state such as files, and if we have a way to reconstruct its state, we can go back to an earlier safe point and restart the execution.

Application state captures a broader set of runtime information. Depending on the programming model, different parts of the application state can be embedded into the structure of the program and user-defined variables. Two of the most popular models in writing large-scale applications are the BSP and dataflow programs. In a BSP program, most of the state management is given to the user. Because dataflow programs model the application as a graph, part of the state is captured in the graph.

Stateless Programs

There are many instances where the stateless nature of programs is exploited to develop robust applications resilient to failure. As discussed earlier, we need application state to recover from failures. If a program has no state associated with it, it can be restarted after a failure without any side effects to the system.

In most cases, by stateless programs we mean programs that do not keep state in the main memory. Such programs keep the state in a fault-tolerant distributed storage such as a distributed file system or a database. This allows the program to be started from the last saved state in the storage. We can see this approach used in some components of distributed frameworks to provide fault tolerance.

When discussing data analytics, the term *stateless* appears especially in the streaming dataflow programs. In some situations, it is possible to develop dataflow applications without keeping the state at the user level. This does not necessarily mean there is no state associated with the program, only that it is embedded in the dataflow graph.

Batch Systems

Batch systems are required to process all the data available. It is hard to define batch applications that process data partially in case of failures. Because of this, a dependable batch system must process the complete dataset amid failures. If it does not, the output may be incorrect.

Batch systems can choose how far back they want to recompute if a failure happens. This decision depends on the failure rate of the system and the importance of completing the computation on time. One extreme approach a batch application can use is to run two (or many) instances simultaneously. Given that these application instances run in nonoverlapping computers, if one fails due to hardware failure, the other can still succeed. This is an easier-to-understand approach with no effect to the application performance but requires double the resources.

Streaming Systems

Streaming systems are more sensitive to failures than batch systems due to latency requirements. The purpose of streaming systems is to process data as it arrives and produce results within a reasonable time. Because of the time-sensitive nature, streaming systems must recover faster. Because data is in flight and can be lost permanently amidst failures, they must provide guarantees on data processing.

There are many streaming applications where it is acceptable to lose a few messages every so often. Furthermore, stringent processing guarantees are expensive in terms of overhead for normal message processing latency. Because of this, streaming systems work with a range of processing guarantees amid failures.

Processing Guarantees

Stream processing engines in general provide three types of processing guarantees. They are "exactly once," "at least once," and "no guarantee." These guarantees are related to the fault recovery methods implemented by the system, which have been categorized as precise recovery, rollback recovery, and gap recovery.

In precise recovery, there is no evidence of a failure afterward except some increase in latency; this provides "exactly once" semantics. With rollback recovery, the information flowing through the system is not lost, but there can be an effect on the system other than an increase in latency. For example, information may be processed more than once when a failure happens. That means rollback recovery can provide "at least once" semantics. With gap recovery, the loss of information is expected and provides no guarantees about messages being processed. In practice, there are a surprisingly large number of streaming applications that can work amid few message losses once in a while.

There are several methods of achieving processing guarantees in streaming environments. The more traditional approaches are to use active-backup nodes, passive backup nodes, upstream backup, or amnesia. Amnesia provides gap recovery with the least overhead. The other three approaches can be used to offer both precise recovery and rollback recovery. All these methods assume that there are free nodes in the system that can take over the responsibility of a failed task.

Before providing processing guarantees, systems should be able to recover from faults. If a system cannot recover automatically from a fault while in operation, it must be manually maintained in a large cluster environment, which is not a practical approach. Almost all the modern distributed processing systems provide the ability to recover automatically from faults like node failures and network partitions.

Role of Cluster Resource Managers

Cluster resource managers play an integral part in providing for distributed applications to be fault tolerant. They monitor the available resources, as well as applications running on them for possible runtime issues. Also, when failures crop up, they allocate new resources for the applications to use.

Some resources can encounter partial failures that are harder to detect. Partial disk failures rank high among these. In normal circumstances, resource managers can periodically check whether all the disks are working and mark those that are not as failed. Sometimes hard disk failures are only visible to applications writing to specific parts of it. In those cases, the resource manager may not detect the failure by itself. The only way it can do so is when the task fails multiple times on the same resource. At that point it can try to schedule the task on another resource. This is called *blacklisting*.

Resource managers monitor applications for excessive resource usage and can terminate parts of the application that has such usage. A good example is excessive use of memory due to programming and configuration errors or trying to use excessive CPUs than what is being allocated to the application. When a network partition happens, resource managers must intervene to localize the applications to the reachable areas of the network.

So far, our discussion assumes there is enough working nodes in a cluster when a failure happens so that an application can continue. If multiple nodes fail or a network switch has issues, we may have to wait until the cluster is repaired.

Checkpointing

Checkpointing is a commonly used mechanism in data analytics systems to recover from failures without any data loss. In short, a checkpointing application saves a snapshot of its state to stable storage regularly. In case of failure, the application goes back to an earlier checkpointed state using the saved information. This allows it to restart from a point other than the beginning. This is an example of rollback recovery.

To roll back to an earlier state, this state must be a globally consistent one. Otherwise, the application would be giving incorrect answers or would not work at all after the rollback. If the clocks on different computers are perfectly synchronized, they could take snapshots of the state at precisely the same time, avoiding any communications as they do. But in practical systems, clocks are far from synchronized, and we cannot rely on them to make such decisions.

State

We can think of a program as an entity that changes its state by taking certain actions. In a serial program, these actions consist of internal computations. In a distributed system, they include message sending and receiving. At any given moment, the state of a process is defined by all the actions it has taken previously. In a distributed application, the local state is the state of a single process.

Consistent Global State

Global state is the collective state of all processes plus the states of the communication channels between them. In a distributed system, it is not possible to start from any global state as there are message dependencies involved. A global state from which we can restart an application is called a *consistent global state*. The first step in a checkpointing implementation is to find these globally consistent states.

A consistent global state can be taken only when the system is running without any failures. Furthermore, a globally consistent state cannot include events that have no origin. Since internal events happen within a process, they always have a cause-effect relationship. The previous rule applies to messages between systems. In a globally consistent state, there cannot be a "message received" event without a "message sent" event. This is illustrated in Figure 9-1. In this picture, two processes called P1 and P2 take snapshots at time t1 and t2, respectively. P1 sends a message M to P2. The dotted line shows where the snapshot is taken at each process. On the left, process P2's state includes the receive event of the message but the sending event of the message is not included in the P1's state, leading to an inconsistent global state. On the right, the receiving event is not included in P2's state.

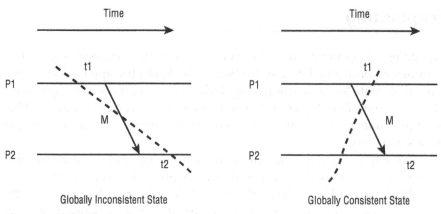

Figure 9-1: Globally consistent state

We can name a set of requirements needed to achieve a globally consistent state.

- Any message that is sent by a process before recording its snapshot must be recorded in the global snapshot.

- Any message that is sent by a process after recording its snapshot must not be recorded in the global snapshot.

- A process must record its snapshot before processing a message that was sent by another process after recording its snapshot.

Uncoordinated Checkpointing

Distributed systems can choose between coordinated checkpointing or uncoordinated checkpointing. With uncoordinated checkpointing, the processes take snapshots of their state independently of others. If the state of one process depends on the state of another, this can cause a failure scenario where a series of cascading rollbacks lead it all the way back to the initial state of the application, wasting time and resources. This is called the *domino effect*. Let's examine this phenomenon with an example. In Figure 9-2, two processes P1 and P2 take checkpoints denoted by C without any coordination. There are messages sent between these processes as well. Now say P2 crashes after taking $C2_2$ checkpoint. First, it tries to go back to $C2_2$ checkpoint. After this checkpoint, P2 is expecting message m3 from P1. Because of this, P1 needs to go to $C2_1$ checkpoint. When P1 goes to this checkpoint, it expects message m2 from P2, so P2 needs to go to the $C1_2$ checkpoint. Now P2 expects message m1 from P1, and P1 needs to go to the initial state to send this message, rendering any previous progress moot.

As we can clearly see, uncoordinated checkpointing is inefficient as there is no synchronization between the processes. When recovering, it can send the application back many checkpoints. Also, when a failure happens, the algorithm needs to figure out a valid state by restoring through multiple checkpoints, which can be expensive.

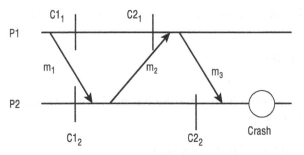

Figure 9-2: Domino effect

If there is no communication between the parallel processes, uncoordinated checkpointing works perfectly. All the complexities come from the fact that processes depend on each other for completing computations.

Coordinated Checkpointing

In data analytics systems, coordinated checkpointing is more common. This allows applications to create a globally consistent state. Various distributed parts of the application must come to a consistent state before they start the checkpointing. To achieve this, there are many algorithms available.

Chandy-Lamport Algorithm

The Chandy-Lamport algorithm was one of the earliest algorithms developed to achieve a globally consistent checkpoint in a general distributed system. The Chandy-Lamport [2] algorithm assumes certain properties in the system.

- Communication channels between processes are first in first out (FIFO) ordered.

- Communication channels are reliable, and messages are not duplicated.

- There are no failures in the system.

- There is a communication channel between any two processes in the system.

All these assumptions are true for a data processing application running inside a data center with a TCP/IP communication between them. The algorithm works by sending markers among different processes that indicate them to a checkpoint. This marker contains a token that identifies the checkpoint. For a given checkpoint there is a process called the *observer* that starts it. This process sends the initial marker to all the processes. When a process sees a marker for the first time, it takes a certain set of actions, and when it sees a marker again, it takes another set of actions. The following is a description of how the algorithm functions:

1. Marker sending rule for process *i*

   a. Records its state

   b. For each outgoing channel on which a marker has not been sent, sends a marker with the same token

2. On receiving marker for process *j from process k*

   a. If state is not recorded:

      i.   Records the state of the channel from *k to j* as empty

      ii. Follows the marker sending rule

      iii. Start recording messages from all other processes except *k*

   b. If state is recorded:

      i.   Finalize the state of channel from *k* to *j* and record it.

3. Snapshot

   a. All processes have received a marker (recorded state) and all processes have received a marker from all other channels (recorded channel states).

   b. Use a central server to create the global snapshot from the local snapshots.

The Chandy-Lamport algorithm is designed for a general distributed computing system. In pure form, it is an expensive operation as it requires every process to send messages to every other process as well as saving channel states. There are other algorithms designed to work under different assumptions. Other programming models, especially with batch data processing systems, present opportunities to greatly simplify achieving a global consistent state.

Batch Systems

In batch systems that work according to the bulk synchronous paradigm (BSP) or Dataflow, there are natural globally synchronized points. These points are visible when the program is created. Batch data processing systems use communications that involve multiple parallel tasks. These types of communication are called *collective operations*. Unlike in peer-to-peer messaging, when a collective communication operation finishes, it can be viewed as a synchronizing point for the tasks involved. As a result, we can checkpoint at these points without relying on another algorithm to synchronize the processes.

Let's take the popular shuffle operation occurring in dataflow systems as an example. A shuffle operation involves multiple source task instances, and one instance can send messages to all the receiving task instances. When this operation finishes at each parallel process, we can guarantee that there will be no more messages related to this operation in the system.

```
// read a set of files from the folder
DataSet d = readDataset("fileFolder");
d.partition(); // alltoall operation
```

When the AllToAll operation finishes, it creates a globally consistent state across all the parallel workers. If we create a checkpoint at this point, it will be consistent. This is shown in Figure 9-3.

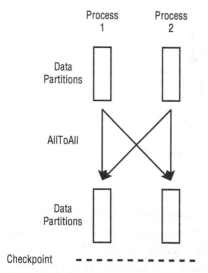

Figure 9-3: Program synchronization point

In this case, we are taking messaging one level up from peer-to-peer messaging to collective communications. Once the AllToAll operation completes, it receives all the messages relevant to that operation. If everyone checkpoints after AllToAll operation is done, no one will receive messages that were not included as a send event in the global state.

To handle a failure while taking a snapshot, processes can contact a central server to commit the checkpoint. If some workers do not contact the central server within a given period, the program can assume the checkpoint failed. When all the processes contact the manager about successful saving of the checkpoint locally, the manager can commit the checkpoint as a valid one. This is shown in Figure 9-4.

Batch frameworks take these to their advantage to avoid complicated messaging and saving of channel states.

When to Checkpoint?

An application must decide when to checkpoint and what to save as checkpoint data. The time to checkpoint can be controlled by the user or the framework. In practice, we have seen that batch applications give the control to the user, while streaming applications automatically checkpoint with user-configurable parameters.

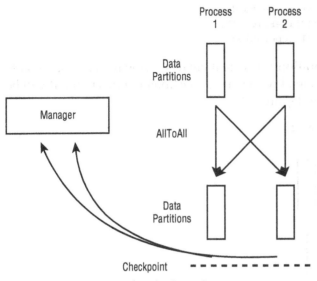

Figure 9-4: Program synchronization point

When we configure the checkpointing, it is important to keep a balance between performance and frequency. Consider an iterative application with a `for` loop that runs for 10 iterations. Each iteration of the algorithm takes about 10 minutes to run and produces a large amount of data. Without any checkpointing application, it takes 100 minutes to run. Now assume checkpointing this data takes about 2 minutes. If we save state every iteration, the application will add 20 minutes because of the checkpointing. In a failure scenario, it will take at most 132 minutes to complete because it must go back one iteration.

If we save the state only at the halfway mark of iterations, it will add only two extra minutes. The downside is that we need to go to the beginning or the halfway mark in case of a failure. So, in a failure scenario, the application can take up to 152 minutes to complete. Now if we run this application every day and a failure occurs only once a year, it may be better to choose the halfway mark to save a snapshot. If failures occur often and we cannot afford to run the application for 152 minutes, we can choose the more frequent checkpointing.

Snapshot Data

One approach to implement checkpointing is to save everything in memory to a fault-tolerant storage such as a distributed file system. Saving the complete memory into disk can be a time-consuming I/O-intensive process. Also, we need to keep in mind that not everything in memory is part of the state and that some data in the main memory can take up more space than when we save them to disk. So, this naïve approach can lead to inefficient checkpointing.

Applications choose the minimum information required to start the program from the time the checkpoint happens. Usually two types of information are saved:

- **Framework-level information**—This includes things like checkpoint IDs and internal variables.

- **User data**—This includes state of the operators as well as data. In practice, most frameworks avoid saving communication channel states.

We cannot save the checkpoint data to local hard disks in case the complete node becomes unavailable. As such, we need to save the checkpoint data to distributed storage that functions despite failures, such as a distributed file system or a database.

Streaming Systems

There are many streaming systems available that can process streaming data in real time. Message brokers are an integral part of streaming systems where they act as sources for the processing system. Streaming systems model a computation as a dataflow graph, and streaming data flows through this graph. The computations at the nodes of the graph are user defined.

Case Study: Apache Storm

Apache Storm was one of the first open source streaming frameworks that introduced failure recovery with few message processing guarantees. With Storm, applications can choose best-effort, at-least-once, or exactly-once processing guarantees. It uses an acknowledgment mechanism to keep track of the messages that are fully processed. If a message provides a failed ACK (acknowledgment) or the ACK does not come in a specified period (time out), Storm will replay the message through the dataflow graph.

Figure 9-5 shows the Storm architecture, where it has a cluster management process called Nimbus and a set of worker processes called supervisors. The communication between Nimbus and supervisors happens through ZooKeeper, which is a fault-tolerant service that supplies functions such as distributed synchronization and storage.

Storm streaming applications are programmed as a graph with nodes having user code and links standing for communications between the nodes. From this user-programmed graph, a physical graph is created at runtime according to the parallelism that is placed on compute resources and executed in an event-driven fashion using the supervisors. There are designated sources called *spouts* that produce the data. Every message inserted into the rest of the graph by the

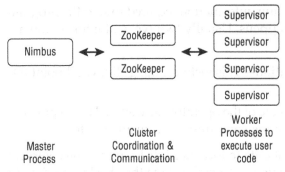

Figure 9-5: Apache Storm architecture

source can have an ID. The remaining graph nodes are compute tasks called *bolts* that take in messages coming from its links and produce messages in turn.

Message Tracking

The sources in Apache Storm need to keep messages in memory until they are acknowledged as having been processed successfully. Once a message is acknowledged, the source can release it from the memory. Upon arrival of a message, a task can produce one or more messages. These new messages are children of the originating message. The child messages can go to other tasks and spawn more child messages. This process creates a tree structure. Storm tracks this tree and determines when a tree for a message completes. After the tree is finished, the source is notified that the message is done processing. At this point, the source can release the message.

Figure 9-6 shows this process, where there is a source and two tasks. The figure shows the actual message transfer between the instances of the tasks. A message m originates from the source and is sent to the first task instance. Source needs to keep track of m in memory or at a message broker until the acknowledgment arrives. Upon processing of message m at task 2, two messages called p and q are produced and sent to two instances of task 2. Task 2 is the last task. After it processes the messages, it sends acknowledgment for p and q. Once acknowledgments for p and q arrive, m is acknowledged. At this point, we can stop tracking m at the source. If a failure happens at any of these steps, a failed ack will be sent. Failures are detected as timeouts to acknowledge. In Storm acknowledgments flow through separate tasks called *ackers*, and we omit that from our figure to simplify the process.

When a message fails at a downstream task in the dataflow graph, Storm will replay the message from the source. This means the upstream tasks can process the same message twice. Because of this, messages can be processed more than once and hence the at-least-once processing guarantee. If the acknowledgment mechanism is turned off, the messages can be lost should a failure transpire.

So, it is a best effort with no guarantees on message processing. Since source tasks can also fail, Storm needs a message source that can replay messages such as Apache Kafka or Apache Pulsar to provide the at-least-once processing guarantees. This design can lead to many acknowledgments being produced by the system for applications with wide dependencies.

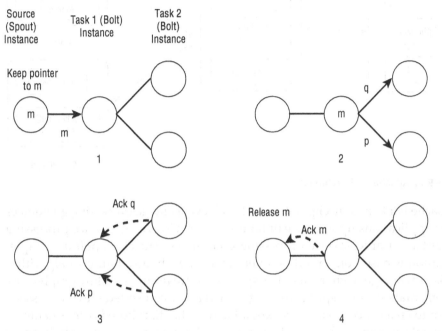

Figure 9-6: Apache Storm acknowledgments

Failure Recovery

When a failure happens in a worker, Storm restarts the worker. If a node failure should occur, Storm assigns the tasks of the node to new nodes. All this is done by the Nimbus process. Nimbus is stateless, and its state is kept in Apache ZooKeeper, which acts as a fault-tolerant key-value store. Should Nimbus fail, it can restart with the state saved in the ZooKeeper. This stateless design allows Nimbus to be fault tolerant.

Case Study: Apache Flink

Apache Flink [3] is another popular streaming engine. Flink streaming applications are developed as dataflow graphs. We can use a typed Java data transformation API to program an application. Figure 9-7 shows the Flink architecture. It consists of a `JobManager` and set of `TaskManagers`. The `JobManager` acts as a coordinator for jobs, while `TaskManagers` execute the application logic. `JobManager` instances consist of a `CheckpointCoordinator` that helps with handling faults.

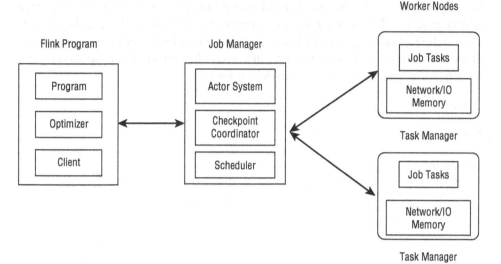

Figure 9-7: Apache Flink architecture

Apache Flink uses checkpointing [4] to achieve message processing guarantees for its applications upon notice of failures. It provides exactly once processing guarantees or at least once processing guarantees. The checkpointing implementation is based on a modified version of the Chandy-Lamport algorithm to take advantage of characteristics specific to streaming dataflow graphs. The implementation uses a special message called a *barrier* inserted into the message stream to create a consistent checkpoint across the distributed components.

The data stream needs to be checkpointed at a source external to Flink. There are message brokers such as Apache Kafka and Apache Pulsar that possess this capability to checkpoint and replay messages. Flink only checkpoints the state of the operators and does not need to checkpoint the channel states.

Checkpointing

The Flink checkpoints are aided by a manager program that handles the two-phase commit protocol when checkpointing. Barrier messages are inserted into the sources by the JobManager. In this case, JobManager is the observer process of the Chandy-Lamport algorithm. These barriers carry the checkpoint ID. When a barrier message reaches a dataflow node in the graph, it will checkpoint its state to a permanent storage. State includes user data along with system data. This is the pre-commit stage.

Once the barriers reach the end of the dataflow graph, they inform the Job-Manager. At this point, the state of the operators is saved in persistent storage. When JobManager receives messages from all the leaf nodes of the graph, it completes the checkpoint as a valid one. The state back ends are configurable with Flink supporting storages such as a file system (HDFS) or a RocksDB database. Figure 9-8 shows this process. JobManager sends the barrier message, and when the sources receive this message, they checkpoint at the message queue and pass the barrier to the downstream tasks. In the second diagram, the sources acknowledge the manager with the queue positions, and the barriers reach the second task. These tasks save the state to the stable storage and forward the barrier to the third task. Additionally, the second task acknowledges the manager about the checkpoint. Once the barrier reaches the last task, it saves its state

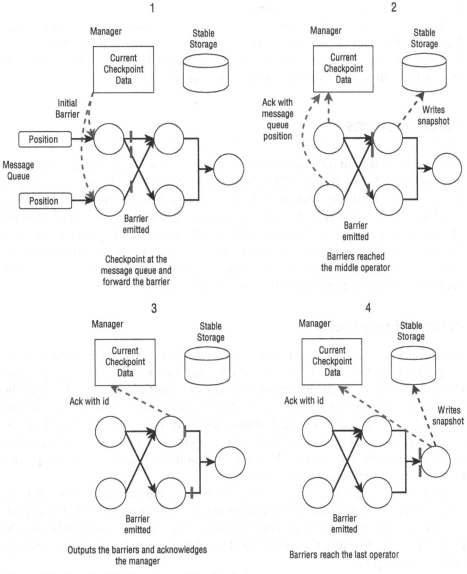

Figure 9-8: Apache Flink barriers and checkpointing

to stable storage and acknowledges the manager. At this point, the manager gets ACKs from all the tasks, and it can commit the checkpoint as a valid one.

If the system fails at any of these points, the ongoing checkpoint will be invalidated, and the system will go to the earlier valid checkpoint.

Failure Recovery

When a failure happens, the tasks are restarted with the state from the latest successful checkpoint. The sources start reading the data from the last checkpointed location of the message broker.

Flink does not store messages (data) and instead only stores the user state. As such, it has a low overhead compared to the message tracking scheme used by Apache Storm. Furthermore, Apache Storm needs to keep track of each message, while Flink only tracks the barrier messages.

Batch Systems

Batch systems do not have a method of message processing guarantee as they process datasets as a whole. Either it processes the whole dataset, or it fails to do so. Unlike streaming systems, where it can take a best effort to recover from a failure, a batch system cannot recover without restoring the complete state. The state can be large, and having active backups is not an option. Because of this, they must use some form of checkpointing to recover from failures. Owing to the nature of parallel communication involved in batch systems, there are natural synchronization points the program can agree on.

Iterative Programs

A program can have local iterations or parallel iterations. Local iterations are simple loops that work only on the data from the local process. The parallel iterations involve synchronization of data from multiple processes inside the loop, as shown in Figure 9-9. We have data that is updated inside the loop and data that is not updated. The global updates are done using distributed operators that synchronize data in multiple computers. This updated data is used in the next iteration until it ends. We can checkpoint at the end of the loop after this data synchronization has occurred.

An iterative program can have many loops before it terminates. Depending on the amount of work inside a single loop, it may be better to avoid checkpointing every iteration. In most practical applications, an assessment between the probability of failure and the cost of checkpointing is considered for determining when to checkpoint.

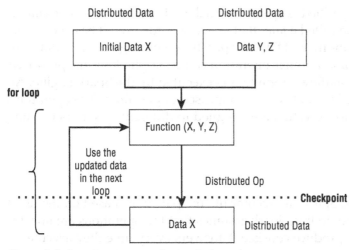

Figure 9-9: Iterative program checkpointing

Case Study: Apache Spark

Apache Spark uses a combination of checkpointing, recomputing, and write-ahead logs to achieve fault tolerance. Spark employs a driver program to control the distributed computations. This driver program submits computations to the cluster and waits for them to compute, as shown in Figure 9-10. It can send as many computations as needed. The computations are specified as a set of transformations on datasets. Spark RDD [5] is the data abstraction for general computing, and Spark DataSet is the table-based abstraction for structured data processing (SQL).

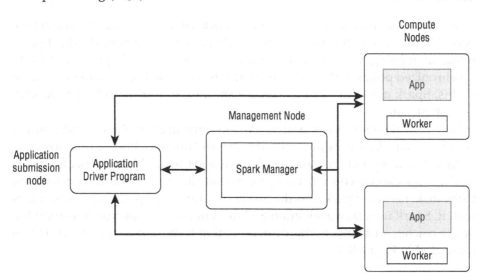

Figure 9-10: Apache Spark architecture

Computations are specified as operations on the data abstractions. For example, RDD has an operation called a *filter* that selects records from it based on some criteria and creates another RDD. An operation working on some data can produce more data, and another operation can be applied on this produced data. This creates a dataflow graph that is executed by the Spark engine. All data, whether it is RDD or datasets, is comprised of partitions. The operations are carried out on partitions that are assigned to different executors running in the cluster.

RDD Recomputing

When a failure arises, Spark can recompute the partitions based on the user-defined operations. To do this, Spark assumes that the operations are nonstochastic and that they produce consistent answers every time they execute on the same data. Also, it assumes operations are stateless and do not keep state outside of the Spark environment.

If an executor fails, the partitions assigned to it are lost. Spark can assign these partitions to other executors and run the computations again. This works well for jobs that have no dependencies to other datasets. If a calculation depends on partitions of other datasets that reside in different executors, Spark may need to recompute these data as well to reconstruct the lost partitions. This can easily roll back the application to the beginning, rendering the fault tolerance useless in terms of recomputing. As we have seen with the uncoordinated checkpoints, this method is susceptible to the domino effect.

Checkpointing

To avoid the domino effect, Spark allows users to checkpoint datasets so that they persist in the disk. In this way, a recalculation can proceed from the checkpoint rather than going back to the beginning. The checkpoints happen at globally synchronized points in the program, which is controlled by the driver. Because of this, Spark does not need to execute another algorithm to find a globally consistent state.

Let's look at how Spark persistence works with an example. The code shown next is a Spark Java program with the persist function. Persist functions can be used to checkpoint the data to stable storage (disk). When the persist call is made, Spark executes the dataflow graph inside its executors and saves the data to the disk. Because Spark uses the driver program, the operation synchronizes with it. Spark uses lazy evaluation and does not run the instructions until the driver reaches an action. In this case, the action is the persist command. This is illustrated in Figure 9-11.

```
JavaSparkContext sc = new JavaSparkContext(conf);
JavaRDD<String> input = sc.textFile(prefix, parallel);
JavaRDD<String> filtered = input.filter(filterFn);
// persist the data to the stable storage
JavaRDD<String> persisted = filtered.persist(StorageLevel. MEMORY_AND_DISK());
// use the persisted values
persisted.map(mapFn);
```

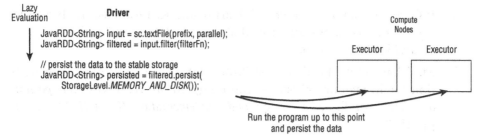

Figure 9-11: Spark persistence

If an error occurs in the cluster while executing the functions after persisting, the driver program will retry the operations using the persisted data. Should the driver program fail, Spark cannot recover this application.

Recovery from Failures

In case of a failure, Spark will use the executors in different machines to resubmit the failed dataflow graphs. The program state is kept only at the driver program. The executors are stateless. So, if a calculation fails at an executor, the whole calculation can be started from the last checkpoint.

Summary

In this chapter, we discussed common faults occurring in data processing systems as well as how to recover from them. We studied fault tolerance techniques used by several popular systems. Even though there are many algorithms available in the literature to recover from faults, the current systems take advantage of application characteristics to simplify the fault-tolerant mechanisms.

References

1. V. P. Nelson, "Fault-tolerant computing: Fundamental concepts," *Computer*, vol. 23, no. 7, pp. 19-25, 1990.

2. K. M. Chandy and L. Lamport, "Distributed snapshots: Determining global states of distributed systems," *ACM Transactions on Computer Systems (TOCS)*, vol. 3, no. 1, pp. 63-75, 1985.

3. P. Carbone, A. Katsifodimos, S. Ewen, V. Markl, S. Haridi, and K. Tzoumas, "Apache Flink: Stream and batch processing in a single engine," *Bulletin of the IEEE Computer Society Technical Committee on Data Engineering*, vol. 36, no. 4, 2015.

4. P. Carbone, G. Fóra, S. Ewen, S. Haridi, and K. Tzoumas, "Lightweight asynchronous snapshots for distributed dataflows," *arXiv preprint arXiv:1506.08603*, 2015.

5. M. Zaharia *et al.*, "Resilient distributed datasets: A fault-tolerant abstraction for in-memory cluster computing," in *9th {USENIX} Symposium on Networked Systems Design and Implementation ({NSDI} 12)*, 2012, pp. 15-28.

# CHAPTER 10

Performance and Productivity

As important as it is to know the technical intricacies of designing high-performance large-scale systems, it is equally important to understand how to quantify performance and find bottlenecks. In this chapter, we will look at different performance models, profiling techniques, and factors affecting them. Productivity goes hand in hand with performance, so we will dive into details such as the pros and cons of programming languages, libraries, and special hardware as well.

Performance Metrics

Understanding the performance of large-scale data-intensive applications is necessary to decide on the resource requirements of applications. The performance of a cluster is not the sum of its individual parts. There are metrics developed to measure the performance of hardware so we can specify the requirements to the vendors.

Furthermore, we need to measure the performance of our applications to see whether they are efficient in using the available resources. In a distributed setting, resources can be wasted easily, and finding issues is a labor-intensive process. There are standard metrics used by application developers to measure the performance of distributed parallel applications.

System Performance Metrics

There are metrics developed to measure the performance of clusters that run large-scale computations. We use these to find out the general capabilities of a cluster.

- **FLOPS**—Even though there is no single number that can accurately represent the performance of a computer system, floating-point operations per second (FLOPS, flops, or flop/s) have been used widely as a yardstick of computational performance. Top500,[1] for example, lists the world's best-performing computer systems sorted by their peak FLOPS. FLOPS are specified as double precision and single precision for 64-bit and 32-bit floating-point number operations.

- **Rmax and Rpeak**—When listing FLOPS, it is usually presented as two numbers: the theoretical maximum FLOPS and the maximum FLOPS achieved by a certain computational benchmark. These are commonly referred to as Rpeak and Rmax, respectively. Rmax is evaluated using the LINPACK [1] benchmark here.

- **Input/output operations per second (IOPS)**—IOPS (pronounced "eye-ops") is the amount of input/output operations a system can perform per second. IOPS are further divided into sequential and random IOPS. Sequential IOPS are usually far greater than the random IOPS of a system.

- **Performance/price**—With public clouds and large amounts of data, users are looking at more business-oriented performance metrics such as performance compared to the cost of the solution. For example, large-scale sorting performance can be thought of as how much money we need to spend for sorting 1 terabyte of data in a system.

Parallel Performance Metrics

When computations are split among parallel processes, we can define additional important metrics to evaluate the benefits of parallelization.

Speedup

If the total execution time of a serial program and its parallel version are T_1 and T_N, respectively, then speedup is defined as the ratio of serial to parallel time.

$$Speedup\,(S) = \frac{T_1}{T_N}$$

---

[1]https://www.top500.org/

We denote ideal speedup as $\frac{T_1}{N}$, thus giving a speedup of N for a parallel implementation running over N instances. A speedup less than ideal, i.e., less than $\frac{T_1}{N}$, is called *sublinear speedup*. Similarly, speedups greater than ideal are called *superlinear speedups*.

If an application continues to follow ideal speedup with increasing parallelism, it is said to scale linearly. Should the speedup diverge to suboptimal values, it is recognized as sublinear scaling. As illustrated in Figure 10-1, most parallel implementations aim to stay closer to linear scaling but typically fall back to sublinear performance with increasing parallelism. This is often due to overheads associated with communications in parallel computing.

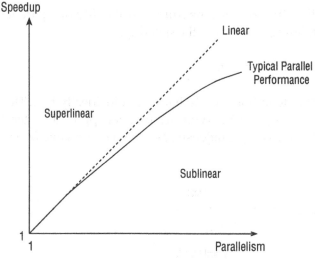

Figure 10-1: Parallel speedup

However, we can occasionally observe applications crossing the linear scaling threshold and obtaining superlinear scaling. While this may sound unrealistic, the main reason why this could happen is due to cache. When the problem domain is decomposed, chances are the data accesses can fit within a cache line leading to better utilization of cache. This would result in less time for operations than estimated when data accesses were to happen through main memory and thus giving superlinear speedup.

Strong Scaling

If parallelism is increased while keeping the total input size constant, it leads to less work for each worker. This type of scaling is called *strong scaling*, and it results in speedup graphs like the one shown in Figure 10-1. This could still lead to diminishing returns or worse than serial performance beyond a certain parallelism threshold. The primary reason for such poor performance is the exhaustion of available parallelism in the program.

Weak Scaling

This is an alternative scaling method to evaluate the scalability of a program without diminishing returns as in strong scaling. It keeps the workload for each parallel instance constant while increasing the parallelism. Ideally, this should produce a flat speedup of 1 for all parallelisms.

Parallel Efficiency

Related to speedup, parallel efficiency is a measure of scalability of a parallel program. It is defined as follows, where S is the speedup:

$$Efficiency\,(E) = \frac{S}{N}$$

A quick examination of this definition reveals that E should, ideally, be 1. This is shown in the dashed line in Figure 10-2. Typically, parallel applications tend to lose their efficiency with increasing parallelism, as shown in the same figure.

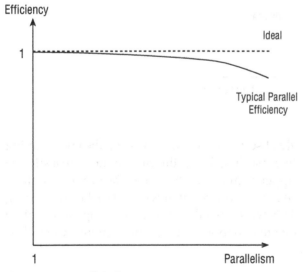

Figure 10-2: Parallel efficiency

We hinted that communication costs are a prime reason for not achieving ideal speedup or efficiency. While this plays a dominant role, it can also be due to poor load balancing, which could lead to slower processes or stragglers that hinder the total parallel execution time. While it may seem simple to avoid this by having a uniform partitioning scheme of the problem domain, it is dependent on the problem type and as such is not always straightforward.

To elaborate, consider a real-world graph, such as a friendship graph. If we were to decompose this among parallel processes, load balancing is unclear, as an equal number of vertices in each process does not necessarily result in an equal number of incoming and outgoing edges. Edges are important as they usually determine the communication volume of a graph algorithm. Therefore, balancing both computation and communication volumes becomes a nontrivial problem.

The third reason for such divergence in performance is tied with the nonparallelizable sections of the algorithm and how scaling is performed. To elaborate, one can think of a parallel program as containing two parts: serial and parallel. The serial part denotes sections like initial data loading or warmup that do not benefit from parallelization. The parallel section refers to parts that can be parallelized. With this model, one can study scaling while keeping the problem size fixed as in strong scaling mentioned earlier. Amdahl's law formulates this scenario and presents an upper bound for speedup based on the serial fraction of the program.

Amdahl's Law

The best way to understand Amdahl's law [2] is to think about a lawn mowing scenario, as depicted in Figure 10-3.

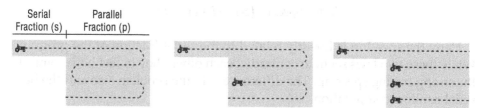

Figure 10-3: An analogy to Amdahl's law

The lawn shown in the picture has a thin section that can be mowed using only a single mower. The large square section may be mowed by more than one mower, as shown in the two- and four-mower configurations. If the area fractions of these serial and parallel sections are s and p, respectively, then for simplicity, we can assume it takes 1 unit of time to go over both using a single mower. Then if we keep increasing the number of mowers, that will reduce the time it takes to mow the large square section but not the thin strip.

This is the same analogy that Amdahl's law is based on. Thus, it states the theoretical speedup you would get is bounded by the serial fraction of the program and is defined as follows:

$$Speedup(S) = 1/(s + p/N)$$

As useful as this definition is, its upper bound has caused much confusion in the parallel programming community, suggesting that massively parallel processing is not worth it. For example, as pointed out by John Gustafson in his evaluation of Amdahl's law, even with just 1 percent serial fraction, the speedup drops to 91 from the ideal 1,024 when run on 1,024 processors.

While this is true, Gustafson from Sandia National Laboratories argues such strong scaling of an application is not done in practice. Rather, he suggests a larger problem size be used when the parallelism allows it. Based on this argument and observing that near linear speedup is possible with practical parallel applications, Gustafson has presented a reevaluation of Amdahl's law. This is known as Gustafson's law, or *scaled speedup*.

Gustafson's Law

The key to Gustafson's law [3] is the idea that we look at a larger problem size than one that could potentially be executed on a single machine and then extrapolate the serial runtime based on the parallel runtime to come up with the scaled speedup formulation given here:

$$Scaled\ Speedup(S) = N + (1 - N)s$$

Here, the speedup is linearly related to the serial fraction of the program. While these two laws seem to contradict each other, they in fact both compute the strong scaling speedup. The difference is in the problem size and the base serial runtime computation.

Throughput

Like speedup and efficiency, the third pillar to quantifying parallel performance is throughput. Throughput is the amount of work completed by an application or set of computers within a given time. The work is defined according to the application.

In traditional computing, we define work as a job, so the number of jobs completed over a lengthy period is defined as throughput of a system. In fact, there is a whole branch of computer science called *high-throughput computing* dedicated to this.

In a batch extract, transform, load (ETL) application, the work can be the number of bytes processed. In a streaming application, work can be defined as the number of events or bytes processed. For streaming applications, we are interested in sustainable throughput over an extended time. Otherwise, an application can show an increased throughput over a small period that it cannot support over an extended period.

Latency

For batch applications, latency is the time it takes for the application to complete. We want our batch programs to finish as quickly as possible. Latency is used for creating more useful measures such as speedup.

Latency is one of the primary performance metrics of streaming applications. We take latency as the time it takes for a message to be ingested and processed by a streaming application. Most of the time, latency is not a constant and may follow a certain distribution such as a normal distribution. In case of a normal distribution, if we take the mean, that means half of the messages finish within the mean time, and half require more time to finish. In many cases, the latency distribution does not adhere to the normal distribution. For most applications, taking the mean is not the best measure of the latency, and instead we take the percentile latency. Mostly we are interested in 50th percentile and the 99th percentile latencies.

- **50th percentile latency**—The median latency, at which 50 percent of messages complete. For example, if 50th percentile latency is 5 seconds, 50 percent of the messages finished within 5 seconds.

- **99th percentile latency**—The maximum latency, at which 99 percent of messages complete. For example, if 99th percentile latency is 10 seconds, 99 percent of the messages finished within 10 seconds. The remaining 1 percent of messages require more than 10 seconds.

Figure 10-4 shows a percentile latency chart for normally distributed latency values. As is evident, after about the 95th percentile, we see a quick increase.

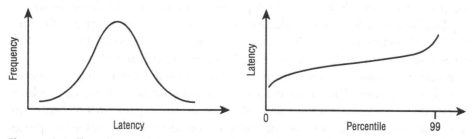

Figure 10-4: The values are following a normal distribution (left); latency percentile chart for this distribution (right)

Benchmarks

Measuring performance of hardware or software systems in a verifiable and comparable manner is a vitally important aspect for users to choose between different options. Benchmarks are developed by independent organizations to create a standard specification for testing these systems. There are a handful of such benchmarks available to measure some of the critical characteristics of data processing systems.

LINPACK Benchmark

LINPACK is one of the most prominent benchmarks in the HPC domain, and it contains three benchmarks: LAPACK [4], ScaLAPACK [5], and HPL. These are dense linear system solvers, so the aim of these benchmarks is to measure floating-point arithmetic performance. HPL, in fact, is the yardstick used in the Top500 supercomputer classification as well. LAPACK is a shared memory implementation of the benchmark, whereas ScaLAPACK is a distributed memory implementation based on MPI.

NAS Parallel Benchmark

Like LINPACK, NAS Parallel Benchmark (NPB) [6] is a benchmark suite to evaluate flops of a system. It contains a collection of pseudo-applications derived from Computational Fluid Dynamics (CFD). While evaluating computer performance, it is aimed at performing parallel computations with MPI and OpenMP-based implementations. Multilevel parallelism using processes and threads were not in the original NPB specification, but rather were later added as a set of multizone (MZ) extensions of three of the applications. Further extensions have been included to measure parallel I/O and data movement as well.

BigDataBench

Unlike LINPACK and NPB, BigDataBench [7] targets Internet services. As of the current version (5.0), it has 13 representative real-world datasets and 27 big data benchmarks. Broadly, these belong to micro, component, application, and HPC benchmarks. Together, they cover areas such as AI, offline analytics, streaming, datacenter, Internet service, HPC, and graph analytics.

In numerous cases, microbenchmarks are presented comparing performance of different systems. Microbenchmarks focus on specific features of products under certain conditions. Often an application uses many features of a software system together. Because of this, the collective performance of individual pieces working together is more important. We should be careful when evaluating systems with microbenchmarks.

TPC Benchmarks

TPC[2] is an organization that defines benchmarks for data-related queries. A hardware vendor or a software project can adopt a benchmark and submit results to TPC. TPC has a mix of SQL query-based benchmarks, as businesses use case–based benchmarks. Two benchmarks related to big data are as follows:

- **TPCx-HS**—This measures the sorting performance of a framework or a hardware configuration.

- **TPCx-BB**—This is a benchmark specifically designed to measure the performance of big data analytical systems. It provides verifiable metrics such as performance, price/performance, and availability.

HiBench

HiBench [8] came out as a Hadoop-based benchmark designed to evaluate MapReduce-style applications. However, it now includes a total of 29 micro, machine learning, SQL, Websearch, graph, and streaming benchmarks. The list of supported frameworks includes Hadoop, Spark, Flink, Storm, and Gearpump.

Performance Factors

Runtime performance of a program is dependent upon many factors. We have touched upon these in previous chapters. Here, we will try to provide a recap of different concepts discussed in those chapters.

Memory

Efficient use of memory is critical for the performance of applications. Memory access patterns and data structures are closely related.

- **Memory access patterns**—Performance is best when we access memory sequentially. The data structures should support the sequential access of memory to gain the best performance.

- **Nonuniform memory access (NUMA)**—If memory used by a single CPU core crosses the NUMA boundary for that CPU core, it can lead to slower performance.

- **Cache**—If the memory access is sequential, that is ideal. If random access is required, the best performance is when we limit random access to the memory in cache.

- **TLB**—Try to keep the memory accesses within the pages that can be loaded into the TLB.

---

[2]http://tpc.org/

Execution

We need carefully written programs to take advantage of the full power of modern CPUs.

- **Threads**—For compute-intensive applications, hyperthreading (creating more threads than the cores) is not useful and should not be applied. In general, if the program is not I/O bound, we should keep the threads equal or less than the number of cores available (oversubscribing hinders performance).

- **Spin locks vs. locks**—If we are using several threads equal to the number of cores, we can use spin locks, which will avoid context switches and thread scheduling overheads.

- **False sharing**—If multiple threads access a shared data structure and modify them concurrently, we should make sure the modifications are not within the same cache line.

- **Stragglers**—The performance of a parallel program is determined not by the fastest process but the slowest one. If the slowest is below acceptable limits, we call them *stragglers*. There is no definitive reason to have stragglers, but often in parallel computing it happens due to load imbalance. It could also be due to resource contention, communication delays, and hardware failures. Detecting stragglers is challenging because determining when to declare a task as slow is ill-defined.

- **Vectorization**—The code can be written to take advantage of vectorization features in modern CPUs.

Distributed Operators

Distributed operators define the performance when we scale applications to a larger number of computers.

- **Serialization/deserialization**—One of the biggest issues with distributed operators is the serialization and deserialization of data structures to and from the byte representations in the network. It is vital to choose correct data structures and serialization/deserialization methods to achieve optimum performance.

- **Network bandwidth**—If the network bandwidth is not enough, the data can be compressed to reduce the amount of data transmitted.

- **Use of correct operators**—Sometimes it is possible to use an operator defined to work on a table in an array. Chances are that the table operator is not optimized for the array. As such, we should use the correct operators for our data structures.

- **Use of hardware**—If available, use of networks such as InfiniBand along with technologies like RDMA can significantly increase the performance. This requires software that works on this hardware.

- **Grouping of messages**—It is more efficient to send larger messages (which can contain small data) than sending lots of small messages.

- **Nonblocking operations**—If network I/O takes longer and the program has other work to do while the operations are pending, it is best to use nonblocking operations.

Disk I/O

Optimized disk I/O can significantly enhance the performance of data-intensive applications.

- **Access patterns**—As with memory, sequential reads and writes are the fastest. If random access is required, it is better to load the blocks into memory before doing random access.

- **Concurrent access**—When the number of processes accessing a disk increases, at some point performance starts to drop sharply.

Garbage Collection

Memory-managed languages such as Java, C#, JavaScript, Python, and Go all come with an automatic mechanism to manage heap space for user-allocated objects. Unlike C and C++, where programmers handle deallocating heap objects to avoid memory leaks, garbage collection (GC) leverages different techniques to automatically identify stale memory and reuse it for future allocations.

The convenience this brings to the table comes with a price, and an especially hefty one in high-performance applications. GC is a "stop-the-world" event. That is, execution of the application is halted while GC is in progress. Java, for example, uses mark-and-sweep to identify objects that have valid references and to remove the rest. Removing the rest means to just mark those memories as reusable.

However, the heap could quickly become fragmented, leaving insufficient contiguous space to allocate objects. GC algorithms, therefore, also perform memory compaction when certain thresholds are met, as shown in Figure 10-5.

To get a closer look at GC, we need to use a profiling tool. We discuss profiling in detail later, but for now we will use the VisualVM[3] tool to monitor a running Java application, as shown in Figure 10-6.

We use the following command to invoke the sample Java2D application that comes with JDK 8:

```
java -Xmx12m -Xms3m -Xmn1m -XX:PermSize=20m -XX:MaxPermSize=20m -XX:+UseSerialGC
-jar Java2Demo.jar
```

---

[3]https://visualvm.github.io/

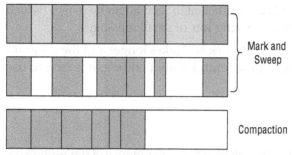

Figure 10-5: Garbage collection

Figure 10-6: Java heap space monitoring

This sets the maximum heap size to 12MB, sets the minimum heap size to 1MB, and adds another 20MB for the permanent generation region. It also instructs how to use the serial garbage collector in Java.

Attaching VisualVM to the running Java application shows an overview of the heap usage in Figure 10-6. The orange bar on top is the max heap size (12MB) we have set. The area under the blue line shows the current heap usage. As shown in the graph, heap usage spikes and drops repeatedly. These drops are caused by GC invocations.

If you would like to get a better understanding of what happens inside the heap space, VisualVM has a plugin called VisualGC that produces more stats like in Figure 10-7. Java breaks up the heap space into different regions such as Eden, Survivor (S0 and S1), Old Generation, and Permanent Generation. Eden, S0, and S1 are collectively known as Young Generation. New allocations happen in the Young Generation and are tenured into the Old Generation if they

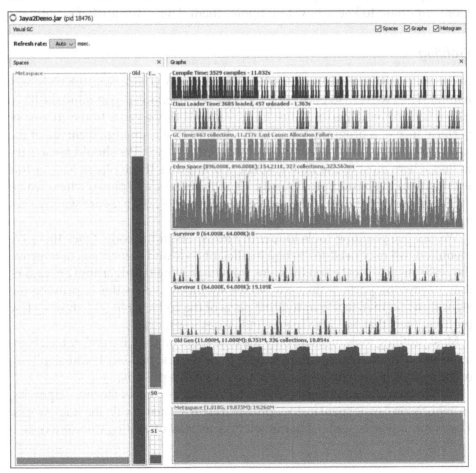

Figure 10-7: Java GC and heap space breakdown

survive a set age limit. We will refrain from going into further technicalities in the Java GC behavior, but note that GC events stop the application, so proper tuning using tools like VisualVM is necessary to improve performance.

Finding Issues

Distributed applications are inherently difficult to manage and run in production. We spend a significant amount of time debugging and improving our applications. In fact, for most applications, this maintenance effort is far greater than the initial development.

Serial Programs

Knowing what can cause performance bottlenecks is important, but it is even more important to know how to pinpoint them. This is the goal of profiling.

Profiling

In general, we take the approach of building error-free code first, which is only natural. Then we turn to perfecting the code. We need to keep in mind the 80:20 rule when applying performance improvements to the code. In the context of performance of a program, we usually observe that a small percentage of the source code is responsible for most of the performance. We should always try to find where most of the time is spent and improve those places first, as this will result in the best improvements. Usually, these are in places where we do repetitive computations. If the code is run only once, chances are we may not gain much by improving it.

We can use profiling tools to identify hot spots in the code. Once these are identified, we may need to change inefficient code and algorithms to improve the performance. Most often the gains from improving the algorithm are greater than improving parts of the code, so we should first consider improving the algorithm and then tackle individual parts of the code. Table 10-1 shows a few profiling tools that we often use to find issues in programs.

Most profiling tools measure only the time spent on the CPU and not the communication times. It is important to determine those separately before applying profiling tools to determine the best improvements possible.

With frameworks handling the bulk of the operators, most of the time improving an application can be spent inside optimized code written within the frameworks. This is one advantage of using frameworks instead of writing our own code.

Table 10-1: Profiling Tools

PERF TOOL	LANGUAGES	DESCRIPTION
JProfiler[4]	Java	Java profiler
VTune[5]	C, C++, C#, Fortran, .NET, Java, Python, Go	Collection of profiling tools with sampling, instrumentation, and processor trace technologies
perf tools[6]	C/C++	Linux utility for low-level hardware events
Valgrind[7]	Any language	Supports both finding issues such as memory leaks and performance problems
gprof[8]	Languages supported by gcc	Profiling tool for Linux/Unix systems

When digging deeper into performance issues, one tool we often turn to in Linux platforms is the perf tool. It exposes some valuable low-level details about a program, including hardware counters such as cache misses and TLB misses for understanding the performance. Usually, we come to this level of performance optimization after fixing our algorithmic and programming issues that can be detected by language-level profilers.

Scaling

We choose to run our data analytics on larger numbers of computers because some problems cannot be supported in a single computer or we need to increase the performance. If the performance does not improve adequately when we increase the number of resources, we need to investigate and understand the limits of our programs in terms of algorithm and implementation details.

Strong Scaling

Strong scaling is the hardest to achieve. Ideally, when parallelism increases, the program should have a linear performance increase, but this is seldom the case in practice.

- The serial part of the program that is common to all the parallel processes is large. When we increase the parallelism, only the parallel part of the code sees an improvement, while the serial part stays the same. This leads to diminishing speedup when increasing parallelism.

- The communication cost is too high due to more nodes being added to the calculation.

---

[4]https://www.ej-technologies.com/products/jprofiler/overview.html
[5]https://software.intel.com/content/www/us/en/develop/tools/oneapi/components/vtune-profiler.html#gs.51o1nq
[6]https://www.brendangregg.com/perf.html
[7]https://www.valgrind.org/
[8]https://sourceware.org/binutils/docs/gprof/

By measuring the time it takes for the serial part of the program versus the parallel part, we can get an idea about the scalability of a program. Combining this with communication time can give us an upper bound for the scalability of the program. Beyond this, when we increase parallelism, we will see a reduction in performance gain (speedup).

For most ETL applications, the biggest factor is communication because the computations are mostly data parallel. For machine learning applications, it can be a combination of both.

Weak Scaling

If the program does not show good weak scaling characteristics, that means the algorithm has a higher communication cost when it scales to more nodes. In a well-optimized system, it is harder to avoid this. The solutions may include increasing the network bandwidth or decreasing the amount of data transferred through techniques such as compression.

Debugging Distributed Applications

Debugging distributed applications requires practice and knowledge. There are many situations in which we may need to debug an application to figure out an issue, such as the following:

- The program runs but does not supply the correct answer.
- The program produces an error.
- The program does not progress.

Developers take different approaches to find an issue in a large-scale program. Here is a set of steps we usually follow to figure out issues in large-scale distributed applications. The first step is to run the application with a small dataset (scaled-down problem) and parallelism of 1 (no parallel parts). This is the serial execution of the program and it should provide the correct answer. If we get the same issue in this mode, we are lucky and can attach a debugger to the program to find the issue as we would for a serial application.

If the error does not materialize in this way, we find ourselves in a much more demanding situation. At this point, there are several common issues with distributed programs.

- The parallel version of the program is incorrect.
- The program is given a data input with some unexcepted values. These can be in a large dataset and may not be present in our small test.
- The program can have concurrency issues. There are two types of concurrency issues in distributed programs. The first comes from the internal threads of the application. The second can derive from distributed communications.

At this point, we can reexamine the design of the parallel program to make sure it is correct. The easiest way to find data validation issues is to properly log the errors and validate the data in the source code. Most likely we missed a parsing error in the program or read a value incorrectly.

If we are facing a concurrency issue, it may take a lot of effort to find the problem. Most of the time, the applications developed on top of task-based systems do not face these issues because the concurrency and communication are handled by the system. This is one of the biggest advantages of such systems over handling concurrency by the user. If we get such an error, we are limited to a few options for finding the issue, including the following:

- Review the potential problem areas of the source code. We can use log files to get an idea about the sections of the code that were executing when the error happened.

- Adding logs may change the execution of the program, and the issue may become harder to reproduce. We must be careful here.

- If we have multiple threads in a single process, try to reduce the number as much as possible to limit the number of moving parts.

If the program does not progress, it is much easier to debug since it must be in a deadlock situation or an infinite loop. All we need to do is get a stack trace of the processes that cannot progress. The stack trace of the program will show the method call stack of the threads.

In the case of a deadlock, multiple processes or threads within a single process will be waiting for each other without making progress. For an infinite loop, a few processes or a single process may be stuck in a loop. When taking stack traces, it is important to take multiple examples at various times to see whether processes are truly stuck at the same place.

Programming Languages

The choice of programming language mostly comes down to software developers and users in terms of what languages an organization is familiar with and software ecosystems. By *ecosystem*, we mean the set of software libraries and tools written in the same language integrating with each other. Today, Java, C/C++, and Python are the most popular languages for data analytics. Scripting languages such as Python are easy and productive to use, although they are known to not perform well for large-scale problems. System-level languages such as C/C++ are far superior in performance but lack the ease of use and flexibility of Python. Java is a language that falls somewhere in the middle of C/C++ and Python, but it has its own set of advantages and disadvantages when it comes to large-scale applications.

C/C++

Before the Java revolution, the C/C++ and Fortran languages were the only choice available for writing parallel applications that ran on thousands of computers. Since the programmer can control every aspect of a C/C++ program and access the low-level hardware functions, they are well-suited for writing frameworks targeting high performance.

For scientific applications, C/C++ and Fortran are still the major languages in use today. Java is rarely seen in large-scale scientific applications, and there are some Python interfaces built around C/C++ codes. There is a rich set of libraries and tools available in C/C++ that can work at large scale. Billions of dollars have been invested in these libraries over the years to make them run as well as possible on different hardware platforms.

The biggest disadvantage of C/C++ is that they are not popular among many programmers who are tasked with writing data analytics programs. C/C++ applications tend to be harder to write and debug. They need programmers with deep knowledge about the system and can take longer to write. Because of this, most enterprises do not choose C/C++ as their preferred choice for writing data analytics applications unless there is a pressing need for performance.

Table 10-2 summarizes the frameworks used for data-intensive applications, languages in which they are written, and APIs they support. If we look at the APIs available, Python stands out as the common language supported by all the frameworks.

Java

Java is the language in which the big data revolution began. As such, there is a vast array of tools available in Java. Further, it is a rich language popular in enterprise use cases, and there is an abundance of software developers who are

Table 10-2: Frameworks and Languages

FRAMEWORK	LANGUAGES	LANGUAGES OF APIS
Hadoop	Java	Java, Python
Spark	Scala/Java	Scala, Java, Python
Flink	Java	Java, Python
PyTorch	C++	Python, C++
TensorFlow	C++	Python, Java, C++
OpenMPI (MPI implementation)	C	C, C++, Java, Python, Fortran

comfortable with it. Java is also surrounded by numerous libraries. A carefully written Java program can achieve reasonably good performance compared to well-optimized native code. In some cases, Java can even outperform native code due to its JIT compilation capabilities.

Memory Management

The biggest advantage of Java over C/C++ is its automatic memory management. Ironically, this is also Java's main weakness when it comes to large-scale problems. Java garbage collection can come in the way of distributed operations within multiple processes. This is illustrated in the hypothetical scenario shown in Figure 10-8.

Imagine a scenario where we are sending a message from Process 1 to Process 4 through Processes 2 and 3. We first send the message to Process 2 where it gathers some information, then to Process 3, and so on. When Process 2 receives the message, the GC kicks in. The same thing happens in Process 3. Without

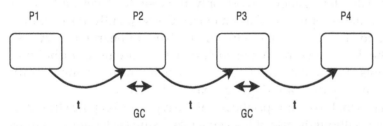

Figure 10-8: Effects of garbage collection for distributed messaging

GC, it takes 3t to send the message from Process 1 to Process 4, and with GC it takes 3t + 2GC to send the message. If there are many processes and garbage collection takes a considerable amount of time, this can lead to a huge delay for the message to reach the end. While this takes place, the last process can be idle, wasting valuable computing time.

Further garbage collection can affect parallel programs where the time to compute depends on the slowest process (stragglers). If a process takes more time because of garbage collection, the whole program will be slow.

Owing to the effects of garbage collection, Java-based frameworks try to minimize the heap memory usage as much as possible. The way this is done in current systems is to allocate critical memory regions outside of Java's heap space and manage those as we manage a C/C++ program memory. Figure 10-9 shows how the memory of an Apache Spark executor is partitioned. The storage memory and execution memory can be in the heap or allocated off-heap.

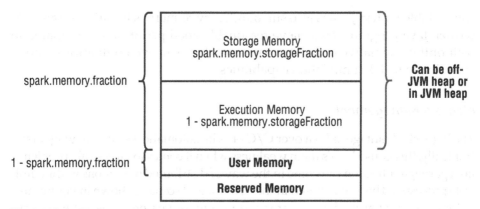

Figure 10-9: Spark memory structure

Data Structures

The built-in Java data structures, such as lists and maps, are all based on generics. Unlike C++ templates, Java generics work only at the syntax level, and underneath this, everything is represented as an object. Consequently, for primitive types they need to keep the actual value of an object in heap memory and maintain it in the data structure. When such structures are used for holding enormous amounts of data that need to be traversed, it can create unnecessary small objects in memory that can trigger garbage collections.

There are libraries that work on specific primitive types for keeping structures like lists and maps without the use of Java generics. Using such data structures can reduce the pressure on the Java garbage collection. Also, there are off-heap data structures, such as those provided by Apache Arrow, for keeping data without getting garbage collection involved.

Interfacing with Python

One of the biggest drawbacks with Java is providing efficient Python and C/C++ APIs for frameworks written on it. Doing so is technically hard unless they are supported over a messaging protocol such as a REST API, which is not suitable for data-intensive applications.

To support Python APIs, we can start a Python process and a Java process separately and bind them together using a network connection. The code we write in Python is sent into the JVM and executed within. There is a serialization cost for sending objects and data between the two processes. This is the approach taken by Apache Spark for developing PySpark, which is a Python API on top of the Apache Spark Java/Scala API. Figure 10-10 shows the architecture of PySpark, along with different processes in Python and Java.

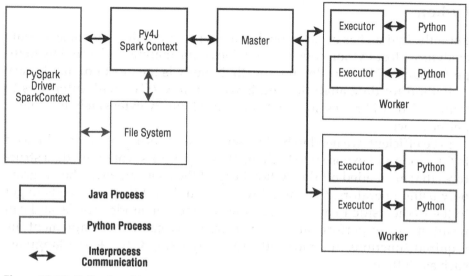

Figure 10-10: PySpark architecture

The user writes a Python program. Spark uses the driver model for executing the jobs. For a Python program, the driver consists of a Python process running the user code and a Java process connected to this Python program. This Java process runs the actual driver program by accepting commands from the Python program. The two processes communicate via sockets, and objects are serialized from the Python program and sent to the Java program. The Java program runs Py4J,[9] which helps it to understand the Python objects inside the Java program.

A Spark program consists of system-defined operators and user-defined functions. For example, reading a CSV file is an operator in Spark, which is written in Java. It is the same for a partition operator. A Map function is a user-defined function that has Python code written by the user. Now, when the program is given to the cluster to be executed by the Spark executors, it will consist of these Spark operators and user operators.

In the cluster workers, Spark creates a Java process called the *executor* and a Python process for executing the user-defined functions. The executor is the normal Java program executor that runs the Java operators. Python-based functions are executed inside the Python process by sending data from Java to Python and taking results from Python to Java.

Obviously, this is a complex approach for supporting a Python API in a distributed Java program. It requires us to start twice the normal processes and do added communications between them. These communications need data serializations and deserializations as well.

---

[9]https://www.py4j.org/

Python

Recently, Python has become the dominant programming language for data analytics. Most Python code that involves data analytics is backed by high-performance C/C++ code underneath. NumPy is the most popular library in Python for data analytics and is written in C/C++ with interfaces to Python. Other libraries such as Pandas use NumPy extensively to achieve performance.

To be efficient, we need to build a set of operators a program might need in C++ code and expose it to Python. These operators work with data structures that are loaded off the Python heap. If the user can write the program only using operators, this model works well. But if the user needs to get to the Python side to apply custom user code, the model breaks and can result in slower performance. In such cases, we can either implement the required functions in a more effective way using C/C++ or a language such as Cython.

C/C++ Code integration

Python provides a C API for developers to write extension modules or embed Python with C/C++ libraries and applications. This is a low-level API used by demanding applications that requires total control. Cython[10] and pybind11[11] are two much easier ways for interfacing Python with C/C++ code since both use the Python C API underneath.

Cython is a programming language on its own that supports the full Python syntax. In addition to this, Cython can directly call C/C++ code inside its own. Cython code translates into a Python library that can be invoked from the Python interpreter. This allows easy integration of Python and C/C++ code.

pybind11 is a lightweight version of the Boost.Python library. It exposes C++ code to Python and vice versa. The user inserts special code segments to the C/C++ code, and these are used by pybind11 to generate Python code that can invoke the C/C++ functions.

As in the Python APIs to Java frameworks, we can build Python APIs to C/C++ programs using Cython or pybind11. Unlike in Java, both Python and C/C++ code runs in the same process space. If a program consists of user-defined functions and system-defined operators, the same approach we discussed for Java applies. The only difference is that instead of communication between a Java and Python process, we can use the same process space to pass values from Python to C/C++ and vice-versa.

---

[10]https://cython.org/
[11]https://pybind11.readthedocs.io/en/stable/

Productivity

We have many expectations when developing large-scale data-intensive applications. The following are some key attributes that drive the decisions around data-intensive applications:

- **Productivity**—The developers should be able to design and develop applications and support them. Cost is a relative term, and for some applications it is okay to choose costly approaches that give the required performance and flexibility.

- **Flexibility**—We should be able to work across different systems and data formats that are designed to work well on specific applications. This allows systems to evolve and change without locking into technology stacks.

- **Performance**—Organizations want to get the best performance out of the available compute resources. This is especially important in organizations where the time needed to extract knowledge is critical. Also, not getting adequate performance means wasted resources and higher costs. If we have already purchased a big cluster, it might not be that critical in terms of costs. But with public clouds, performance is important because we pay for time and the amount of resources used.

When designing data analytics applications, we are often faced with the choice of the following:

- Programming languages
- Frameworks
- Operating environments

Scripting languages such as Python are productive compared to low-level languages like C/C++. In an ideal world, we would be programming everything with Python-like languages with the performance of C/C++. The data analytics world is heading there thanks to machine learning and deep learning frameworks. There was a lack of C/C++ high-performance codes in the ETL area, but that gap is also being filled by new frameworks.

Choice of Frameworks

We need different frameworks for data-driven applications because the frameworks are specialized in specific application domains. Table 10-3 summarizes the strengths of some of the frameworks available for data-intensive applications.

Table 10-3: Frameworks and Target Applications

FRAMEWORK	APPLICATIONS AND FEATURES
Apache Hadoop	Batch ETL applications, the first open source framework designed for ETL applications, fault tolerant.
Apache Spark	Batch ETL applications, SQL support, many distributed operators compared to Hadoop, fault tolerant.
Apache Spark Streaming	Streaming applications without low-latency requirements, high throughput, fault tolerant. Higher latency.
Apache Flink	Streaming applications, batch ETL applications, SQL support, streaming and batch applications in a single engine.
Apache Storm	Streaming applications, one of the first open source frameworks for stream processing.
PyTorch	Specifically designed for deep learning.
TensorFlow	Specifically designed for deep learning.
Rapids cuDF	Pandas like DataFrame on GPUs at scale.
Cylon	Pandas like DataFrame on CPUs at scale.
MPI	In-memory applications, scientific simulations, machine learning, low-level APIs that give the best performance. Harder to program, not designed to support ETL applications.

At the end of the day, it is inevitable that we need multiple frameworks and libraries to support our data-intensive applications. It is important to understand the cost of using these systems together to achieve our goals.

Having data structures that can work across systems without heavy performance costs can help us in scaling our use cases. In heterogeneous systems, the data conversion costs can be a large bottleneck if not chosen correctly. Because of this, it is important to use common data formats that can work across multiple frameworks and languages to achieve this. Apache Arrow is a columnar data format supported across multiple frameworks. The NumPy data structure is also used widely among different systems. Figure 10-11 shows a data format–centric view of programming languages, data processing engines, and machine/deep learning frameworks.

Minimizing the number of programming languages used can help us create rich libraries and tools that can be used across our applications so that developers can work in a more homogeneous environment.

As with any framework, we take note of professional support around frameworks and enterprise solutions such as monitoring.

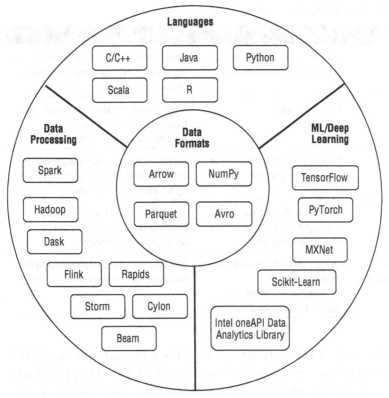

Figure 10-11: Data formats for data processing, ML/deep learning

Operating Environment

The decision to use a public cloud or an on-premises solution is usually an organizational matter. Mostly it is decided by factors such as the ones described in Table 10-4. Data-intensive applications demand high-end computers with larger core counts, more memory, higher network bandwidth, and faster disks. Because of this, cost can be a determining factor for high-end data analytics.

More and more data analytics problems are moving to public clouds due to ease of use and availability of ready-to-use services coupled with monitoring, fault tolerance, and security features.

CPUs and GPUs

There are a few hardware choices available when running data-intensive applications for public use:

- **CPUs**—The default choice for running applications
- **GPUs**—Became popular with deep learning and now libraries are available for ETL applications
- **FPGAs**—For specialized applications that require best performance

Table 10-4: Cloud vs. On-Premises for Data Processing

FACTOR	PUBLIC CLOUD	ON-PREMISES
Time to market	Can start immediately and scale as the solutions grow.	Need to plan for required hardware up front. Purchasing hardware and setting it up is a lengthy process.
Cost	Pay as we use.	Responsible for the costs such as hardware, power, space, maintenance, and upkeep.
Security	Security is the number-one concern for going to public clouds.	Sensitive information may require extra security that can be provided by on-premises solutions.
Compliance	The cloud should support the regulatory controls of the data stored.	Companies may have regulatory controls that force them to use on-premises solutions.
Availability of rich, integrated software environments	Clouds provide managed data processing environments for all the applications discussed here.	The users need to deploy multiple software stacks and maintain them.

GPUs are dominant in deep learning applications. CPUs are still the default choice for processing data, especially for streaming and batch ETL applications. Owing to relatively less use of FPGAs, we will set it aside for the time being. There are many possibilities available for creating a data-intensive application environment with CPUs and GPUs, as shown in Table 10-5.

Table 10-5: CPUs and GPUs for Data-Intensive Applications

CONFIGURATION	DESCRIPTION
CPU clusters	Clusters with CPU machines for batch ETL and streaming applications.
CPU clusters + GPU clusters	A CPU cluster is used for data processing tasks, and the GPU cluster is used for deep learning tasks. The GPU cluster gets data from the CPU cluster.
GPU clusters	GPUs are used for deep learning as well as ETL operations surrounding deep learning.
CPU and GPU mixed clusters	Every CPU node has a set of GPUs. These clusters can interchangeably use CPUs and GPUs for ETL operations and GPUs for deep learning tasks.

In some cases, we are given clusters with certain configurations, and it is our responsibility to find the best frameworks and applications to solve our problems with that hardware. This is the case in academic settings and government-funded clusters such as supercomputers.

Normally, we can define the parameters of the hardware for the applications we are going to support. In this case, we can choose the hardware that suits the application best.

Public Clouds

Public clouds offer services for storing data and processing them. The services are usually pay-for-use. These solutions have features such as monitoring of services and built-in security and fault tolerance. There is a good correspondence between many services offered in different public clouds for data analytics. Figure 10-12 shows a general cloud data pipeline.

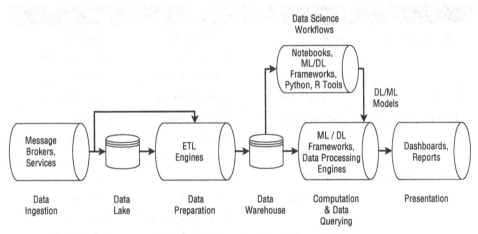

Figure 10.12: Components of end-to-end data pipeline

A cloud data pipeline usually starts with data ingestion frameworks such as message brokers. The data coming from message brokers is stored in cloud storage services that are designed to handle large amounts of row data. The data preparation layer provides both batch and streaming engines for processing this data and storing them in a more structured manner for other services to consume at the data warehouse layer.

This structured data is used by data scientists for exploratory data analysis to create models, which produce real insight into the data. Finally, the presentation layer has services capable of generating graphs, reports, and dashboards to visualize and present data.

- **Data lakes and data warehouse**—Data lakes contain data in raw form as it is received from sources. Data warehouses store cleaned data in more structured formats that are ready for querying and use by ML/DL frameworks.

- **Data preparation vs. computation**—Data preparation deals with large amounts of data both in streaming and batch forms. Computation involves applying algorithmic models to data as well as querying data for analysis.

- **Data science workflows**—This is sometimes referred to as *exploratory analytics*. The data scientists explore the data and employ various mathematical models to extract knowledge. This is a highly iterative process with a great deal of experimentation.

Table 10-6 summarizes data analytics tools in Amazon Web Services, Google Cloud Services, and Microsoft Azure. All the clouds provide similar methods to accept the data, store them as raw data, and then process and store this as structured data. In many cases, open source products are used underneath the cloud services.

Table 10-6: Cloud Services for Data Pipelines

	AWS	AZURE	GCP
Data ingestion	Kinesis	Azure IoT Hub	Cloud IoT
	IoT	Event Hub	Cloud Function
	Lambda Function	Azure Function	PubSub
Data lake	S3, S3 Glacier	Azure Data Lake	Cloud Storage
Data preparation	Data pipeline	Data Explorer	DataPrep
	Glue ETL	Databricks	DataProc
		Stream Analytics	Dataflows
Data warehouse	Redshift	Cosmos DB	Cloud Datastore
	DynamoDB	Azure SQL	Bigtable
	RDS	Azure Redus Cache	BigQuery
	Glue Catalog	Data Catalog	Data Catalog
	Kinesis Streams	Event Hub	PubSub
	Neptune		MemoryStore
			CloudSQL
Compute and queries	Kinesis Analytics	Azure ML	AutoML
	EMR	Databricks	DataProc
	Glue ETL		DataPrep
	SageMaker		DataFlow
	TensorFlow on AWS		DataLab
	PyTorch on AWS		
Data science	SageMaker	Azure ML	DataLab
	SageMaker Notebooks	Azure Notebooks	Data Studio
			Colab
	TensorFlow on AWS		
	PyTorch on AWS		
Presentation	QuickSight	Power BI	DataLab

Cloud services are inherently designed to work across multiple organizations and users. This is called *multitenancy* in cloud computing. Normally, when we set up data analytics solutions on our own, multitenancy is not needed. Cloud vendors also race to include high-performance deep learning solutions as services. From virtual machines equipped with high-end GPUs to complete software ecosystems, quite a few solutions exist in Amazon, Google, and Microsoft clouds.

The basic offering is the IaaS solutions that come with high-end accelerators. All three vendors provide the latest GPUs in various VM categories. Also available are FPGAs, which can be used in application domains such as bioinformatics, stream processing, and security to speed up computations. Custom accelerators are being deployed as well. Amazon, for example, recently introduced its Inferentia chip, which is designed to accelerate deep learning inference. Google has also had TPUs for similar purposes for a while.

Cloud providers also enable machine learning software as services. Amazon's flagship machine learning solution is SageMaker. Google's competing offer to artificial intelligence is Cloud AI, while Microsoft Azure provides Azure AI. As the solutions from these services are rapidly evolving, we will not go over the fine points of each. However, they currently provide similar services, described as follows:

- **Data labeling**—This involves adding different types of labels to various data such as images, texts, and videos. For example, images could be labeled for bounding boxes, classified as something or not, labeled as cat or dog, or even used to label the semantics to display whether the image is showing something happy or sad. These types of tasks require manual labor, and it is extremely important to get quality ground truth data to train other machine learning models. Therefore, these platforms allow data labeling tasks to be easily automated and distributed to a collection of human workers of choosing.

- **Prepare and analyze data**—Initial data needs to be prepared to be fed into different models. These are usually known as *data wrangling tasks*. From simple query extractions to complex mappings, the cloud providers support data wrangling tasks through their AI solutions.

- **Build, train, and deploy**—This is the core of any AI solution that practitioners seek. The most common form available in all three of these providers is the support to have notebooks. A user can build, train, and deploy a custom model easily on the cloud provider's IaaS using this technique.

Future of Data-Intensive Applications

Data-intensive applications have become ever so important in the last decade. The Apache Hadoop era is ending, and we are moving toward a more fragmented but rich set of tools for data analytics. New data processing frameworks are being developed to facilitate different classes of applications.

With the ending of Moore's law in sight, high-performance data-intensive applications are moving toward custom hardware solutions. Already there are deep learning workloads that run on hardware specifically designed to run them optimally. FPGAs and GPUs are attracting users who are looking to run their data-intensive workloads faster and more efficiently. Programming platforms such as Kokkos [9] are facilitating the creation of data-intensive applications that can run on any hardware.

From the beginning, Java was the language of choice for data-intensive applications. Some Java implementations are being replaced by high-performance implementations with system-level languages such as C/C++. Faster networks, faster disks, CPUs with large number of cores, and cheap main memory are putting more and more pressure on data-intensive applications to utilize them efficiently.

For the foreseeable future, deep learning will be one of the driving forces behind data-intensive applications. Many tools are being developed around deep learning frameworks to use them efficiently and at scale. More people are moving their data and analytical workloads to public clouds where there are managed services for on-demand processing of data.

Integration between different systems and applications is a key to successfully develop rich applications. Workflow systems are emerging to fill this gap in data-intensive applications. Overall, the data-intensive applications are increasingly becoming diverse and mature with experts from different domains working together to solve harder problems with the help of data.

Summary

At the dawn of data-intensive frameworks, performance and productivity were at odds with each other. The programming models were productive, but performance was not adequate. At the time, there were few frameworks available, so users did not have much of a choice. Now, frameworks are catching up with performance and even pushing the boundaries of usability and productivity. New frameworks are emerging that embrace performance and efficiency while keeping productivity as well. All these are built on the success stories of the products that came before them. It is indeed an exciting time for data-intensive applications and the users.

References

1. J. J. Dongarra, C. B. Moler, J. R. Bunch, and G. W. Stewart, *LINPACK users' guide*. SIAM, 1979.

2. M. D. Hill and M. R. Marty, "Amdahl's law in the multicore era," *Computer*, vol. 41, no. 7, pp. 33-38, 2008.

3 J. L. Gustafson, "Reevaluating Amdahl's law," *Communications of the ACM*, vol. 31, no. 5, pp. 532-533, 1988.

4. E. Anderson *et al.*, *LAPACK users' guide*. SIAM, 1999.

5. L. S. Blackford *et al.*, *ScaLAPACK users' guide*. SIAM, 1997.

6. D. H. Bailey, E. Barszcz, L. Dagum, and H. D. Simon, "NAS parallel benchmark results," *IEEE Parallel & Distributed Technology: Systems & Applications*, vol. 1, no. 1, pp. 43-51, 1993.

7. L. Wang *et al.*, "Bigdatabench: A big data benchmark suite from internet services," in *2014 IEEE 20th international symposium on high performance computer architecture (HPCA)*, 2014: IEEE, pp. 488-499.

8. J. Pješivac-Grbović, T. Angskun, G. Bosilca, G. E. Fagg, E. Gabriel, and J. J. Dongarra, "Performance analysis of MPI collective operations," *Cluster Computing*, vol. 10, no. 2, pp. 127-143, 2007.

9. H. C. Edwards, C. R. Trott, and D. Sunderland, "Kokkos: Enabling manycore performance portability through polymorphic memory access patterns," *Journal of Parallel and Distributed Computing*, vol. 74, no. 12, pp. 3202-3216, 2014.

Index